To
Change
a Mind

A Division of Booklight, Inc.
2011
Lantern Books
128 Second Place
Brooklyn, NY 11231
www.lanternbooks.com

Printed in the United States of America

Library of Congress Cataloging-in-Publication Data

McKinnon, John A., M.D.
To Change a mind : parenting to promote
maturity in teenagers / John A. McKinnon.
p. cm.
Includes bibliographical references.
ISBN-13: 978–1-59056–234–5 (alk. paper)
ISBN-10: 1–59056–234–8 (alk. paper)
1. Parent and teenager. 2. Adolescence.
3. Emotional maturity. 4. Adolescent psychology.
I. Title.
HQ799.15.M384 2010
649'.125—dc22
2010029711

To Change a Mind

Parenting to Promote Maturity in Teenagers

John A. McKinnon, M.D.

Lantern Books • New York
A Division of Booklight, Inc.

For
Fiona, Moira,
and Julia

What kind of a thing is it Matty's parents want of him? . . . They want him to stop doing certain things he does and start doing others. But . . . it is more than behavior. . . . What [his parents] want . . . is for his mind to be different. They want him to . . . change his mind.

—**Robert Kegan**, *In Over Our Heads*
(Cambridge: Harvard University Press, 1994, pp. 16–17)

Contents

Acknowledgments

It is still apt, after writing this second book, to say again what I acknowledged after writing the first: After thinking about a problem for many years it's difficult to know just where an idea came from, what friend gave it a hearing, what colleague contributed the kernel of a new concept. These contributions go far beyond those specific ideas or words that call for footnotes. Some come back to me from my own psychiatric training thirty years ago. I still vividly recall my first adolescent patients at the Yale Psychiatric Institute, and, along with their faces, I still recall some of the ideas my teachers had about them, albeit these ghostly remarks surface in memory long after some of those mentors have gone to their graves. Over the years, no doubt, other contributions have come from the staff at Montana Academy, who have said clever or enigmatic things with which it may have taken me years to come to terms.

No doubt the most valuable intellectual contributions have come from close professional friends, whose ideas and words by now have become impossible to distinguish from my own thoughts and diction. No longer able to disentangle which idea was whose and which was my own, and long since ceasing to care, I acknowledge my debts to John Santa, Ph.D., Dennis Malinak, M.D., Rosemary McKinnon, M.S.W., and Carol Santa, Ph.D., my partners at Montana Academy. And I particularly thank my friend and colleague Peter Banys, M.D., who's shared many of my most memorable and instructive conversations over the years, ever since we met as freshmen in college during our own adolescence.

With great affection I acknowledge the true inspiration for this book: the students of Montana Academy and their parents. They have honored us over the years by trusting us with their children. Inasmuch as we have a daughter who was sometimes so sick that we had to leave her in a hospital in the care of others, Rosemary and I have always known what this trust means. For this reason, perhaps, many of those parents and their children have become lasting friends, who continue to send warm regards and news of their doings, like manna, into our lives. I also acknowledge my debt to those who didn't remain enduring friends, who departed Lost Prairie with the sad or bitter belief that we'd failed them. This is the debt clinicians always owe to those who don't do well, who teach us, too, albeit painfully, what we don't know and cannot remedy.

I owe a debt of gratitude again to Gene Gollogly of Lantern Books, who agreed to publish this second book. I appreciate the alchemy of my editors, Kara Davis and Martin Rowe, who again transformed my work into a tangible, well-designed book. I'm indebted to my friend, Candace Gaudiani, who read my original manuscript, years ago, and recognized that it contained two books, not one. And I'm grateful to my eldest daughter, who lent her acute mind and sharp pencil to this manuscript, too. Its residual flaws, awkward diction, unsound grammar, and failures of imagination are all my own, of course. I know that, once again, she did her best.

Because I have been at work on this book for a decade, I'm reminded, last but by no means least, that this book about parenting emerged from the ongoing life of a family. It was never just about what I learned about parenting in my training or in psychiatric practice. For a start, it always had to be about what we had learned, as parents, about our own daughters. In this sense, this book is the fruit of a man's lucky experience of shared parenting with a loyal friend and skillful, loving mother—my wife, Rosemary. Its best ideas were shared ideas. And in the end I have dedicated this book to my children. They play bit parts in the book, in ways I hope will amuse them. Over the years of its writing, moreover, I was often reminded of my debt to them. One daughter, for example, complaining about another, many years ago, asked me why I hadn't done better as a father. With disgust she asked, "Aren't you the guy who wrote a book about how parents should deal with a misbehaving teenager [like my sister]?"

She'd stumbled upon an important truth, of course. And so with gratitude to them all, I acknowledge, here and now, what I implicitly admitted, then and there, when I asked her in return: "Where do you suppose I learned what's in that book?"

Author's Note

Whenever a clinician describes a professional experience, he risks indiscretion. To avoid this, I've chosen to present composite cases, rather than to detail the lives of actual teenagers and parents. These composites are true to life, insofar as I could make them so. They are typical and plausible. Yet none is a portrait or even a good likeness or deft sketch of any particular person. None contains details that will permit the reader to identify any particular person—other than myself. Any resemblance to any person known to the reader will be unintentional and coincidental.

I ought also to note that, as a matter of taste, I've chosen to alternate the use of personal pronouns that imply gender. Rather than invariably use the masculine form or repetitively employ an awkward locution, such as "him or her," I've preferred to alternate "him" in one context with "her" in another, to use "he" on one occasion and "she" on another, so as not to distract the reader with a clumsy diction.

Preface

This is the second of a pair of books, the second half of a discussion that became too unwieldy to fit inside one cover. I divided the original hefty manuscript into a pair of trim books. In the first, *An Unchanged Mind: The Problem of Immaturity in Adolescence* (published by Lantern Books in 2008), I suggested that a child's psychological development can be disrupted and delayed. The result is a relative immaturity that presents in adolescence as a global dysfunction—at school, at home, and socially, among age-mates—and multiple symptoms and misbehaviors.

An Unchanged Mind described and made sense of this common contemporary problem. This second book describes what, in our experience, has been the solution: parenting. Its dual prescription is just as relevant to the rearing of normal teenagers, however, and I hope it will prove to be a help to all the other adults who inhabit the village it takes to transform an infant into a socialized adult. Although this discussion is the sequel to *An Unchanged Mind*, it can also stand alone. Its discussion of two fundamental parental tasks, recognition and limit-setting, starts at its own beginning, and readers who haven't read the first book can proceed to chapter one without risk of confusion. On the other hand, those who wish to understand the problem they're trying to solve may find helpful the earlier book's description of psychological development and its explanation of relative immaturity in adolescence.

When teenagers fall behind in maturation, the restoration of developmental momentum often requires an extra step beyond what normal parenting requires—a two-step remedy. When an obstacle blocks a teenager's progress relative to age-mates, then as with a train stuck on a mountain behind an avalanche, the first problem is to remove the hindrance, to clear the track. To free up a stuck adolescent may in some cases require professional diagnosis and specialized treatment. But plowing the track isn't enough. The second problem is to restart the locomotive and put the train back on schedule—a task that, in the case of delayed maturation, neither pills nor brief psychotherapies can accomplish. The heavy lifting that's required turns out to be simpler and also more complicated: simpler in the sense that it isn't high-tech, and only requires deft, sustained, parenting; and complex, in that even parenting a normal teenager isn't entirely uncomplicated. However, the remedy for that second problem isn't fundamentally different from the dual effort required of *all* parents—and so these two tasks are the subjects for this volume: how to jump-start and push a modern teenager to move on up the grade.

I have long wanted to make this book available to parents of teenagers who have fallen behind in psychological maturation. In particular, I have for many years wished I could provide it to parents of students arriving at Montana Academy, a residential therapeutic school where, for more than a decade, I've worked with struggling, stuck teenagers and worried moms and dads, who, from thirty states and overseas, have brought their splendid sons and daughters to work and play with us, and to grow up, on a ranch in a remote valley west of Glacier Park. I mention this because I want you to understand that this book is about what we do.

If you're a parent of a normal teenager, I trust that you'll discover that this book is also about what you do to help a teenager to mature. I should mention here that this book isn't a commercial for Montana Academy. I wrote it because of a wish to help *all* the worried parents (and concerned relatives and friends) whose teenagers have needed professional help or were sent "to wilderness" or have enrolled in one of the nation's competent therapeutic boarding schools—of which there are now quite a few. Whether you're the mother or father of an adolescent who makes parenting look easy or the freaked-out parent (or concerned grandparent or family friend) of a teenager who makes child-rearing seem difficult or impossible, I hope this book will help you. It's about what you're trying to do; what teachers and neighbors and relatives hope you're doing; what therapists would be glad if you did; and what clinical and academic staff at therapeutic boarding schools need badly for you to do and to help them do. For this book is simply about parenting. It's about what we all must do to help young people grow up.

1   Two Parental Tasks

WHY SHOULD parents care about maturation?

Aside from what, to a parent, feels like a natural pleasure in a child's progressive steps forward in development, there are also strong reasons for parents to believe that maturity makes many desirable kinds of success and happiness more likely. There are equally strong reasons to suspect that arrested development and perpetual *im*maturity make some forms of failure and unhappiness all but inevitable.

Much is at stake, then. Unfortunately, despite its profound importance in children's lives, progress in growing up is not automatic. Psychological maturation is by no means assured. Its completion is by no means inevitable.[1]

The evidence for this is all around us. A glance at any good newspaper reminds us that fully mature men and women are exceptional, not the rule. The inborn human potential for mature personality development isn't always realized. Childish adults abound. They diminish our communities, drag down our collective productivity, and poison our shared society with selfish narcissism. Often enough, their follies play out in public and can hardly be ignored. We live with their incompetence, endure their crimes. For this invidious immaturity among our fellow citizens, we bear great social costs.

Here, however, the stakes are personal. For mothers and fathers who want the best for their children, promoting maturation matters, as do love and hope. Maturation bodes well for the future, and immaturity does not. A failure to mature, and a consequent perpetual *im*maturity, leaves a son or daughter to make do with a stunted personality—to which, over a lifetime, a mediocrity of thinking, education, and career, repetitive troubles with friendship and love, and ultimate personal unhappiness, all may legitimately be ascribed.[2]

1

Two parental tasks are key. To grow up, children need accurate adult *recognition* and firm *limit-setting*. The adults who are in a position to accomplish these key tasks, particularly in the first decades of life, we call *parents*.

To be clear, when I use these words—"parent" or "parenting"—I refer to a constructive influence that adults exert upon children or teenagers, and specifically I refer to recognition and limit-setting. In other words, I don't just mean the biological act of conceiving a baby. I mean nurture, not merely nature. In this sense, some parents also happen to be biological progenitors, but in this book we're not describing genetic influences, but the powerful role parents play in providing or choreographing a young person's psychological experience. It is in this profound sense that it "takes a village" to rear a child. When I refer to parents and to parenting, then, I'm talking about all the constructive recognition and limit-setting provided by adults who inhabit that village, and so participate in the rearing of children and teenagers.

Both recognition and limit-setting are necessary, albeit neither alone suffices to accomplish the ultimate parental goal, which is to transform an infant into a mature adult, an alchemy we call maturation. By maturation we mean nothing less than the gradual elaboration of character. And by character we mean the durable structure of a personality, upon which, over a lifetime, the quality of a person's thinking, education, career, friendships, capacity for love, and ultimate happiness largely depend.

It is useful to speak of two parental tasks, even though the very concept of parenting covers such vast territory, and even if these "tasks" are neither separate nor unrelated, but rather the *yin* and *yang* of one parental effort. Even so, to think in terms of two broad, fundamental parental tasks puts the focus where it needs to be: upon what helpful adults can do. For there are psychological problems parents cannot solve, potential obstacles to a young person's maturation that require specialized intervention. Yet, once those obstacles have been mitigated or removed, parenting is what restores a young person's arrested developmental momentum. No matter the cause of a developmental delay, parenting is what can be done to help. This is no small matter, for there appear to be no other sources of leverage. Despite the wonders and high-tech razzmatazz of modern neuroscience, there's no pill or neurological intervention that effectively promotes emotional growing up. For better or worse, we must rely upon old-fashioned parenting, which remains indispensable.

For this simple reason, parents may find it useful to contemplate what parenting *is*. Parents may wish to consider what it is that young people need from them, if they are to make reliable progress toward psychological maturity. To say that these two kinds of experience are indispensable doesn't guarantee, by any means, that young people always find parenting available. For many children, these two tasks only name what is painfully missing, and explain a young person's blighted, stunted personality development. In some families, in some communities, and in some cultures, most adults are stressed or absent, and parenting a rare resource.

Moreover, not all that parents do is useful parenting. Some of what parents happen to do in their lives makes little contribution to maturation, however friendly and well-intended those efforts. Strenuous pursuit of a career is one of these extraneous efforts that rarely contributes much to a child's maturation. Or again, adults who rear young people make other contributions, such as earning family income to put food on the table and to provide clothing and shelter. Adults living with children amuse, paint window trim, mow the lawn, pay taxes, vote in school board elections, shop and cook, and yet, in none of these roles—as jester, handyman, kitchen help, or conscientious citizen—does a parent necessarily propel onward a young person's maturation.

In sum, by "parenting" I mean what adults do directly that helps children grow up. The dual effort I will describe surely is all but universal among adults who rear children and teenagers. Parents may parent well or badly, may get better at it, may make more or less time for it. Yet parenting is what mothers and fathers of normal children do. Parenting is what mothers and fathers (and surrogate parents) do for troubled teenagers, who may also participate in local outpatient therapies, take prescribed medications, or get sent away to wilderness programs and therapeutic boarding schools. Parenting is what parents have succeeded in doing when their successful children make child-rearing look easy. It is what parents are trying to do when child-rearing becomes extremely difficult, when intrinsic (e.g., ADHD or somatic illness) or extrinsic (e.g., a death or divorce) obstacles disrupt a teenager's progress, and mothers and fathers (or surrogate parents) struggle to restore developmental momentum. Parenting is what other adults in other roles (grandmothers, neighbors, teachers, coaches, therapists, probation officers) also may contribute as they inhabit the village it takes to transform an infant into a mature adult.

Let me say it again. In this transformation, two parental tasks are critical. We begin with *recognition*, not because it's more important, but only because it comes first. After that, we'll turn to *limit-setting*, which depends upon recognition, but also makes its own equally important contribution.

Part 1
Recognition

2   A Need to Be Known

> **rec og nize** to know again, from Latin *recognoscere*
> *re-*, again + *cognoscere,* to get to know.
> *American Heritage Dictionary*[3]

> Mirror, Mirror on the wall . . .
> Snow White, *Grimm's Fairy Tales*[4]

How simple it sounds: to recognize *re* + *cognoscere* = again + to (get to) know. The act sounds so trivial that it's difficult to imagine how recognition could make such a critical contribution. It sounds so abstract that it may be hard to believe that something so ethereal sustains the morale of human beings at all ages, from the cradle to the grave. The word sounds so insubstantial that it may seem odd that, in its absence, children and teenagers fail to mature properly.

And yet, a lack of recognition disrupts development. Clinically, we notice that a shortage of recognition weakens a young person's sense of self, deflates her self-esteem, and robs her of a confident sense of purpose. The corollary is: when maturation goes awry, recognition is half the remedy. When a young person falls behind in the process of maturation, and so begins to fail in all the venues of modern adolescence, recognition creates the basis for restored momentum.[5]

And that isn't all. For all its critical importance in the maturation of children and teenagers, recognition isn't only of use to the young, any more than air is. To the end of the life cycle, recognition sustains grown-up work and love. We never outgrow our need for that mirror. It consoles stressed adults, just as it reassures children. It creates and deepens friendship and intimacy. By acknowledging the fine job a woman does, her boss, clients, employees, patients, and colleagues sustain her sense of purpose and buoy her satisfaction. By providing affection and gratitude, grown-up children and old friends preserve the dignity and morale of an aging man. And the abrupt loss of that mirror may cause an isolated adult to lose his bearings, his heart, even his mind.

It may be difficult to take recognition seriously, too, because it sounds easy. Most adults probably believe they acknowledge others naturally, without plan or having to try very hard. Yet it surprises some busy parents to discover how difficult it can be to find time to do it at all, much less do it well. This is because recognition is a skill that can be improved. It doesn't just happen. It may be done well or badly, or not at all.

Recognition is central to some of our most telling interpersonal interactions. It is at the core of a parent's loving relationship with a son or daughter. It is the art of the therapist, the heart of the doctor–patient relationship. These relationships involve skilled recognition, which doesn't become possible without self-reflection, informed empathy, and practice. Inasmuch as recognition is one of two essential tasks for any parent who wants to transform a self-centered infant into a competent adult, its features are worth careful consideration.

The Act of Recognition

For a start, recognition is an act, not just an insightful thought. Although it must begin as a thought, an adult's recognition of a child isn't a secret knowledge. Recognition is a relationship's currency and must be spent, for it has little value if it's hidden, like coins hoarded in a mattress. A parent's mute grasp of a teenager's predicament or state of mind isn't yet an act of recognition, for an unexpressed understanding provides little emotional sustenance to a child. A parent's unexpressed understanding is recognition that hasn't yet happened. For instance, it isn't recognition when a mother merely feels proud about her son's performance in school, or when a father merely mentions his worries about a lonely daughter starting a new school to his acquaintances in the car pool. A sad girl has to learn somehow that her watchful father has noticed her unhappiness and understands it, so she isn't alone in her despair.

This isn't to say that recognition needs always to be spoken or written down in so many words. Among lovers and friends, parents and children, recognition requires but a look or a touch. Yet a son won't feel his mother's pride unless she lets him learn of it in some way. To have an impact, a parent's knowledge must become known. Ideally it gets expressed with tact at a moment when there aren't distractions, and so provides to a listening child an adult's interpretation of what his performance portends. When that mom took the trouble to read her son's report card with him and to say, "That's my boy!" he truly had received his report card. Before she saw it and said so, all he had was a scrap of paper and a little ink.

All Our Lives

The experience of recognition presumably begins in the moment when we're born to the light, when one of us becomes two, and our mothers look into our eyes and we are seen to be. We then know, in some infantile fashion, that we exist. And recognition is reciprocal, even then. In that moment, a woman rediscovers herself, too, as a mother—as *our* mother. Fathers also rediscover themselves. This was an unexpected lesson I learned each of the three times a nurse passed to me a tiny daughter. Under that little girl's trusting gaze, all the cockiness of a young physician cracked open and fell away, and I was undone, forever changed. Each daughter transfixed me with a calm, avid stare. I saw that she *knew* me. And in those diminutive mirrors I, too, recognized the new man I had become: her dad.

Yet this recognition was only the start. Each of my daughters would need, again and again, just as I myself have needed all my life, to be seen anew, to be found worthy, to be re-defined: to be *known + again*. All our lives we need to see ourselves reflected once more in the mirror of the other, to be acknowledged, understood, liked, even loved, and so to recognize who we are, and to be reminded that we're not alone.

To look into the mirror of the other isn't an entirely passive experience. We must permit others to see us, let them look behind our masks, or risk that we'll always be strangers to ourselves.[6] What we seem to long for and need all our lives are echoes of that experience in our first months of infancy: a parent's reassurance. As we grow up, our friends give this gift. Having none, solitary children create imaginary friends, to pretend, in play, that they're heard and understood. As we mature, we hope to fall in love. And what is love if not an experience of recognition, in which we let ourselves be seen as openly as we dare, more honestly than we permit others to see us? In love, we hope to be understood, and known, and loved anyway.

And this isn't all. Troubled human beings look for recognition in the intimacy of the hour spent in psychotherapy. What is psychotherapy if not the experience of recognition by a respected other? And for millions of believers across the planet, what is the experience of prayer if not a plea for transcendent acceptance that passeth understanding? In encounters with the deity, what *ich* receives from *du* is empathic, all-knowing recognition.[7]

$$\sim$$

Apparently, we never outgrow this need to be known, although what knowledge we need changes through the life cycle. As infants, we know we're understood by parents who correctly interpret our inchoate cries—feed us when we're hungry, or change our nappies when we're wet and cold. As toddlers, we sense that we're understood by parents who let us try, but keep us safe. In school, we're recognized in new ways, beyond the perimeters of our homes, by special adults who acknowledge our new mastery with gold stars on spelling lists and wolf badges awarded at gatherings of the pack. In adolescence, when we enter an even wider society, a multi-faceted social mirror reflects back a complex social persona, which hints at the shape of a first, coherent adult identity. Affectionate adolescent relationships with mentoring adults, fostered by mutual recognition, provide leverage for grown-ups, aside from family, to exert a parental influence. Such relationships make it possible for teachers, coaches, friends' parents, therapists, and other mentors to mirror and sustain a young person's growing confidence in a social persona and capacity for accomplishment beyond the nuclear family. These relationships are created by mutual recognition. In fact, recognition *is* the relationship.

For it goes both ways. Adults need recognition, too. Working adults hope for career recognition, and find themselves reflected in transcripts, reference letters, performance evaluations, promotions, and raises. Teachers need recognition from students, lawyers from clients, physicians from patients. Young adults find it in reciprocal adult relationships, in friends' jokes, and in the adoring eyes of lovers. What is a wedding but an act of mutual recognition? And in new families, a husband receives his wife's admiration for reciprocal teamwork; a wife receives the awe and gratitude of a husband for children.

Then there are children. Surely, when a dad grasps a daughter's loneliness in the schoolyard, she finds herself less alone. But his love is repaid when she situates him in his paternal role, and so makes sense of his life, too—no small gift. Most of us need sometimes to be reminded why we bother to get up in the morning, why we work so hard, why we endure the slings and arrows of outrageous modern life. Even though children cannot fully grasp an adult's inner world, a toddler's Crayola portrait tells his parents what he makes of them, and reminds them that they have a job to do, that their specks of consciousness have a purpose, that they're not alone, either.

We need it to the end. Beyond retirement, when employment can no longer provide a daily reflection, grandchildren may sustain a pensioner's morale. A new collaboration with adult children may give purpose to an old woman's final years. And, if we're lucky, at the end we may close our eyes under the affectionate gaze of those who still know us, and will soon miss us, who care enough to hold our hands until we let go.

Beyond death, many believe that we meet our maker on judgment day. In that mythic encounter of *ich* with *du*, we receive a final summing up—of what we have become or failed to become; what was accomplished or left undone. We are said to learn whether it was good enough. If we've been lucky in our lives, this won't be the first time we were understood and loved; or forgiven our trespasses; or the only time we ever knew who we were, what we had become, what we deserved, and where we were going. Those of us who have been fortunate will have been recognized many times before.

"Watch Me!"

Parents recognize children in all sensory modes: rocking a tired baby, touching an infant's body in the bath, bouncing a toddler on one knee, winking to a five-year-old strutting about in mommy's heels, clapping when a schoolboy wins a spelling bee, and shouting when the center forward kicks a goal. In whatever modality, recognition feels like a synthesis, an assembly of various elements into one gestalt. To be recognized in this coherent way has an all-at-once, visual quality.

11

For small children, it often *is* to be seen: to have dad's full attention, to catch a glimpse of mother's watchful eye. Most parents will recall those brief occasions when this visual exchange became vivid and poignant, when a fallen toddler glanced up anxiously from the rug to discover from us whether she was all right or not. At those times, if parents stayed cool, she went back to her play unperturbed. If an adult got upset or looked anxious or scared, then the child burst into tears and had to be consoled. I recall that with each of our daughters in those toddler years, there were memorable dramas that turned upon this act of recognition—when one daughter climbed to the high platform of a playground slide and called back down to me: "Daddy, *watch* me!" If, talking to a friend, I carelessly glanced away as she let go and went down, her face fell, and she arrived in the sand pit distressed and petulant, her features crumpled with disappointment, wailing reproachfully: "Daddy, you didn't watch!" Then she was up and running for the ladder, calling to me, "Daddy, *this* time *watch* me!"

In such moments, a father learns that, for all their independence, children don't only want to exist alone, to go their own way, to live by themselves, or play a solo part. Neither do teenagers wish to be trees crashing down in empty forests, wondering if anyone noticed. They don't want to wonder whether the events in their lives truly happened or had meaning; worry whether they, themselves, actually exist; or feel uncertain about whether they stand or fall. They want us to be there, to watch them, to hear them perform, to touch them with a reassuring hand. They hope for a little applause. But even beyond accolades they need us to listen and to register what they say, respond to what we see them do, and make them feel, beyond their own powers to explain themselves, that we know about their triumphs and tribulations, that we understand their hopes and humiliations, that we get it about them.

This experience—of being seen and heard, of feeling understood—is deeply meaningful to human beings at all ages and stages. A parent's gaze transforms a task, an event, or accomplishment, and makes it real, important, and true. Each of my daughters felt this so strongly that, until she saw me watch her go down the slide, until I called, "Yes, you *did* it!" she had not yet, in some important sense, gone down the slide. Put another way, what each of my daughters wanted and needed was not merely an experience of going-down-the-slide. She wanted to have that experience in the memorable context of her daddy's love and pride in her. What she craved, beyond the exhilaration of going down, was the experience of daddy-watching-me-go-down. This witnessed success felt real, fully accomplished, and would be filed away as a defining moment in the brief conjunction of our lives. It would be a sweet collaboration, a triumph of her courage in my watchful presence, a memorable metaphor for our shared sojourn in dappled Eden. Each of my daughters in turn wanted to be transformed from a tremulous-little-girl-a-bit-scared-and-all-alone-at-the-top-of-the-slide into a glowing-little-girl-whose-daddy-was-proud-of-her-because-he-saw-her-go-down.

Teenagers, who are usually more self-conscious than toddlers, can be reluctant to express this need directly. Children may fail to do this at any age, just as a fish sees no need to explain its mortal need for water. So small-fry don't say in so many words, "I need your recognition, Dad, so could you please show up?" Yet children long for this recognition, and rarely fail to signal in some way that it matters that their parents turn up: to admire a finger-painting tacked up on a classroom wall, to hear her sing "The Volga Boat Song" with the choir, to see him dressed up as a Halloween goblin, to listen to her recite the Torah at her Bat Mitzvah, to hear him take the Boy Scout Oath, to see her kick a goal, or to watch him swish a jumper from the top of the key. Children need parents to watch them do homework, to witness wolf badge rites at solemn gatherings of the pack, to admire gold stars on spelling lists, to ooh and aah at blue ribbons won at science fairs.

This is because a parent's presence, her willingness to watch and see, can transform a young person's experience. No doubt this is why attentive parents spend so many hours of their lives hunkered down on cold bleachers or seated in dim auditoriums, watching soccer matches or listening to recitals. It's difficult to overstate the power of parental recognition over a son's or daughter's experience of self. This power endures for a lifetime. And, however diffident they may be, teenagers want and need this, too. This is why they need to find pictures of themselves when young pasted into the family album: swinging a bat, sporting a first bikini, uniformed as a Boy Scout, or dressed up as the belle of the ball. This is why, when a capped-and-gowned son marches into the stadium to "Pomp & Circumstance," or a veiled beauty floats down the aisle to the "Wedding March," we'd better show up. If we still can walk or crawl, even if we have to be carried in, we'd better get there. Why? Because if our relationships retain even a whiff of the old magic, even our grown-up children won't feel they've truly done it unless, out of the corners of their eyes, they see us watching them go down.

Empty Chair

Recognition isn't always a cheerful theme. Not for everyone. Like food, there can be too little of it, and the experience of starving can leave a hunger that lasts a lifetime. Even a relative lack of recognition can be wounding. Years ago, one of my daughters counted the framed photos in our family gallery and, crestfallen, asked: "Why aren't there as many of *me*?" One of my college classmates, a stand-out basketball star when an upper-classman at his high school, never recalls his triumphs without remarking sadly that his parents never came to see him play. Both memories retain equal valence: his pride in having played for the state championship; and his grief, which forty years and the deaths of both parents hadn't assuaged, that they failed to find their way to the bleachers to watch him do it.

Recognition relies upon relationships. This being so, and humans being fallible creatures, recognition sometimes may not happen at all. For all sorts of reasons, parents turn up missing. Whatever the reason or the excuse, however, a lack of affectionate mirroring isn't without consequences. As my once-athletic friend reminds us, the absence of parental recognition can become a sad, perpetual memory, even one of life's recurrent leitmotifs. When parents fail to show up to watch a game or clap for the orchestra or applaud a daughter's solo in *Carousel*, the absence can leave a painful empty place in a young person's recollections, a tender vacuum in an adult's memory, and an ache in an old man's reveries. Surely, any number of explanations or excuses can be made for that empty chair; that seat at the head of the table at Thanksgiving left vacant by a deceased father; that numbered auditorium loge unfilled by a parent too busy presiding over patients in the hospital or doing deals in Dhaka; that unoccupied bleacher which a sick parent no longer had the strength to climb; that small school desk left vacant on parents' night by a dad too drunk or a mom too lazy to rise from the couch. Whatever the explanation, that empty chair left a young person at risk of feeling abandoned and invisible.

Clinical Observations

Does it matter? How necessary is recognition? Is it necessary to life, like air, or merely decorative and pleasant, like frosting on a cake? To answer, we cannot experimentally prevent recognition in selected research subjects, any more than we could ethically choke off oxygen. Yet misfortune provides natural experimentation, whose results may be reported in the news or studied systematically and presented as clinical observation. It turns out that, in the absence of recognition, children suffocate psychologically. So do adults.

Among institutionalized infants, who were provided adequate nutrition and immaculate nursing hygiene but separated from their own mothers and unable to make relationships with busy care-givers, René Spitz (1945) described a progressive profound pathology characterized by weepy withdrawal, weight loss (rather than gain), insomnia, recurrent infections, retarded emotional and intellectual development followed by actual decline, frozen facial expression (a faraway look, as if dazed, not registering what went on around them), and increasing difficulty making human contact. Over time this "anaclitic depression" became more dire and less reversible. If not reconciled with their mothers in three months, these children descended into an ominous condition Spitz called "hospitalism," characterized by motor retardation, complete passivity, vacuous facial expression, defects in eye coordination, spasticity of body motion (which persisted after extensive rehabilitation), and bizarre finger movements similar to decerebrate or athetoid posturing. The first-year mortality rate was thirty percent. It got worse. In children with hospitalism who survived, there was a progressive deterioration in intelligence, so that by the fourth year, Spitz reported, the "average developmental quotient was in the moderately to severely retarded range."[8]

In the same era in which Spitz described anaclitic depression and hospitalism, visitation policies in London's pediatric wards (e.g., no parent visits to toddlers "for the first month") provided another natural experiment that couldn't have been better designed to demonstrate what a lack of adult recognition portends in children. In a series of poignant documentaries filmed on these wards, James Robertson recorded the rapid collapse into anaclitic depression of toddlers separated from their parents for days and weeks. These grim sequences are painful to watch, particularly because the nursing staff make little attempt to rescue these sad children from despair. About his own first film, *A Two-Year-Old Goes to Hospital* (1952), Robertson recalled:

> I was struck by the undercurrent of unhappiness in children in hospital wards. . . . [T]he unhappiness of very young children is so painful that the staffs were turning a very blind eye to it.[9]

A reviewer of a later Robertson documentary, *John* (1969), describes the film's mapping of

> a well-adjusted boy's experiences in a residential nursery while his mother is giving birth to a sibling. Competing with more boisterous children, he struggles to form attachments with besieged nurses. His changing reactions to his father's visits mark his building distress.[10]

Robert Karen described this seventeen-month-old boy's collapse:

> His distress building after the third day, he becomes gradually more isolated and moves about aimlessly. The nurses . . . miss his signals of despair. He seeks comfort from a large teddy bear. . . . On the fourth day a nurse who had comforted him two days earlier returns, but he is no longer interested in her. His crying loses its edge of protest, becoming weak and pitiful. By the time the nurses recognize the seriousness of his condition, it is too late to help, especially since none of them is available for the continuous attachment he needs. By the fourth day he is refusing food, and by the eighth he hasn't eaten for several days.[11]

By the time his mother returns, "John" has curled up in the fetal position under a table. He has had to be force-fed.

It might be argued that this rapid deterioration is simply grief, not a lack of recognition. Certainly Spitz, Robertson, and their eminent colleague, John Bowlby, emphasized the "separation," which interrupted an important "attachment" to particular parents. But Robertson strongly hints at a second relevant factor: a lack of recognition. In the absence of their own parents, these children didn't simply collapse. They first tried to engage Robertson's wife, who sat in as an observer. The boy also "struggle[d] to form attachments with besieged nurses," and, when rebuffed, looked for "comfort from a large teddy bear." These children try frantically to locate substitute sources of consolation.

Karen suggests, as did Robertson, that it mattered greatly that nurses didn't "recognize the seriousness of his condition," because they might have offered needed "help," which Karen describes as "the continuous attachment he needs." That is, even in the absence of those particular parents for whom the children grieved, they might have been helped by an alternative source of affectionate understanding. Robertson urges that medical staff needed to *see* the children, rather than turn "a very blind eye" upon their anguish. What these sad children needed was individual attention, because each child's care was "shared by so many people that no one had a continuous impression." Each child, belonging to all the staff, belonged to none of them. In the institutional setting, no one adult saw a child clearly.

In her wartime nurseries, Anna Freud tested this hypothesis, i.e., that an attentive staff's warm recognition could prevent anaclitic depression, even in the continued absence of a child's own parents. The misfortunes of war brought evacuated children from heavily bombed areas of London to her Hampstead nurseries, where distant parents were welcome to visit at any hour. But some parents couldn't get to Hampstead— and Freud began to recognize in her small, frightened, lonely residents the signs of anaclitic depression and hospitalism:

> [T]he familiar difficulties of traumatized and institutionalized children began to be apparent. . . . [S]ome children showed a delay in their development in terms of wetting and soiling, aggressive behavior and tantrums or emotional withdrawal and self-stimulation (e.g., head banging). . . . [W]hile the physical and intellectual needs of the children were being met, . . it was the emotional needs of the child . . . [that were] unsatisfied.[12]

So Freud and her colleagues provided individual recognition in place of those missing parents. They created "artificial families"—four or five children assigned to a surrogate "mother," who took center stage in the children's emotional lives. Promptly this stand-in mom developed a close relationship with each of her "children." The results were unsubtle and remarkable. A startled Freud wrote that the result seemed "astonishing in its force and immediacy." Each child "quickly [was] able to overcome developmental delays (such as in relation to feeding or sleeping) and developed an emotional 'aliveness' that is so often absent in institutionalized children."[13] Despite the children's persistent grief and nostalgia about their own absent mothers and fathers, and notwithstanding the profound continued impact of the disrupted parental attachment, this experience of affectionate recognition had a remarkable restorative effect.[14]

Solitary Confinement

We may be inclined to think adults don't need recognition, or need it less, inasmuch as some adults choose to be alone, e.g., an anchorite in a desert cave, or Trappist monk self-confined within the sworn silence of a monastery. Yet these examples hint at how voluntary solitude may be so readily endured. Presumably, neither one feels utterly alone or wholly ignored. The monk must feel the presence of and see other monks who, even in that remarkable silence, understand him implicitly. Presumably, the anchorite feels the omnipresence of an Other who knows him perfectly, hears his prayers, grasps his every thought and feeling, and forgives him his trespasses.

But what about an adult whose solitude comes involuntarily, whose isolation from others leaves him to believe that all who cared for him now have given up on him—that the sunlight of recognition has gone into permanent eclipse? Sadly, this experiment has been carried out again and again, most recently in secret CIA prisons, and at the US Naval base at Guantanamo, Cuba. In an essay in *The New Yorker*, Atul Gawande, a Harvard surgeon, describes the sustained absence of recognition, the loss of "social interaction," in the experiences of prisoners subjected to solitary confinement. Citing the reports of military POWs afterward that social isolation was "as torturous and agonizing as any physical abuse they suffered," Gawande adds with some irony that "what happened to them *was* physical."[15] If they had endured a week or more of solitary confinement, American aviators shot down over Vietnam came home with "diffuse slowing of brain waves" in systematic EEG studies, suggestive of tissue injury.[16] Moreover, in studies and reports from POWs, civilian prison inmates, and kidnap victims—all of whom were subjected to solitary confinement—Gawande finds pathologies resulting from this loss of "sustained social interaction" that include: emotional lability, disorientation, deflated mood, chronic fatigue, lost purpose, changed personality, cognitive dulling, and hallucinosis.[17]

Misrecognition

In sum, the loss of recognition is a disaster for infants and small children, and it's profoundly disturbing to grown-ups, too. What about when "recognition" is present, but wildly inaccurate?[18] What happens when others' responsive acts of recognition fail to get it right—when recognition is a malicious insult, rather than a hopeful and kind reflection? What about parental "recognition" that fails to acknowledge that a child is a separate person whose views are entitled to be different from her parents', when she's made to feel she has no right to nourish ambitions not congruent with her parents' dreams?

Surely, there isn't one answer. Some recognition errors are trivial, even comical. On the Broadway stage and in fiction, for example, misrecognition may create slapstick or dramatic irony. In their plays and operas, Shakespeare and Mozart disguise their heroes and heroines to create comedy or bathos when identities are switched or mistaken.[19] In Evelyn Waugh's novel *Brideshead Revisited*, the protagonist, Charles, comes down from Oxford to stay with his father in London, and the skinflint father resists his son's pressure for money. When Charles brings home to dinner an old, vague acquaintance named Jorkins, who is as English as Stilton cheese, his father torments his son by attacking his friend with sardonic misrecognition. As Charles explains:

> My father . . . made a little fantasy for himself, that Jorkins should be an American, and throughout the evening he played a delicate, one-sided parlor-game with him, explaining any peculiarly English terms that occurred in the conversation, translating pounds into dollars, and courteously deferring to

him with such phrases as "Of course, by *your* standards," . . .
so that my guest was left with the vague sense that there was a
misconception somewhere as to his identity. . . ."

The old man starts in on Jorkins immediately:

> "Good evening, good evening. So nice of you to come
> all this way."
> "Oh, it wasn't far," said Jorkins, who lived in Sussex Square.

By the end of an evening of this, Jorkins takes his leave, so dumb-
founded and intensely uncomfortable that he can hardly speak. Even at
parting, Charles' father will not relent:

> "Good night, Mr. Jorkins," he said. "I hope you will pay us
> another visit when you next 'cross the herring pond.'"[20]

Outside the theater or novel, misrecognition is not so funny. When
children subject a child to contemptuous distortions, this hazing can have
darker results: deflated self-esteem, burning resentment, even homicidal
or suicidal rage. When adults have been subjected to contemptuous ste-
reotypes, treated by neighbors as if various ugly slurs were true of them,
solely because of their race or creed—as black citizens were misrecognized in the Jim Crow South, as Jews were reviled by Nazi Brown Shirts,
as Catholics were attacked in Londonderry, or Palestinians in contemporary Jenin—the psychological results are no different. The consequences
can be enduring, violent, or willingly suicidal.

Yet misrecognition can be hard on people even when it isn't
intended or malicious, when it's simply mistaken, a matter of ignorance.
As an example, here's an eloquent letter from an Argentine woman, a
good friend who once lived with our family as an exchange student. Years
later, when she married a Dutch engineer and moved with him to Hol-
land, she wrote this description of her reception:

> I went out to find a job and got slapped. According to job
> agencies all I can do for work is clean a house or ring a cash
> register—that's it! No matter my years of education, all the

languages I speak, or my job experience—I'm not fit! Much as I don't want it to affect me, it does—I'm humiliated. . . .

As an immigrant my biggest problem is this loss of identity, not knowing my place anymore. I used to be the daughter of X, the sister of Y, president of the local AFS chapter, a university student, a volunteer at the hospital—so people knew me, understood what I was doing, got what I was talking about. If I said, 'I'm this, the daughter of my father,' then people knew what to expect from me. Here, I don't have any of that. People don't know me. Even when they read my resume they don't know half of what it refers to, or what it means. So it's hard, because what I already had built—which by the way was very good—is lost. . . . The loss of all that has made me feel very lost. I don't know how to face it. It confuses me.

In a way, this dislocation gives me a new clean sheet. I can be whoever I want. But the security of my old identity is what I find myself missing and wanting, not a new clean sheet. I had no problem with who I was before—why the need to build a new me? And a pinch of prejudice—because I'm Latin American and therefore, apparently, I am uneducated and stupid.[21]

This is the anomie of a fish out of water. Certainly, this wonderful young woman knew that Europeans could be reasonable and affectionate. After all, she'd married one. Yet it was awful for her to discover that her new compatriots didn't get it about her. In the distorted mirror they held up, she could not recognize herself. In that fun-house reflection she felt humiliated, misunderstood, disrespected, slapped down, held in contempt. Clearly, more than her feathers had been ruffled. She felt unhinged, and she suspected she was going a little nuts. She feared a loss of her sense of identity, for she no longer knew her place. This dislocation was not geographical, but emotional. The sustained experience of other people's misrecognition made her feel disoriented, *confused*, and *lost*.

Recognition in Character Development

At all stages of life, recognition fulfills a fundamental human need to be acknowledged, known, seen clearly, understood. Children need parents to recognize them from the first moments, hours, and months of their lives. Whether, and how, their parents address this need will have a powerful shaping influence upon the personalities of children and teenagers and the adults they become. Its absence, or distortions, will have important, durable, pathological consequences.

In normal teenagers, the repeated experience of accurate, optimistic recognition creates the core of adult identity. Children who grow up knowing who they are, where they belong, and where they're going, simply become confident adults who've always been grounded in their lives. Children who grow up confused, lost, invisible, or unrecognized in the eyes of important adults take that empty dysphoria (feelings of discomfort, unhappiness, and worse) into adult life, too. When all goes well, then, the experience of recognition becomes character structure. We say that a teenager, or an adult, has *self-esteem*, by which we mean she can face new challenges confidently, that she will risk trying, because she has grown up and thinks effectively like an adult; but also because she carries those formative experiences of orienting, confidence-building recognition within her—from infancy into the third decade of life. When all goes well, then, a young adult's emergent personality demonstrates a reflexive trust in the world; a confident sense of autonomy; a capacity for vigorous initiative; an ability to work and sustain effort; and the gumption to have ambition. In normal development, in sum, recognition shapes a confident, coherent sense of self.[22]

All does not always go well, of course. Not every child is born with the same neuropsychological equipage, and what I will call "intrinsic" obstacles or "equipment" problems (e.g., autism) can make it difficult or impossible for a developing child or teenager to make developmental use of recognition, even when parenting is available and exemplary. Or again, what I call "extrinsic" family disruptions (e.g., divorce, death of a parent) can distort parental recognition or, over the short or long term, make it unavailable. What happens to a child when his family cannot parent him depends greatly upon luck and upon other adults who inhabit the larger village it takes to raise a child. Yet, beyond the coping resources or economic fortunes of any family or village, large-scale disasters (e.g., flood, famine, pestilence, war) disable whole adult communities, and make effective parenting unavailable across entire communities or regions of the planet. This generational implication—of a disrupted maturation among a society's affected children and teenagers—provides the truly worrisome subtext for much of the world's news.

Although we're here primarily concerned with individual families, it's also true that larger recent social and economic trends have complicated parenting—and put the parental task of recognition into conflict with other adult time-demands, distractions, and goals. Divorce, blending, single parenting, and overseas adoption have changed the shape of the family, making moot any attempt to generalize about a "typical" family and transforming the terms in which recognition must be framed. The economic liberation of women has made two-career families commonplace, if not now financially obligatory, and so we have outsourced beyond the family a good deal of parenting. What does it mean that, in urban and suburban communities, few parents provide communal supervision, as mothers did when I was a child: so that children felt known, and recognized, wherever in the neighborhood they happened to wander and play? And what sort of relationship—and mutual recognition—does a toddler or schoolboy have in front of a television or computer screen?

None of these broad social questions, as yet, has a definitive answer. From the point of view of a teenager and his mom and dad, moreover, these aren't even relevant questions. For here the question is: What can a parent *do*, or do better? And, for a start, the answer is: make time, pay attention, and recognize.

In modern, stressed families, accurate recognition can become unavailable—and struggling teenagers may go un- or misrecognized. Not every father makes the time to recognize his children, or does it very well. Not every mother preserves an emotional boundary between her own motives and needs and a daughter's independent development. In the glare of parental narcissism, a son may never feel that his own ideas, predilections, and passions find an expression that his parents respect—and so feels that he's only his parents' show poodle. Lest we imagine that such problems occur only in other people's families, I must add with humility that even well-meaning, educated parents find it difficult not to inflict this kind of self-alienating influence upon teenagers. Perceptive, affectionate sons and daughters wish to please, to make their parents proud, and, out of love and sometimes far from consciously, try to turn themselves into marionettes for a parental puppet show. Too readily, sometimes quite wrongly, they imagine that this is what their parents want of them.

This situation is tricky for parents, who may be unaware of the power of their own dreams and prejudices. The problem isn't always obvious, for when choosing to please or placate their parents, teenagers and young adults persuade themselves they're making independent choices. Alice Miller[23] described such emotionally gifted, intuitive children who create "false selves" to fit their parents' (perceived) needs and wishes—and so pass a kind of narcissistic pathology from one generation to the next. Why pathology? Why should our children not become what they see we want them to become? Because this fraudulence consigns the adult that a son or daughter will become years later to an unhappy alienation: from academic studies (carried out to please mom); from a career (pursued so as not to disappoint dad); from a spouse (picked to suit a parental conception of the sort of mate one *should* want); and so from himself or herself, inasmuch as it later becomes difficult or impossible to rediscover the thread of a buried curiosity or passion or dream that got abandoned long ago.

In sum, when it comes to parental recognition, the stakes are high. If our children aren't understood, and don't *know* they're understood—that their own predilections and dreams will be of interest and respected—they'll carry this lonely inner emptiness into their adult lives. To please us, despite our distortions, they may live a lie, and the theme of fraudulence will become the leitmotif of their soap operas. Insofar as we matter to them then, our failures to see them clearly can become darkly consequential in their lives.

3   How to Recognize

WHAT DOES it mean to recognize? How is it best done? This chapter will rehearse what I've learned, sometimes the hard way, about how to acknowledge teenagers and make them know they're understood. To begin, I urge that parents make the time and find the occasion to say what needs saying, and then consider how best to say it.

Make Time, Find the Occasion

To a parent who cannot make time to parent, no other advice about parenting can be of any use. I realize that this sounds peremptory. Yet few parents know better than I do how awkward it can be to delay the call of a promising career, put aside a demanding patient, fend off a paying customer, or set aside the work that pays the bills. I'm sympathetic, in short, with those who find this prescription difficult.

Yet if we really cannot make time, perhaps we really ought to hire a nanny to rear our children. And this might be a reasonable alternative, some experts have suggested, so long as (s)he is affectionate and competent and willing to parent our children, and will stick around, without disruption, until they're grown up and ready to leave home.[24] But why bother? Why would anyone want to conceive and give birth to children only to let someone else parent them? And how can we afford a nanny? Very few of us have that kind of ready cash. But if we don't intend to make the time to parent our children, and we cannot provide a long-term nanny to take our place(s), how can we justify their deprivation and suffering? Or justify making our neighbors put up with our incompetent, boorish, selfish, or antisocial offspring? When you think it over, parenting seems like one of those things we ought to do ourselves, beginning to end, and do very well, or not bother to start.

So what does it mean to make time—and how much? My answer would be: enough to recognize them, and set limits for them. We begin with recognition. For this there's a simple metric: the quality of our relationships. About a daughter, we might simply ask: Do I know where she is, what she's doing, and with whom? Is it all right with me? Or again, about a son we might just ask: Am I on his wavelength? Does he know what I think, or care? Does he know me or want time with me? Or, to put it the other way round, has my teenaged son (or daughter) gone incommunicado, or vanished into an alternative world of shadowy friends—i-chat, video games, angry music, or intoxication—so that I'm irrelevant? If so, is this inaccessibility a parody of my own, and how long have we been alienated? How intractable is this estrangement?[25]

Probably every busy parent struggles with this first problem: to find time. If we have once been available but then begin to fail to find time, and if we still matter, then a son or daughter may well try to tell us so, and so recover our attention. This message may be indirect, or take the exasperating form of misbehavior, which may prod us to drop whatever else we're doing, and yet a son or daughter still may not be clearly heard. To recover the relationship we're at risk of losing, we must hear the message. If it's ignored, then young people soon give up and look elsewhere for the recognition they need.[26]

Sometimes a son or daughter's attempt to get her mother or father's attention can be so deft as in retrospect to be funny. During the strenuous first year after we opened a therapeutic school for other parents' troubled teenagers on a remote ranch, I began to neglect my own teenagers. This was no mystery. I was working all hours, arriving at the ranch early in the morning and coming home at midnight. We'd just begun, and so I had to keep my day job. I took no time off, and I forgot what a weekend was. The cell-phone or pager summoned me day and night. I had no time for myself, let alone for anyone outside the perimeter of work.[27] And so one winter morning on my way to the door I kissed a daughter's cheek, and heard her mutter, "Oh, by the way, Dad, I decided not to apply for college."

This stopped me. "You have?"

"Yeah," she said. She saw that I was still thinking about visitors I was scheduled to meet at the ranch house in an hour, and she rolled her eyes. "It's okay, Dad, I know you're too busy to talk."

"You're right," I said, "I don't have time right now. . . ."

She turned away, and I saw that she was weeping.

"You free for dinner tonight?" I tried.

"No, I can't, Dad, not tonight."

"Tomorrow?"

"No, Dad. I have volleyball practice every night. Tomorrow, I'm studying for the chem final with Krista and Bo, so . . . the whole week I'm busy. I really don't have much time for you right now, Dad."

"You don't?"

"I really don't."

This turned out to be true. The scheduling was difficult, because our lives had become so contrary. When I was home, she was gone; when she was home, I was at the ranch. Finally, we found the only solution: breakfast on Sunday mornings, when her friends would be asleep, and the students at the ranch weren't yet demanding my attention.

I ran for my 4x4 and sped down the winding highway. We'd found a time to catch up with one another; but for some reason I felt slapped. Something was bothering me. But in the white silence of a Montana winter it still took half the ride to the ranch to recognize her bitter parody— of me. For a year I'd been saying it to her, and now she said it to me: *I really don't have much time for you right now, Dad.*

Choose the Moment

Effective recognition is well-timed. Arranging this isn't always easy. Unfortunately, we learn about a teenager's admirable behavior or wretched sneakiness at inopportune moments: in a crowd of his friends, at a sibling's birthday party, or when all the adults and adolescents are rushing out the door to other pressing appointments. Whether the task is to recognize or to set limits, adults should try to choose the moment for greatest impact. Sometimes that time may be now. When setting limits, often there's no time like the present. Or again, it may also make sense to acknowledge now, in public, a daughter's constructive contribution. Certainly, there may be no time to wait when a son's misbehavior endangers the family or threatens another person. But it may also be wise, at times, to wait until the time is more ripe, until a teenager is less weary or distracted or overwhelmed, and better able to concentrate upon what an adult has to say.

In particular, parents should determine the concentration of shame. We must ask ourselves: Do we need to humiliate a teenager, or not? Is this the moment for recognition to be heard? Young people don't listen well when they're anxious, grieved, or angry, so it may be best to make our critical remarks privately, to prevent humiliation or make sure we're heard.[28] Proud or tender comments associated with very strong feelings may also best be discussed privately, where they remain intimate, and so special. On the other hand, some affirmations are best delivered noisily, in public, where a crowd may amplify a toast or shout its approbation. There are no easy rules, other than the obvious. Keep private what should remain confidential, and make public what ought to be public. Consider carefully which is which.

Make It Clear: We're in This Together

Ideally, recognition mirrors a trustworthy and affectionate relationship: *us*. It ought to reflect not just what *I*, as a parent, see in *you*, but what *we* mean to one another. When we're on good terms with a teenager, that glass reflects the ways in which we *like*, *admire*, and *love* one another. But ideally we recognize also that we need each other. It's particularly important that teenagers, who still need our parenting, *need* us. There'll be a time, soon enough, when an adult son or daughter no longer needs us much, but insofar as we're still at work on the dual tasks of parenting, trying to create competent young adults, it's important that we both feel that we're in this together.

For this reason, parents ought to insist upon interdependence and not be too quick to cede to teenagers a parent's proper control over the family's resources and parameters of a teenager's life—e.g., the use of a family car, possession of a cell-phone, and the freedom to leave home. For various reasons, parents too often quickly give teenagers carte blanche, often merely on the basis of age, rather than upon a sustained demonstration of consideration and good judgment, or other hallmarks of adolescent maturity. In families in which parents can afford such privileges, teenagers may be given cars and cell-phones whose bills parents routinely pay. In underprivileged families, when parents are stressed (e.g., by poverty or the outsized task of single-parenting), teenagers may simply come and go without permission.

Whatever the reason, such concessions empty parent–teenager relationships of the need for collaboration that's necessary for useful parenting. A parent needs control over family resources and a teenager's degrees of freedom not just to be able to say "No," if necessary, but also to be able to give a meaningful "Yes." To concede a teenager a car, a cell-phone, and permission to come and go at will is to turn a son or daughter prematurely into a roommate, rather than a teenager with parents. To illustrate the difference, consider two brief conversations, which, as it happens, have much the same practical result, albeit they don't at all reflect the same kind of parent–teenager relationship:

(A) *Son*: "Bye, Mom, I'm gone."
      Mom: "Where are you going?" (*the door slams, no reply*)

(B) *Son*: "Mom, may I use the key to your car to go over to
             Chloe's house to study? I swept the garage already.
             It's okay with her mom that I come over, and I'll
             be back by 9 p.m., if that's okay.
      Mom: "Sure, here are my keys."

The first (A) is the announcement of a pseudo-adult who thinks his mother is a roommate, and he's leaving home as he likes and when he likes, and needn't ask. The second (B) is a considerate collaboration between a parent and son whose drill clearly implies that if the request were more complex, involved a risk, if the chores weren't done, or there were any other parental concern or another need for the car, then his mother could ask for clarity and get it, or just say "sorry, no." Yet, even where there was no impediment, the medium of this conversation communicates implicit messages, which begin with: *We're in this together*, but also include: *Our relationship is important to us both*, and *Our collaboration is a pleasure, and I'm glad to say "Yes."*

Speak with (True) Empathy

True empathy is a father's putting himself into a teenager's shoes, imagining what she thinks and feels. True empathy requires a parent recognizing that a son is separate and thinks differently than his mother does, and that a daughter isn't just a stand-in for her dad. This is more difficult than it sounds.

29

I call this mistake *pseudo*-empathy, because it sounds like true empathy, but isn't. Pseudo-empathy is what a four-year-old feels when she says: "My beagle loves cotton candy, too." Pseudo-empathy is what teenagers feel when they discover that a pal likes the same music, and so assume that he feels *just like me* about everything. The logic of this narcissistic *faux* understanding of another person (or creature) takes the form of a fallacious syllogism:

<blockquote>
You like Metallica.
I like Metallica.
So you are (and feel and think just the same as) me.[29]
</blockquote>

Immature teenagers err in this way when they assume that any other teenager with a Mohawk, a skateboard, or a joint must be a soul mate. This illogic may be amusing when it stuffs a pet with cotton candy or creates a gaggle of teenagers all wearing Metallica T-shirts or sporting Mohawks. It's less funny when adults ingratiate themselves with teenagers by claiming some common predicate. The distinction sounds subtle, but in the end it's not. To see that this is so, compare:

(A) I once was a teenager, too—and so, although now I'm an adult and parent, who thinks like an adult, I recall when I thought as you do now—so I get it about how you feel.

(B) Yo, I was a teenager, too (like you), and hey, we all smoked a little dope, right?—so I'm hip. Hey, pass me that joint, will you?

The distinction between pseudo-empathy and true empathy is profound. True empathy doesn't assert that we're the same. Rather, it's an act of imagination, informed by experience, about how the other might feel, even though you're a different person, with different thoughts and feelings. True empathy doesn't require that you think the same thoughts, share the same convictions, or feel the same way (or share a joint).

As teenagers mature, we hope that they become capable of true empathy. We hope a girl may understand friends who aren't like herself; that a boy may imagine what it might be like to be a girl; a Prep can imagine what it might feel like to be a Goth; a brother can understand what he means to his little sister; and that an adolescent may imagine how an adult—a teacher, coach, cop, even a parent—might feel.

Mature adults will be able to mobilize true empathy for adolescent children, then, and so recognize that sons and daughters are separate from themselves, and may well not think or feel about the world the same way.

Recognize You Are Separate—and an Adult

Parental messages, then, include: *We're in this together* and *I understand how you feel,* but *We're not the same,* and *I will see things differently than you do, at times, because I'm an adult.* If an adult loses true empathy, or never mastered this capacity to be separate, then she loses (or never had) the capacity to function as a parent. Childish parents over-identify with teenagers, and so lose the capacity to disagree or to impose constraints. A father of one of my young patients, for example, saw a highway police-man pull in behind one of his sons, who was driving drunk, and got out of his car to argue with the trooper. Other chase cars were called to the scene, and the father was threatened with arrest. Afterward he told his son, "It was all I could do not to clock that SOB." Such a "pal" proved incapable of setting limits for his son (see chapters six to eight), and so was also incapable of helping his son to grow up and take responsibil-ity for his actions. Worse, by siding with a grossly misbehaving son or daughter, a childish parent undermines the constructive limit-setting of teachers, coaches, cops, or other parenting adults.

In a way, this question—as to whether a parent is an adult, and on the side of responsible expectations for teenagers—isn't only a matter for individual families to consider for themselves. It's a political ques-tion, too, for the nation's parents. How closely do we identify with our arrogant teenagers and their self-preoccupied, entitled narcissism? How willing are we to join adults to protect the ideal of a civil society? Whether or not some of us misbehaved in our own youthful years, or defied uni-formed authority in the name of principle, neither our moral transgres-sions nor our past political gestures make a son or daughter's wretched behavior smart, honorable, or legal. Our adolescent moral judgments need not prevent us from thinking like adults now.

Moreover, when we think like adults, separate from our own teen-agers—however much we love them and however empathic we can be about their feelings—we know that we have no right to permit, much less to encourage, a son or daughter's contempt for legitimate authority. If we stay adult, we know we have no business winking at a teenager's mistreatment of other adults.[30] If we hold on to an adult vantage, we'll keep in mind that when a teacher disciplines a son who's disrupted his algebra class, the teacher is prodding him to grow up, and thus our ally in the parental enterprise. We put aside our own past adolescent antipathy for unreasonable authority and recall that *we* are now the adults, and we must firmly support reasonable authority.

So long as we're thinking like adults, then, when a trooper cites a daughter for speeding, we recognize that he's pushing her to grow up, reminding her that reasonable civil rules apply to her. Thinking like adults, we recognize that his stopping her may save her life. This doesn't mean that we don't feel empathy for a teenager's distress when (other) adults confront her misbehavior. Of course she doesn't like it! Yet we must join other reasonable adults in solidarity by insisting that our adolescent children gain control over themselves, accept legitimate rules, and become responsible citizens. To do so, we must remain separate and adult, even while we feel true empathy for an adolescent point of view about the world. If we can do so, we can be loyal and loving parents, but yet provide and support limit-setting that helps teenagers grow up.[31]

We must permit teenagers to become separate, too. I've just argued that, as adults and parents, we should preserve our separateness and not apologize for, or give up, adult feelings and judgments. I've suggested that our capacity to function as parents depends upon this separateness and this unapologetic, mature point of view. Yet we must also recognize a teenager's right to become separate and think differently than we do. They needn't always do it our way. To please us, they needn't always like what we like or hate what we hate; they needn't adopt all of our values; and they shouldn't be bullied into living our dreams. At the other extreme, to recognize them only when they reflect ourselves in a funhouse mirror of pseudo-empathy, to acknowledge them favorably only when they identify with our hopes for them to redeem our own failures, is to urge upon them a false self. This is destructive misrecognition. It's one way that parental narcissism introduces the leitmotif of fraudulence into their lives. It does them harm.[32]

Instead, we need to help our teenaged children separate from us and become themselves. Gradually letting go of the leash occurs in a series of acts of recognition that acknowledge separation and individuation. Parents help children separate by recognizing when they become capable of independent decisions and have a right to make them; by taking those independent decisions seriously; by recognizing that it's already up to a teenager to choose between x and y, and that, soon enough, they may earn the right to choose what to do about z, too. For example, about a particular sexual behavior, x, we may say explicitly to a daughter:

> You know what we think about x. But you have to think x through for yourself. We won't be there when you decide what behavior in yourself you respect and what you don't. You'll have to choose for yourself.[33]

Or again, when a teenaged boy announces he's going to break up with a girlfriend we happen to like, we have to recognize that this is his decision, not our own:

> You sound upset, but decided. Surely, you have to choose for yourself whom to commit to. Having been through this ourselves, you both have our sympathies.

Keep an Adult Style and Sense of Proportion

When we talk with teenagers, our style should be adult: confident, sensible, dignified, realistic, unapologetic about authority, assertive without bullying, good-humored but not silly. Our diction and tone should reflect a grown-up perspective, an adult common sense, self-discipline, and respect for others' feelings and rights. We should treat ourselves with the same respect we want teenagers to show us, and we should never wheedle or beg, never permit teenagers to bully us, never tolerate bald expressions of contempt. Our style should be the medium that conveys an important message: confident grown-ups behave like this.

We should preserve an adult sense of proportion. A teenager's durable self-esteem derives from parental recognition of legitimate accomplishments, not from much ado about nothing. It's a mistake, for instance, to express exaltation when a girl merely acquiesces in a simple request, accomplishes a chore, or only does her duty. It's a fine thing when a boy does his homework, but also expected, not an occasion for swooning. We should be glad he's done it; we may recognize his self-discipline, if that's what's required. But we needn't pretend he's done us a favor by doing his algebra. We should calmly expect teenagers to do their part, never acquiescing in a teenager's demand for a bribe for doing what is expected or for participating graciously in family life. It's nice when a teenager is punctual, and perhaps worth noting if it's a new accomplishment, but it's also a simple courtesy, not a remarkable gift to the world. In sum, proportionate parental expectations create a family culture whose baseline expectations include good manners, cheerful promptness about chores, a courteous diction, and proper gratitude for what has been received. By making too much of small accomplishments, we debase the currency of recognition.

Speak Courteously

Adults should treat teenagers with respect. Even when critical or angry, we ought to make sure our recognition and limit-setting remain courteous. We needn't be ingratiating, or make nice. Yet we also ought not to patronize teenagers or belittle them with contempt or sarcasm. They are young and less mature, it's to be hoped, than we are. This is as it's supposed to be, not an occasion for adult self-congratulation. Because young people identify with us, they're likely, in the end, to become a lot like us. If for no other reason, we're well-advised to follow the golden rule, and *not* do unto our teenagers that which, in future, we'd hate to think they might do to our grandchildren.

That said, we needn't candy-coat what we despise. I needn't yell to describe an ugly act or nasty attitude in unflattering terms. I needn't call a boy a jerk to refer to his jerk behavior, nor call a boy stupid to label his lack of consideration moronic. I use frank adjectives to describe cruel acts or an unseemly discourtesy, but I keep separate the young person in question, who continues to lift my hopes, from that specific misbehavior or rudeness that's provoked my scorn. I preserve this distinction, because I want a boy to make the same distinction between his worthy self and his unseemly actions. I want a girl to feel confident of my affection, even as she learns of my disapproval for her arrogant behavior. I want a boy to register my implacable opposition to his bullying, but not miss my still-current expectation that he'll soon become a compassionate young man.

In this distinction there's an implicit offer: that I'll admire a young person who renounces a wretched attitude and refrains from ignoble acts.

In expressing disquiet or scorn, be careful about irony with young people. Think twice about sarcasm, except with very grown-up teenagers. It's fine to be witty, even funny, if you know how. But interpretation of double-meaning requires cross-contextual (abstract) thinking, which is unavailable to young children and may not be available either to immature teenagers. To them, sarcasm is baffling or worrisome, not amusing. Instead, a still-young teenager may sense adult hostility, or feel offended, but miss the fun. For the same reason, avoid cruel or barbed jokes until you're sure that young people can defend themselves from witty thrusts—and parry.

Be Frank without Lying, Guessing, or Making Nice
A parent's recognition should be tactful, but honest. If we expect teenagers to be frank, we must not lie to them. For instance, it's beyond tactful to admire a daughter's new hair-do (painted half green and half orange) unless you actually do. Nor is it any good fawning over a boy's virtuosity on the violin if he has none, or laughing at a girl's jokes if you find them unfunny. Nor is there any use pretending you're enthralled by ideas that actually bore you. Tact is one thing, fibbing another. To be trusted, we must demonstrate integrity, admit mistakes, accept corrections when we've misunderstood, and apologize gladly when an apology is warranted. On the other hand, there's no need for abject *mea culpas* or groveling reparation when we occasionally err. A mistake requires an apology: once. Try not to go on and on.

For the sake of factual truthfulness, avoid scattershot appreciations and condemnations. Don't accuse a teenager of "always" doing anything. If you exaggerate or fulminate, they'll simply lose faith in your probity. It's better to avoid error, for sons and daughters know when you get it and when you don't. It's a particularly serious mistake to guess wrong about a teenager's motives, for she'll know immediately if, for example, she's shy about expressing herself because she fears you'll misunderstand her experience, and, instead, you construe her silence as an admission of guilt or an "attempt to gain power." When you're wrong, and particularly if you're angrily vehement about it, your accusation isn't recognition, but instead a hostile misrecognition. It will wound, invalidate your perceptiveness, and be experienced as an assault. Moreover, there's no point. No one expects you to be omniscient. You needn't guess or try to read a young person's mind. If you don't know, you can simply ask.

Recognition deals with questions that are too weighty to be addressed in slapdash or phony ways. To have its remarkable impact, recognition about where a son stands, who a daughter has become, or how a teenager fits in must be the truth. The recipient will appreciate tact, but will prefer silence to a lie. No matter what the stage of life, human beings have little use for ingratiation or false reassurance. Some may prefer flattery to candid criticism, but flattery isn't recognition. A falsehood is misrecognition, and the recipient knows the fraud. Surely, we want from our parents love and tact, but not mendacity or pap. We pray to be forgiven our trespasses, not to be lied to about them. We want a compassionate reflection of the truth.

Be Precise

To provide accurate recognition is a tall order, for the truth isn't always obvious or unsubtle. Acts, objects, and words don't have only one meaning. Sometimes a cigar is, and sometimes it's *not*, just a cigar; before we make pronouncements, we'd best know the difference. For example, when a boy brings home a C on a big math test, his C can have a variety of meanings. One mother, who sees her son's long face but accurately perceives his academic diffidence, might offer this precise recognition:

(A) Yes, trigonometry is difficult. But let's not kid ourselves, shall we? Talking on the phone with Jill for two hours every night doesn't constitute the discipline that earns an A. You're old enough to know better and bright enough to do better. In this case, you deserved a C.

Yet another mother, seeing the same long face in a very different son, might with equal precision offer a very different interpretation of the same C on the same math exam:

(B) Yes, I'm sorry, too. Math is difficult for you, and yet you're ashamed about that C. I must tell you, however, that I'm not upset about that C, and I'm not ashamed of you. You did your best. I watched you work at it manfully every night. So yes, it's a C. But you did your best, which is all your father and I expect. Actually, we're proud of you.

Use "I" Statements

As I've suggested, it's generally unwise to tell a teenager what she thinks or feels. If an adult guesses, the risk is a bruising misrecognition. On the other hand, if an angry adult just wants to score an insult—e.g., "You think you're *so* smart!"—then that accusation will do. Certainly, this is an insult, not accurate recognition. In fact, those words offer a deliberate *mis*recognition, which is what makes them insulting. They suggest that a daughter not only thinks she's smart, but that she's mistaken, and is instead kind of stupid. Yet the accusation is also almost certainly untrue. For among all the plausible thoughts a daughter might entertain in the context of an ugly spat with her mother, *I'm so smart!* surely isn't high on the list. If a parent wants to enrage a daughter, however, this jibe will probably accomplish the aim. But to what purpose?

It's also unwise most of the time to instruct a teenager about what to believe or feel. Such pushing—e.g., "Surely you don't believe *that* nonsense!" or, "How could you possibly love *him*!"—only incite ping-pong exchanges: *I do, too!*—You can't!—*Yes, I can!*—No, you can't!—*Yeah? Watch me!* If the goals are recognition and a relationship, then parents would do well to spare their offspring those clever lectures about what they should think or would believe if they had any sense—i.e., if they were you. The whole point of recognition is that a daughter may become separate and different, and might not see it all your way.

So, rather than "You" statements, we'd do well to use "I" statements—even if we think we might be able to guess what a teenager thinks or feels. An "I" statement takes the general form: "When you do (or say) *x*, I feel (or think) *y*."

Without presumption, a mother can safely bring up a son's taunt or nasty comment, assuming she can bring herself to describe to him what he did in a neutral, tactful way. It should be possible to be precise and beyond refutation, for after all, both parties saw or heard *x*. There's little point in disputing whether *x* happened, assuming *x* can be described in a non-provocative way. But the rule is that the one making an "I" statement may describe only her own feelings about *x*. She may not comment about what the other person thought or felt or believed or intended, because she doesn't know for sure.

The "I" statement invites an informative reply, such as: "Well, to tell you the truth, when I did (or said) *x*, I was thinking (or feeling, or intending, or hoping, or meaning) *z*." Or it might take this form: "Well, when I did *x*, you did (or said) *y*, and then I felt *z*." Such reciprocal "I" statements have a chance of starting a discussion, rather than provoking shame, defensive denial, and counter-accusation. Here are a few more examples of "I" statements, which invite emotional exploration, rather than merely angry ripostes:

- "When you shout and slam the door and rush away, I feel sick at heart."
- "When you refuse to speak to me, I feel like I've lost a friend."
- "When you lie to me, even once, I suddenly believe I can never trust you again."
- "When you roll your eyes, I feel like a bug you just stepped on."

Notably, "I" statements aren't only useful in conversations about wretched behavior or hurt feelings. They needn't only embody criticism or introduce a sore subject. They serve just as well to express admiring recognition, and are particularly suited to this task. Inevitably, they express recognition within the relationship, as what *I* notice about *you*. Here are a few examples of "I" statements that support and encourage mature virtues:

- "When you come home with a report card like this, I want to run out on the front lawn and sing an aria."
- "When you treat me with such consideration, I realize I'm living with a gentleman."
- "When you bring home friends like Nora and Sarah, I feel confident that you're on the right track in your social life."
- "When I watch you help your little sister with her homework, I find myself filled with admiration for your patience and kindness."

Find the Constructive Motive

How does an adult talk with a teenager about behavior that's compounded of motives we should discourage and also those we applaud? A boy's rudeness may be witty, for example; a girl's presumptuousness may be an act of loyalty to her brother. A boy's hostility may be the first honest feeling he's expressed since his mother's death; a girl may sneak out after curfew to console a sad friend. Surely it's our goal in recognizing teenagers not only to step on disgraceful behavior but also to support what's constructive and mature. This isn't always so simple. Indignant about the medium, we may miss the message. A flash of our own negative feelings may blind us, and we fail to see that a son's defiance is also an attempt to make up his own mind; that a daughter's stubbornness is also an attempt to stick to her guns and do what she thinks is right. Certainly when I've been angry, I've been capable of saying something unidimensional, such as:

- "You're just a brat, and you're grounded!"
- "How dare you speak to me like that?"
- "If you ever cut class again, you're grounded until you're senile!"

Better to recognize both. Nuanced recognition might better sound like this:

- "You've forgotten your manners, but I don't miss the point—that you've also thought about this and know your own mind."
- "I'm offended by your sarcasm, but maybe I deserve your criticism."
- "Okay, I get it. You wanted not to let your friend down. But your mother and I do not accept the idea that a true friend will ask you to cut class—and we do *not* permit you to cut class. So you must find another way to be loyal."

These bivalent comments may unpack confused, chaotic motives, and so acknowledge that it's fine to think for yourself, or to say what you feel, or be a loyal friend, and yet *not* okay to be rude, to treat parents or teachers with contempt, or cut class. Nor are these nuanced acts of recognition the end of the discussion or a reason to withhold consequences. These interpretations don't preclude sanctions. But leaving limit-setting aside, these complex forms of recognition are better than blanket blame, noisy bluster, or reflexive punishment, when more than one intention can be discerned.[34] They invite a conversation, rather than ending one. They recognize mixed motives, and welcome the dimensions of maturity, even as they call proper attention to churlish, unacceptable behavior.

Use Tact: Recognize from "Above"
We ought to expect mixed intentions. There are good reasons for a child or a teenager's compound motives. For as we parent them, and children and teenagers become socialized, they inevitably become conflicted. This is precisely the point and the goal.

At the start, infants aren't born with manners or altruism. They're neither fastidious, considerate, nor capable of planning. To counter this small animal's messiness, selfishness, gross reflexes, and unseemly urges, parents promote a range of socialized counter-motives: to sleep alone, rather than in mommy and daddy's bed; to eat tidily at the table rather than demand to suck at a breast; to pee and poop in the potty rather than in one's bed or pants; to wait quietly, not scream with impatience. Newborn babies seem to be entirely unconflicted, but by the time they become toddlers, children begin to hear parents (and others) say "No." Soon, if all goes well, when tempted by inner urges or reflexes, toddlers anticipate that parental "No" and restrain themselves. We consider a child's acquiescence in these social demands to be developmental milestones, e.g., sleeping through, weaning, toilet-training.

All through grade-school years and adolescence, various kinds of societal norms—home and school routines, manners, mores, rules, and laws—are set in opposition to a young person's freedom to do or say whatever he wishes, whenever he likes. If this parental limit-setting is successful, then young people take these social constraints into themselves. To live in any society with a reflexive courtesy, children and teenagers need parents (and other adults) to do this—to install these constraints as working parts of their personalities. Whether we call these inner constraints good manners, conscience, super-ego, or values, we mean that a fine person comes to be constrained by inner scruples—and misbehaves only at the cost of feeling anxious, ashamed, or guilty. In short, to become a well-socialized grown-up is to become conflicted: to want (naturally) to be selfish, but also to want (as taught) to be virtuous. Well-reared teenagers at once want to behave well and not to. They feel *both* motives and, most of the time, acquiesce in that inner parental "No."[35]

Conversely, to remain *un*conflicted is to be uncouth. To have no inner constraints is to remain selfish, lack courtesy, or be without consideration or conscience.[36] Without this inner governor, teenagers and adults are held back only by enforced rules or laws. Such people without inner scruples are socio- or psychopaths, whose shameless, remorseless acts horrify us and arouse our contempt and hatred. They cannot happily be allowed to live within a safe, decorous social order, and they themselves live in an unstable equilibrium: restive, frustrated, impatient to have what they want immediately, and limited only by calculations about the risk of getting caught and punished.

In the context of a son or daughter's conflict, then, parents help to develop conscience by recognizing both the animal urge and the inner scruple. To help teenagers become socialized, parents admire them as they develop interpersonal grace and poise. In these acts of recognition, tact helps. We'd do well to acknowledge both impulses, even as we support a boy's attempts to act from "higher" motives by recognizing the virtuous side of his conflict—from "above." When a son returns her dropped $20, a mom might recognize his dilemma from "below" by guessing that he wanted to steal it—but she'll support his civil behavior and developing conscience, if she underlines his integrity instead: "Not every boy resists temptation, and is honest—I'm proud of you!"

The alternative (i.e., recognition from "below") tends to underline the selfish, ugly motive, and invites shame, guilt, and anxiety. You may wish to make it plain that you don't miss that nasty motive, but if that is all a son or daughter ever hears, there's the risk that children identify with that repeatedly reflected self-image as "bad." To recognize from "above" instead tends to integrate the conflict—acknowledging the possibility of a disreputable motive, or even its presence when it's also obvious, but reflecting back a boy's triumph over the dark side.[37]

To illustrate the difference, here are a few paired acts of recognition: the first (A) from above; the second (B) from below:

A: "I appreciated the way you kept your temper."
B: "I was late, and you want to strangle me."

A: "I notice that you're doing your best to be polite."
B: "Your rude contempt is obvious."

A: "You're trying to be loyal to a friend, aren't you?"
B: "You're lying to me!"

A: "You're doing your best to keep your dignity and self-respect."
B: "You're over-sexed teenagers who want to have intercourse right now, right here on the dinner table!"

These dual motives can be even better integrated without the risk of making nice—even while recognizing from "above"—if a parent acknowledges both the presence of the nether motive and yet also emphasizes a teenager's incipient virtue, his wish to stay on the side of the angels. These next sentences integrate both A and B, while yet recognizing (from above) a civil response in the context of an acknowledged conflict:

AB: "I've kept you waiting, and surely I've made you impatient. How good of you to keep your temper."
AB: "You're polite about it, although I think you don't like me very much."
AB: "What a loyal brother you are! I suspect you're lying to protect him."
AB: "I get it that you're a sexy teenager, but I'm impressed that you're struggling to keep your dignity and self-respect."

This being said, sometimes a parent should put aside tact and call ugly bigotry or nasty cruelty by its rude name. Sometimes adults should confront wretched behavior from "below," deliberately making recognition the occasion for shame. After all, conscience is constructed from shame and guilt. Surely, sometimes parents shouldn't protect teenagers from a well-earned dysphoria or humiliation. But *when?* When a young person's arrogant, antisocial, or offensive narcissism persists despite more tactful remonstrance; when a young person's words or deeds are profoundly offensive, and oughtn't to be allowed to stand unanswered; or when a young person's misbehavior threatens the family or school or civil order. At such times it's appropriate and useful to disgrace a young person, intimidate a bully, call shaming attention to despicable sneakiness, and make it clear that "no" means "No" and "right now" means "Right Now."[38] When an act of recognition precedes a stiff consequence, recognition should be blunt, and it may make sense not to try to prevent hurt feelings.

Remember: Relationship, Relationship, Relationship

In recognizing sons and daughters, parents should think of the long pull. Our affectionate recognition creates our close relationships with our children, and sustains them. Honest, tactful, well-timed, hopeful recognition will long be remembered. A considerate remark, even a look or an arm around a shoulder, may live in a son's memory for a lifetime. A letter that makes sense of daughter's anguished experience may sustain her self-respect all of her life.

These acts of recognition lie close to the heart of intimacy. They become durable memories of respect and love. Like saved capital, they accumulate interest over time. Years later, that capital may be needed to console, or set a limit. When an adult son or daughter's life goes badly, to help may take all the capital you've stored in that account.

4 Stage and Theme

So FAR my advice has been limited to diplomacy, to suggestions that might just as well serve an envoy to an exotic nation—whose dress, rituals, diction, and emotional preoccupations differ from our own. Regarding those conversations I've urged parents to make time for, I've talked about the process and the approach, or attitude, but not the content. So let's turn now to content. Recognize *what*? If parental recognition is a reliable mirror, what should be reflected back to a teenager? Mirror *what*?

Part of the answer is: himself (or herself). We recognize teenagers so they can see themselves. Do they need this mirror? Yes. Human beings generally, and adolescents particularly, have difficulty seeing themselves. For all their staring at their own faces and bodies in any available mirror, teenagers are no less blinkered than the rest of us. In their narcissism, they fail to see themselves accurately from "outside," to picture themselves as others see them. They become very interested in this view and worry about it most of the time. Yet they can be startled and wounded by an overheard remark.

What parents usefully do with that reliable mirror, then, is reflect back to a teenager an accurate recognition of herself in the context of others. A parent can hardly help but see the wider social context: a parent–daughter relationship; a son in relation to siblings; or a daughter within the family. A teenager who still first thinks reflexively only of *me* finds instead, in the parental mirror, a portrait of *us*. Why is this important and timely? Because the next milestones in the maturation of normal teenagers include a new consideration for others; an achievement of empathy and separateness; and a social dimension to ethical thinking. All these require a novel perspective: myself in relation to others.[39] Moreover, this social mirroring is particularly useful when development has been disrupted and maturity delayed. For this interpersonal perspective is the most obviously missing dimension in the gross narcissism of relative immaturity.

Put Feelings into Interpersonal Context

So, for a start, parental recognition puts a teenager's thoughts and feelings into a social context. In these examples, a father reflects upon a son's experience. Given that a boy may have important emotional experiences at school, on the playing field, during a music lesson, or while squabbling with his mother, the social context can be far removed (in space and time) from the immediate father–son conversation:

- "You sound like you were very proud when you won the dance contest!"
- "Perhaps you felt left out when your sister took center stage."
- "I gather you were embarrassed when your teacher called on you and it became obvious you hadn't done your homework."

When it is, parents have to rely upon a son's account of feelings and dialogue and tone—the context for his own feelings. But this isn't so when a father's conversation with a son *is* the immediate context: *you* and *me*, right *now*.[40] For example, a father might notice and observe his son's repetitive outbursts of anger and put that feeling into the immediate context of their own shared conversations: "You seem to get angry with me whenever I say 'No.'" Because this is still a bit of a guess, a father might respectfully check to be sure: "Do I have it right—is *that* what upsets you?"

After that, the discussion could go in many possible directions, e.g., about a father's duty to say "No"; about a son's indignation or humiliation; about a boy's sadness on not joining his friends; about a boy's memories of other times when he felt the same anger in class or on the playing field when a teacher or coach said "No"; or about a boy's anger that everyone tells him what to do or not do. Any of these possible conversations could begin with this paternal recognition: of a relationship (*you + I*) and a feeling (*anger*).

Here are a few more parental recognition statements, which describe feelings (or thoughts) that occur in the vivid context of a parent–child relationship.

1a "When you call, like this, to let me know where you are going, I know I can trust you."

1b "After you took $5 out of my purse this week, without asking, I realized that I couldn't trust you, even though I wanted to."

2a "When I have to say 'No' to you, you get red-faced and scream at me."

2b "I realize that you probably want to make your own choices, and I think you don't like me to nag you to do your homework, right?"

3a "When you talk with me about your ambitions and dreams, I feel that I still have a special place in your life."

3b "When you leave your dirty dishes in the sink for me to wash, I realize that you must think I'm just the scullery maid around here, and I get grumpy about your contempt for me."

4a "When you bring home a report card like this one, I admire you."

4b "When I come home after you're already asleep, I imagine you feel that I have let you down, and I feel awful about it."

5a "I watched you mow and sweep this afternoon, and I was proud about the manly work you do. Nice job."

5b "When I saw you push your sister on the swing, I was glad to see what a kind, funny, affectionate brother you've become."

Recognize Developmental Leitmotifs

In pre-adolescent children the predictable sequence of stages seems simple. The struggle to grow up seems to involve but one psychological crisis at a time: *trust, autonomy, initiative, industry,* and *identity*.[41] An infant's cries soon reveal whether he can *trust* his caregivers to provide what he needs or must *mistrust* the world's attentiveness. A toddler struggles out of her helplessness to achieve *autonomy*; she soon discovers how well she can manage independently and experiences *shame* when she fails. The preschool (oedipal) child discovers triangular relationships and encounters rivalry, and so discovers whether *initiative* will win the object of his desire or whether his murderous jealousy only poisons and paralyzes his ambition with guilty *inhibition*. The schoolgirl finds out in the kitchen, in the classroom, and on the playing field, whether her *industry* creates something admirable, or just leaves her, once again, feeling *inferior*.

Reciprocally, the parental task is to orient differently to each stage, to recognize the central theme and attend to an infant's helplessness; a toddler's demand to tie her own shoes; an oedipal boy's wish to have his mommy for himself; and a schoolboy or schoolgirl's drive to master the soccer ball, the fried egg, the 12 times multiplication table, and the spelling list. So long as development isn't disrupted, a parent's recognition needs at each stage to center upon one of these leitmotifs.

This is a useful over-simplification in comparison with the complexity of adolescence. Teenagers make parental recognition more challenging. First, they struggle all over again with all these pre-adolescent themes, and then they add a crisis peculiar to their own developmental stage: *identity*.[42] In the presence of all of these thematic possibilities, it requires a discerning parent to recognize in a daughter's emotional experience the specific theme that has sounded.[43] It's necessary to make the time to listen, as I've suggested, and yet time alone isn't sufficient to this puzzle. To make teenagers feel understood, to be able to understand their experience, we also must be ready to make sense of a teenager's experience in pre-adolescent terms, while simultaneously our teenaged children assemble an initial young-adult identity.[44]

Given this complexity, the risk of misrecognition becomes acute. It's easy to get it wrong. Teenagers struggle again with small-fry themes, but they don't look like small-fry. Given a very grown-up appearance, it can be difficult to discern that a teenager is feeling as helpless as an infant or as clumsy as a schoolboy. They get caught up in complex triangular relationships, as when they were five, but now with greater risks. All the while, they're supposed to master pre-collegiate academic subjects, hit a fastball, drive on the interstate, and log onto Facebook.

Somehow, in the midst of this elaborate game of charades, teenagers must struggle to cobble together a first attempt at an adult identity. They're most successful at doing so when parents and other adults help them by recognizing the outline of this synthesis, letting teenagers know what they recognize. The integration of identity happens, in part, in the minds of parents (and other adults and influential peers), who discern the emerging shape of a young person's identity and hold up a reliable mirror. To help in this way, parents need to have in mind earlier developmental leitmotifs, which recur during this period of adolescence. Various experts have described useful developmental lines or predictable sequences of maturational stages. These needn't all be rehearsed again.[45] Nonetheless, here is a schematic description of one classic sequence of pre-adolescent and adolescent psychosocial crises:

Psycho-Social Crises

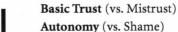

1. Infant   **Basic Trust** (vs. Mistrust)
2. Toddler   **Autonomy** (vs. Shame)
3. Pre-School   **Initiative** (vs. Guilt)
4. Schoolchild   **Industry** (vs. Inferiority)
5. Adolescent   **Identity** (vs. Confusion)

For parents to help teenagers grow up, the trick is to recognize these themes, talk with them usefully but tactfully about these leitmotifs, so as not to patronize adolescents, who tend to bridle when treated like infants or toddlers. To illustrate how these emotional themes may be recognized without references to early childhood, I've provided below mirroring comments in this developmental sequence. They allude to early developmental themes (e.g., trust vs. mistrust), but don't do so in a way that accuses a teenager of childishness.[46] This is the point: to refer to these relevant themes, because they'll resonate with a teenager if they're accurate, but to do so without attacking a young person's self-respect.

This adolescent echo of early childhood themes may seem odd. Why should this happen? Some authors have suggested that the dramatic endocrine transformations of puberty and the striking psychological innovations of adolescence together provoke an emotional renaissance, a reworking of all the old familiar melodies in the new key.[47] Recognition helps accomplish this reworking—a task that may become more clear if we reconsider those childhood themes in the context of a teenager's new experience.

Trust (vs. Mistrust)

This infantile theme becomes a powerful leitmotif again as puberty unsettles what once were secure childhood assumptions. Moreover, teenagers can think differently, and they sort themselves on the basis of concrete predicates into new groups of *us* who, on the basis of these differences, are dubious about trusting *them*. Among these aliens are adults. Moreover, as teenagers feel the urge to pleasure themselves in forbidden ways, they're tempted to sneak around adult prohibitions, lie about where they are, what they're doing, and who they're with. They may conspire against curfews and other lines drawn by adults in the sand, and trust can become a casualty.

Pubescent teenagers also discover a new form of helplessness. They can no longer trust their own bodies, which begin to look different, do what they never used to do, and behave in humiliating, unpredictable ways. A boy is helpless to prevent his voice from cracking in English class just as he must stand up to read Romeo's lines. He cannot prevent a zit from erupting on his nose the night of his first date. A girl no longer recognizes her own silhouette, and this transmogrification provokes a lot of unwanted male scrutiny. She bleeds without warning and, it seems, always in public. Neither gets the dreamed-of body. His is too short, weak, round, or skinny. Hers is so flat she feels invisible or so voluptuous she wants to hide. Heaven forbid that she should just trust her appetite, lest she be led into temptation and delivered into a larger dress size.

Nor can boys or girls trust their social reflexes or rely upon old interpersonal rules, which reliably guided their behavior on the playground. With puberty and junior high come radical changes in mores, new groupings, new inclusions and exclusions, and redefinitions as to who can (and cannot) be trusted. New infatuations, passions, and cliques sweep away old friendships. A boy must figure out anew who'll stand with him; a girl must figure out who will tell, be true, or cheat. Teenagers perennially invent new diction to describe timeless adolescent sins: to "rat," to "dump," to "talk shit."

Yet mistrust alienates adolescents from adults, too. In the 1960s we warned one another not to "trust anyone over thirty." As I recall, adults didn't trust us, either. They learned they couldn't always trust the probity of teenagers, or their sexual restraint. For their part, teenagers grow wary of the guardians of rules, curfews, and prohibitions, and if adults become contemptuous of adolescent nonconformity, teenagers notice adult faults, too. Adolescents discover ideals and, because abstract thought is a recent acquisition, they imagine they invented peace, love, justice, tolerance, and integrity. Compared to these ideals, of course, adults regularly disappoint. Beyond the fenced yards of childhood, teenagers discover injustice and all the iniquities that adults have failed as yet to remedy. When able to think cross-contextually, they discover adult hypocrisy.[48] They see that grown-ups waste limited resources, pollute the planet's water and soil, and refuse to clean up their messes. Teenagers are shocked to discover that evil abides, children starve, women are brutalized with impunity, and one tribe slaughters another. They figure out that adults start wars and then send their sons and daughters to kill and die in them. How odd that adolescents find it difficult to trust adults!

While trust is the leitmotif of infancy, teenagers aren't babies. As parents recognize this old infantile theme, which was an issue at a time of helplessness, they ought not to encourage teenagers to expect all their wishes to be granted, nor permit teenagers to make parents into servants or allow them to expect to make no effort of their own, or demand that adults solve all problems or provide all resources. To baby a teenager is a destructive act of misrecognition, for teenagers aren't infants. To acquiesce in this childish wish that adults take care of all problems is simply to allow a teenager to remain a child.

The proper parental message to a teenager, when the leitmotif is trust, conveys an adult promise to be there, pay attention, and help (insofar as it's really needed). Yet this message needs an adolescent corollary: "You're no longer a baby, and you mustn't expect me to wait upon you, or do for you what you ought to be trying to do for yourself." To illustrate, here are the two parental comments (from above) that touch upon trust (and mistrust):

- "When you call like this, to let me know where you're going, I know I can trust you."
- "After you took $5 out of my purse this week, without asking, I realized that I couldn't trust you, even though I wanted to."

And here are a few more examples of parental recognition centered upon trust:

- "Sure, you're nervous about the race, but I'll be there to cheer you on."
- "Sure, I get it (*on the phone*): you forgot your homework again. I see it here on your desk, where you left it this morning. You need me to bring it to school. But listen carefully. I'll drive back to school and drop it at the office, where you can pick it up. But this is the last time. It's time for this helplessness to stop. You're sixteen years old, and it's time for you to take responsibility for putting your homework in your backpack. Let's agree this is the last time I deliver your homework to school, and the next time *you* take the consequences— and turn it in the next day, marked down as late."
- "Gee, you had to wait for me. Rounds took longer than I thought. Sorry to let you down. I'm here now, though, ready to listen. Let's hear what got you so upset. Maybe we can figure it out together."

Notably, in the second example, an act of recognition ("Yes, I get it, . . . you need me to . . .") has been paired with a set limit ("But it's time . . ."). We'll come back to limit-setting, but here I want to point out that this limit ("This is the last time . . .") is also an act of recognition ("It's time for you to . . . take responsibility . . .") that a sixteen-year-old has no business behaving like an infant and shouldn't expect to continue to be treated as if he were helpless. In the third example, a father acknowledges (recognizes) his daughter's disappointment in him—and accepts it.

Autonomy (vs. Shame)

For toddlers, the struggle for autonomy was a big deal. For teenagers, it is again. Like toddlers, teenagers demand to tie their own shoes, dress their own way, come and go at will, choose when (even whether) to do their homework, and select their own friends. The theme is the same, but we supervise toddlers closely and don't ask them to decide whether or not to play on the highway. Unlike small children, teenagers often decide for themselves what to put on, what to put into or poke through their bodies. They choose lovers and decide what love to make. Puberty makes those choices portentous; modern mobility quickly puts teenagers beyond the reach of adult supervision; and drugs and alcohol are endemic. And so, although the leitmotif is an echo from the toddler stage, teenagers want to make up their own minds and be able to put themselves at risk for a lethal road accident, a rape, a fatal overdose, pregnancy, sexually transmitted diseases, a crime, and, not least, academic failure.

These risks underline the importance of accurate parental recognition about what a teenager is and isn't ready to manage for herself. Some dangers make this parental recognition (and limit-setting) around autonomy a matter of life and death. For those dangers are at issue whenever teenagers push for greater scope to decide for themselves, whenever they ask to have the car keys, to come in an hour later, to go to a party at an unknown location, to set off for the prom in a stranger's car, to hitchhike to San Francisco, or to stay out all night. Parents must recognize in that bid to grow up, in those demands for greater scope to explore or to try or do something novel, young people will always find unknown dangers exciting (if scary). They'll gravitate to risk-taking. But this mustn't mislead parents into thinking, wrongly, that adolescents only wish that adults would say "Yes"—and approve all bids for greater freedom, however premature or hare-brained. It's easy to guess, incorrectly, that young people want no check upon their own autonomy. But they don't, any more than toddlers do. Both are quietly calmed when parents set reasonable boundaries. They're relieved to know that grown-ups are on the job, and to learn where the boundary is.

If toddlers struggle to find out what they can *do*, teenagers struggle over autonomy, in part, to say who they *are*. Their choices must differ from parents' choices, for if not they've not expressed anything unique about themselves. In this way, the toddler's theme (autonomy) shades into the adolescent theme: *identity*. Knowing this, parents may grant teenagers scope to make their own decisions, even if they wouldn't make the same choices themselves—and usefully recognize those legitimate choices teenagers make. The difference may well be the point! If we refuse to grant adolescent children that scope to express themselves, then they may have to take deviancy to an extreme. I saw this, years ago, when walking with my wife past London's Hyde Park Corner. We took a long curious look at a young man in his twenties, who'd dressed in a peculiar fashion: ponytail braided together from hair he'd dyed half green, half orange; a leather jacket festooned with chains and, on the front, painted in white letters: *Fuck You!* Across the back he had painted a red swastika (in London!).

I said to Rosemary: "You know what I'll bet is true about that outfit?"

"I'll bite," she said.

"His mother didn't pick it!"

The proper parental message, when the theme is autonomy, conveys a proud awareness that a son is trying to grow up, that he wants to become sufficiently adult to be allowed to make his own decisions and live his life in his own way. However, to this message, which still would suit a toddler, parents may need to express bluntly an adolescent corollary:

> "You're no longer a little boy, and it isn't enough just to want to make your own choices, or to throw a red-faced tantrum when your parents say 'No.' You must also *be* a young man, and *demonstrate* good judgment repeatedly before we let you drive away in a car or take another parent's daughter on a date or schedule all your own academic tasks. When you behave like a grown-up teenager, we'll carefully let you try making grown-up decisions for yourself, and we will be proud to watch how you conduct your own life in your own way."

The paradigm for recognition (and limit-setting) around the theme of autonomy takes the general form:

> "Sure, when I see that you're ready for *x*, you may try *x*, but not before. When I think you're ready, I'll help you become competent, and I'll be very proud when you can do *x* for yourself."

Put this way, a parent confides a willingness, even impatience, for a teenager to grow up and acquire the greater scope that he wants, too.

Here are two examples of recognition (cited above) that are couched in terms of autonomy. The first is a contextual observation, not at all intended to be flattering:

- "When I have to say 'No' to you, you get red-faced and scream at me."
- "I realize that you probably want to make your own choices,

and I think you don't like me to nag you about your homework—right?"

Here are more examples:

- "I think you'd like to go out tonight, and go whenever you
  like, and not have to ask permission. And you are warning
  me, if I understand you correctly, that you are going to be
  grumpy if I say anything other than 'Yes.'"
- "Sure, I know you are the Daniel Boone of Santa Rosa, and
  you're impatient to learn to drive! But we both will have to
  wait. It's not legal for me to let you behind the wheel until
  you are sixteen and have earned a permit."

When autonomy is the theme, a constructive parental recognition
applauds curiosity, gumption, mastery, and independence. Permission,
when warranted, acknowledges change and growth, for if once he was
helpless, now he's won the right to try. And so we mark and sustain a
child's progress, rewarding maturity with new options, wider choices,
and higher degrees of freedom.

- "You did it!—passed your driver's test! Sure, take a spin to
  visit Peter (but no one else but you can be in the car yet)."
- "I think you're old enough to pick your own trousers, and
  you're the one who has to wear them in public—so choose
  for yourself. Those with the chartreuse stripes? Wow. Well,
  no risk anybody will imagine your mother picked those
  babies!"

When autonomy is the issue, on the other hand, recognition also can be
the prelude to proper limit-setting. Recognition is also implicit whenever
parents rightly say "No." Said another way, accurate recognition isn't just
a reflexive "Yes," never merely making nice. It also must be true—a sound
appraisal that permission is warranted. That permission is only a form
of recognition when it's rightly granted to a son or daughter who's ready,
who's demonstrated good judgment and prudence, and when the risk

is worth taking. Otherwise, it's only adult carelessness—a form of mis-recognition that can only encourage irresponsibility:

> "Yes, dear girl, you're a very grown-up fifteen-year-old. You're smart, witty, and also a knock-out. You do your chores and homework, and I no longer have to ask you twice. So I'm proud of how grown-up you are. But it's just out of the ques-tion—you may not hitchhike to San Jose to attend the Pearl Jam concert!"

Making nice, i.e., giving permission when it isn't warranted, can get teen-agers hurt or killed. A failure to recognize when a son or daughter is *not* ready may injure a neighbor or kill another parent's child. Sometimes, as we'll see again in later chapters, accurate recognition *is* a set limit.

Initiative (vs. Guilt)

The eternal triangle still complicates a teenager's pursuit of the beloved as soon as his initiative pits him against a rival—a three-sided conflict that first complicates the fantasies and strivings of toddlers, but again becomes an adolescent leitmotif. In adolescence, a triangular parent–child alliance can also undermine effective parenting. Children seem to be born knowing how to "split" parents, asking for permission from the other parent (when the first says "No"), or telling one parent something that undermines the other. This gambit is so common parents needn't be shocked when a daughter or son tries it. But inasmuch as splitting under-mines parenting, adults are well-advised, no matter their differences about specific decisions, to deal firmly with these predictable attempts to divide and conquer. The paradigm for parental recognition (and limit-setting) in the context of adolescent splitting takes the general form: "I love you, too, but I won't side with you against your father/mother. We're both your parents, and we both expect you to treat us with an equivalent respect."

The risk of parents getting divided and defeated is greater, of course, when disagreement and bad feelings already have been introduced into a stressed marriage. Daughters and sons are all the more tempted to split fathers from mothers if they've witnessed that discord. This isn't only a trivial or theoretical matter, but a threat to effective parenting. The risk is that parental recognition will be distorted in a bent or twisted marital mirror, and that because parents are at odds, parental limits cannot be set properly or sustained. In modern blended families, teenagers may split a mother or father from a resented step-parent, just as Hamlet did in his mother's bedchamber: "Here is your husband; like a mildew'd ear. . . ."

The disastrous result when parents are divided is a failure of parenting and children who, as a consequence, cannot grow up. To prevent (or remove) this obstacle to maturation, parents must back up one another with their children, keeping sexual and economic squabbling separate from their parenting. This is easier said than done, however. The more strained a marriage, the more implausible it becomes for parents to stick together, support one another's recognition and limit-setting, and protect the other's capacity to participate in these critical tasks. The risk of pathological triangulation, compounded by marital conflict, may be all but inevitable when parents separate and divorce.

Parenting may become a casualty, too, when one parent vanishes, e.g., is disabled by a stroke, stalks out of the family and disappears, gets deployed, or is killed on the highway. Supporting a household and parenting children are weighty burdens even for two healthy parents to carry. When one parent is gone, the remaining parent has to struggle on alone, carrying an outsized burden, which can become an impossible load. A single parent—weary, humiliated, short of cash, lonely or bereft, or all of the above—will be tempted to permit a son or daughter to fill the vacated adult roles: as parent (to younger siblings); as friend and confidante; even as surrogate partner and spouse. Thoughtful and loyal sons and daughters often volunteer to take these roles, and a grateful, stretched single parent may be tempted to acquiesce. Yet for a teenager to become a pseudo-adult is surely to be fatally distracted from her own adolescent developmental tasks, and so this becomes an obstacle to her maturation. Knowing this risk, considerate parents shove teenagers clear of a marital car wreck and, even if divorce or death leaves one parent alone, the survivor tries to prevent a teenager from making this sacrifice.

Among themselves, teenagers become enthralled with the great romance and entangled in triangular relationships. They witness the drama, share the gossip, and as soon as they figure out how, hope to participate in its erotic titillation. As young people compete for relationships, they risk public rejection; they also may harm others who don't deserve to be hurt. In this generation, moreover, the great adolescent romance has become an explicitly sexual drama. Casual "hooking up" risks sexually transmitted diseases and pregnancy. In short, teenagers have much to talk with parents about. Inevitably they have strong, conflicted feelings about these matters.

Whatever a parent's views about sexuality might be, recognition must begin with an understanding that teenagers may have seen and heard about a great deal of explicit sexual behavior among peers, or on the screen, even if they've restrained themselves. An accepting recognition of a teenager's sexual feelings and knowledge shouldn't become an occasion for euphemistic pieties, judgmental lectures, or adult hypocrisy. These will end the discussion, rather than starting one. If we don't know how much a teenager knows or has experienced, it's better to listen, and even ask, rather than opine or preach:

- "I overheard your friends giggling about a pregnant girl at school, but you were kind of quiet. Something you're upset about?"
- "After your last date with Sally, I found this condom in the back seat of my car. Did you drop something?"

When romance isn't yet a subject open to parental discussion, a frank, tolerant, and good-humored willingness to listen and to recognize accurately the feelings that surface, can be the start of a useful conversation.

Industry (vs. Inferiority)

Like younger school children, adolescents are expected to learn, and we expect teenagers to work at acquiring the knowledge and the skills that adults need. We admire industry in teenagers and fear the demoralization that may follow when a young person becomes convinced that when he tries the result is inferior. The paradigm for recognition around this theme takes the general form: "I'm proud of you when you work persistently and hard to learn *x* or create *y*, and what impresses me most is your willingness to stick with it and do your best."

Here are a few examples of what recognition might sound like when a parent addresses a son or daughter around this leitmotif.

57

- "What a splendid effort you all put into the play. We were so proud of your poise on stage, and the acting skills you and your friends demonstrated. Were you pleased, too?"
- "I know what this A in physics cost you, darling. I remember all those Friday nights when you stayed home, how disciplined you've become. This was a whole new level of effort and excellence—and we're proud of you. Did you feel proud of it, too?"

In recognizing the result of a teenager's work and imagination, we must remember that she might not have come to the same conclusion. Nothing is more common than the childish idea that a teenager ought to be able to learn or master or create something the first time she tries, without frustration or long application. So an adult helps make it normal and expected that mastery isn't magic, but rather the result of study and hard work. For this reason, these acts of parental recognition invite a young person's own opinion, rather than merely pronouncing an adult judgment.

No doubt we should support a teenager's industry, but recognition ought not be uncritical. Mindless enthusiasm isn't encouraging, and fatuous praise isn't really praise at all. Tactful honesty is much more valuable to a teenager who wants a true reflection, and much more useful than high-wattage blather. A lack of proportion can be awkward in either direction. There's nothing worse after a game than a parent making his son endure a grim, play-by-play critique, but an unqualified gush of praise falls just about as far off the mark, particularly when a daughter knows full well that her performance wasn't her best. It's accurate to acknowledge (tactfully) when a beginner hasn't yet achieved mastery; it's equally helpful to recognize calmly a teenager's worry about her disappointment in some imperfection that may be put into perspective by a parent's relaxed appraisal. In all these ways, adult recognition helps a young person to endure the anxiety of performance.

Here are some examples of what a parent might say:

- "Some game! But you look glum—you okay about how you played?"
- "I'm very proud of that blue ribbon. You truly earned it—

with discipline, hard work, blood, sweat, and tears. I hope you're as proud of it as I'm proud of you."
- "I'm disappointed in you. I trusted you to mow the lawn before you went out with your friends. I took you at your word that you would, because I couldn't be home in time to check it before you left. So when I came home to find half the lawn un-mowed, the lid left off the garbage can, and the broom not put away, I knew you had *not* done a good job—and that you broke your word to me. Maybe you'd better explain to me how this looked to you. Did you think that was all right?"

All these acts of recognition invite a teenager to say how (s)he saw the same facts. In some cases, the assessments may be blunt; yet they're meant to be the truth. They invite a conversation, even if what will follow (in the third example) could be an unpleasant consequence for an inferior result or for an effort that wasn't wholehearted.

Identity (vs. Confusion)
Finally, we come to the leitmotif that is the psychological theme of adolescence: the elaboration of a coherent sense of self. When it comes to this critical developmental milestone on the cusp of adult life, adult recognition makes a profound and perhaps indispensable contribution. If all goes well, teenagers weave the various childhood themes into whole cloth and create a first synthesis of adult *identity*. If all goes well, this integrated personality provides a solid basis for higher education, the initial stages of a career, and young adult friendship and intimacy. If all does *not* go well, however, the risk is personal incoherence, lack of synthesis, a personality whose center cannot hold together an adult life of work and love. If adolescence goes badly, in this respect, then the risk is *confusion*.[49]

To achieve a sense of identity is both a psychological and a social task: for no teenager can achieve a confident, coherent synthesis alone. Inasmuch as a young person looks outward upon the world, she cannot reliably know how she appears to others without a mirror, and so she must discover the emerging shape of an adult self in others' eyes. To make this complex discovery, she needs a multi-faceted mirror. She needs recognition from smaller children, from friends, and other age-mates.

But adolescents need recognition from valued adults, not only from teenagers. As at no other stage of life, teenagers are attuned to opinions of peers, who observe carefully and judge by implacable standards. Yet much of what other teenagers willingly recognize are self-reflections. Although adolescents ultimately achieve true empathy, as we've seen, much of what they offer is pseudo-empathy, a narcissistic assumption that those who are "like me" think and feel as I do. Teenagers congregate in gaggles of "us," recognizing in other members of the clique, club, gang, or group the concrete predicates (dress, colors, music, pastimes) that link "us." Later, they discover common attitudes that make them realize they share "so much in common."

This being so, a teenager is likely to feel accurately recognized, will feel great about himself and that he knows himself, only if others in his group recognize in him, with warm approbation, what they think admirable about themselves. Adolescent recognition, then, often is pseudo-recognition, and fellow-feeling for those "not like us" (dorks, dweebs, losers, piss-ants, those Goths, or those Preps) can be cruelly lacking. Those who are different are likely to remain *un*recognized (and to feel lost and lonely), or to feel painfully *mis*recognized (disliked and shunned). For this reason, as other teenagers normally mature, troubled immature teenagers gradually seem "different" in just this excruciating way. Thus the social mirroring that teenagers need, if they're to be accepted as they are, may well require adult participation—starting with parents.

Adult recognition is necessary, and accurate parental recognition crucial, even if no longer sufficient. By the time a son or daughter reaches elementary grades, that mirroring audience includes teachers, coaches, scout leaders, and neighbors, as well as age-mates. In adolescence, teen culture itself will powerfully shape a young person's emerging sense of self. The adolescent sense of identity comes together, then, as part of a broad social act of recognition. If a young person finds himself accurately and affectionately reflected in these many mirrors in a way that feels coherent and consistent, and is admired even if he's quirky and unique, then this collective recognition becomes a solid, confident internal self-image: a stable face with which the teenager can meet others; a moral compass at the heart of his own personality.

This talk of "identity" may sound a bit abstract. Yet the search for a recognized sense of self has been so important in all societies that The

Quest holds an important place in all the imaginative arts through the ages. It's the primal drama told in endless variations in many folk tales and fairy stories: a young person departs home, riddles are posed, mysteries pondered, challenges offered and taken, travails endured, beanstalks climbed, glass slippers tried on, journeys taken, cyclops and dragons and goblins eluded or fought to the death, and virtues put to the test. The adolescent quest fascinates us, presumably because it's been our own. So we know that the search concludes, when all goes well, in a return home where the young hero is vindicated and publicly seen to have become adult. In Greek and Roman epics, Ukrainian folk tales, Shakespearean comedies, our own romantic films, the comic or triumphant ending comes when the novice, who departed as a child, is revealed to have come home an adult, a prince now ready for a crown or for a hand in marriage. The boy has wandered the world, a stranger in a strange land, and comes home to be *recognized* as an adult, ready to assume powers and prerogatives and worthy to shoulder an adult responsibility for others.

For parents, then, and for other responsible adults, this act of recognition, which discovers in an adolescent the emerging shape of adult personality, is a crucial social gift given to the next generation. Its blessing takes the general form:

> "We've seen you answer the riddle, slay the dragon, fight the battle, prove your loyalty and fidelity, courage and ingenuity, and we see that, although you've not faced the final adult challenges of your life, you've become an adult, and you're ready for adult roles, work, marriage, and childrearing, ready to take charge of the next generation."

In the modern world the metaphors may be less lofty, and yet an adult's act of recognition has much the same significance to a teenager:

- "Your first date, driving on your own! You look the dashing prince. We're impressed that you've earned your own cash, finished your chores and homework ahead of time, and that we didn't need to remind you. We see that you're becoming a competent young man. So take my car tonight. Here are the keys. And be home by midnight, please."

- "That ponytail looks great, and I like the dress and sandals. I can't wait to watch you march in to receive your law degree. What a smart and competent woman you've become. Your mother and I love the way you put it all together."

A General Approach to Recognition

The subtitles from chapters three and four may serve as the summary of a general parental approach to the adult recognition of teenagers. At this point, they need little further comment.

- *Make Time, Find the Occasion*
- *Choose the Moment*
- *Make It Clear: We're in This Together*
- *Speak with (True) Empathy*
- *Recognize that You're Separate—and an Adult*
- *Keep an Adult Style and Sense of Proportion*
- *Speak Courteously*
- *Be Frank without Lying, Guessing, or Making Nice*
- *Be Precise*
- *Use "I" Statements*
- *Find the Constructive Motive*
- *Use Tact: Recognize from "Above"*
- *Remember: Relationship, Relationship, Relationship*
- *Put Feelings into Interpersonal Context*
- *Recognize Developmental Leitmotifs*

Taken together, this approach to recognition creates affectionate, hopeful, understanding relationships with teenagers. By creating and sustaining relationships, recognition makes limit-setting possible. This is the other parental task—to which we must now turn.

To end this discussion, however, I should clear up one misperception I may have created. In this discussion and in the examples I provided, I might well have left the impression that recognition must be a studied, formal, discursive, portentous, long-winded, and humorless exercise. Nothing could be further from the truth. When all goes well, young people make use of a lifetime's relevant experience, and take seriously much that was added to the mix without any intention of high seriousness. The truth is that as our children grow up and move beyond the perimeter of home, recognition is all around them. It comes at them from all directions as they climb aboard a bus, hang out at a coffee-shop, sit in algebra class, cheer the home team, travel to Brazil, play in a championship game, rise to a debate, attend a party, decorate the gym for the prom, take the SATs, pick up a date or sit home on Saturday night, and take a job or enroll in college. They hear a chorus of offhand, serious, tearful, funny, raucous, loving, or hostile acts of recognition. They're recognized in a thousand small and a few major ways, by grandparents, teachers, neighbors, coaches, pastors, therapists, instructors, cops, and complete strangers. Not least, they're recognized by one another.

The social soup a teenager digests, so as to synthesize an identity, is a rich semantic stew that contains serious judgments, but also accusations, compliments, flirting, and jokes. Much of what matters probably wasn't said on purpose, and may include chance remarks that weren't even intended to be overheard. What sticks in a young person's mind may well include funny stories, jibes, wisecracks, and nicknames, and much that matters will be said with a smirk or snicker, and recalled with laughter. So it makes sense to talk about recognition, to think about its implications, and to do it well rather than badly, albeit not all recognition is planned or rehearsed, or even intended. Yet when all goes well, the absorbed, sorted, and sifted residue creates an adult identity that's strong, coherent, good-humored, and resilient enough to hold together under the weight of the adult responsibilities to come:

- "You're hired."
- "Come for pizza after the game?"
- "You're not going to wear *that* to the prom, are you?"
- "What are you, a brain or something?"
- "No, I don't want to go out with you."
- "Yo, want a beer, dude?"
- "You made the cut, girl—starting goalie!"
- "Sounds like she hurt your feelings."
- "Sorry, can't use you."
- "Nice to meet you—we've heard so much about you."
- "Do you really think that's right to do?"
- "Semester Grade: C."

- "I'm ashamed of you."
- "Billy told me Mike said you had 'great tits.'"
- "How about we pretend we ran out of gas?"
- "Saw you in the yearbook—'Most Likely to make Broadway.' Way cool, dude."
- "Hey, tubby."
- "This is the most original essay from any student in any of my classes: A+."
- "Put your hands on the roof of the car and spread your feet apart!"
- "Nice catch the other night!"
- "You're not practicing enough—you made all the same mistakes last week, too."
- "I think I love you."
- "Are you pissed off?"
- "If your grandfather were alive, he'd be so proud of you."

5 An Invisible Girl: Lisa

I N EARLIER chapters I made a case for the profound role that recognition quietly plays throughout the lives of normal human beings and then concentrated upon parental recognition in the maturation of teenagers. All this may have become a little abstract.

To show its impact upon healthy maturation, I want to present a girl who lost that experience of recognition as she approached adolescence—and then began to flounder as puberty and the greater academic and social challenges of high school complicated her many problems. I met her when her parents enrolled her in the therapeutic ranch school where I practice. Her case demonstrates adult myopia—in her parents and teachers, but also in clinicians, who construed Lisa's troubles in conventional diagnostic terms and tried to medicate her symptoms. In order to demonstrate what so many adults in her life were missing, I will present her case from four vantages: (I) from Lisa's point of view (reconstructed by her therapist); (II) from her parents' vantage; and (III) from the point of view of a psychiatrist, who briefly evaluated her symptoms and provided a formal diagnostic profile and medication prescriptions to match. Finally, I will provide (IV) a coherent, reconstructed developmental history.

I could have presented a less dramatic, less pathological case.[50] Yet to dramatize the importance of oxygen to life it's more convincing to present a case in which air has become unavailable than merely to describe a mild case of asthma. Lisa is a troubled teenager whose unhappiness, deviant behavior, and flailing attempts to compensate for what's missing from her life demonstrate the profound need for parental recognition that every child experiences.

Most children, even teenagers as physically developed and adult in appearance as Lisa, don't usually ask directly for the recognition they need. Yet unrecognized, worried teenagers often dramatize an anguished *lack* of protection or rescue by putting themselves (covertly) into danger, e.g., in suicide gestures or by cutting themselves. These signals are usually indirect, subtle, or even denied. The onus is upon the adults to notice what may be a subtle signal, to see that a misbehaving or sneaky teenager is in trouble without his having to say so. I am reminded of a toddler I once saw stumble into a swimming pool he'd been forbidden to go near. Fortunately, we saw this and ran to the rescue. The ending was a happy one. Yet I've never forgotten the horror of the boy's silence in this mortal danger. When I got to the pool's edge he was just watching me helplessly, his eyes wide with fright, and revolving slowly a foot beneath the surface. Had we not seen him totter across the lawn, headed for trouble, he would have died within sight of his parents. I recall this near miss, of course, because Lisa suffocates in silence from lack of recognition. She gropes for what's missing and flounders ineffectually. She resorts to disreputable substitute solutions and then goes under without ever asking anyone directly for help. By the time the adults in her life see the danger she is in, it's almost too late.[51]

Before presenting her case, perhaps I should point out that I haven't bothered to explain why Lisa's parents weren't available. I've not blamed or judged them, nor do I invite you to do so. How come they were too busy or oblivious to notice her disarray? I could have provided an explanation for this inattention—such as a conflictual divorce, illness or death of a parent, adult character pathology or mental illness, drug or alcohol addiction, distracting careers, psychological parental trauma, or any number of the larger world events that can disrupt parenting (e.g., poverty, war, famine, or natural disaster). Moreover, there are intrinsic obstacles, neuropsychological "equipment" problems, that might exculpate her parents by explaining why Lisa could be relatively impervious to otherwise-satisfactory parenting.[52] I could have framed Lisa's history along any of these explicit lines.

I chose not to do so. Why? Because I want to emphasize that the reason doesn't matter. It doesn't satisfy a daughter's need for recognition to explain that her father or mother had pressing business elsewhere. With some humility I look back upon times when my daughters needed more from me than they got, when I was a busy doctor and unavailable to them. It didn't much matter, I know now, whether my patients needed me or whether I was earning the tuition my daughters would need for college, years later. With similar logic I make no excuses, lame or otherwise, for Lisa's parents. For Lisa, it could not have mattered less whether her parents were in hot pursuit of a cure for AIDS or merely perfecting their suntans on the Côte d'Azur.

I

Lisa spent a humid Friday afternoon with "friends," whose names she hardly knew. The floating cast of characters hanging out in a remote corner of Cedar Hill State Park, near Arlington, Texas, included unemployed vagrants, stoned young addicts, and other school dropouts like herself, who had nothing better to do.

She drifted home to an empty house and sat alone at her desk watching a Hispanic soap-opera with the volume turned down so she could hear the hypnotic tziak-tziak of the cicadas in the trees outside her open window. When she closed her eyes, her lids pulsed to the insect beat. The locusts seemed to be saying something about her, but she couldn't quite make it out. Hot air drifted in through the screen. On her damp breasts she felt the afternoon's greasy fingerprints. She wanted to shower, but lacked the gumption. She had cadged a joint while a guy fondled her, and so she could still float without heft or effort in the chorus of lonely bugs. On a luminous TV screen reflected in the dark glass of her window, antic actors reenacted her paltry afternoon.

"*¡Déjame! Tienes manos sucias.*"

"*¡No!*"

Beside her, a closed notebook and open textbook pretended to be her homework, in case one of her parents climbed the stairs. Only someone not paying attention would fail to notice that the notebook pages were blank. The risk of discovery was minor, however, for her room was situated high above the main floors of the house, constructed as separate quarters for a servant, and her parents rarely climbed to her aerie. They were busy. Her life and their lives seemed not often to converge. Over the years, it had become their habit to wait for her to come down, but her room was so high above the ground that it required its own fire escape to the garden, and so by this means, in recent years, Lisa came and went without passing through the rest of the house.

Beyond her screen, the cicadas drowned out other suburban sounds, even the barking of dogs. In her dreamy state, she recalled a plot she once saw on TV—and imagined that she was the only living creature left on the planet after everyone else had been zapped by a neutron beam.

"¿No sabes donde están?"

"¡No sé! No sé!"

"¡No sabes nada!"

Below her feet, the house was silent, her parents not yet at home. The cocinera had departed a su casa, leaving the usual note: "La cena está en el refrigerador."

Time passed. Lisa's mood shifted. She showered like a somnambulist, soaping herself mechanically again and again. But moments later, back in her desk chair in jeans and a clean black T-shirt, she couldn't recall how she'd gotten there. Had she taken a shower? She felt unreal. Yet this wasn't new. She knew how to come out of it. She fished from her purse a brown half apple she kept in a baggie, and, as in a dream, she removed a razor blade embedded in its pulpy flesh and watched its edge bite into her forearm. In the bright light of her Mother Goose lamp, she saw blood seep from a new line she cut in parallel to others, already scabbed or healed white. She felt relieved by this dramatization of her solitary distress. She didn't mind the dull ache, which was better than nothing, better than emptiness. Unhurried, she mopped the blood with tissues she wadded into her wastebasket.

Startled when her bedroom door opened, she palmed her cut arm.

"Lisa?" Her mother came behind her and put a hand on her shoulder. "I just stopped in to say goodnight."

"Hi, Mom." Lisa closed her eyes with pleasure and anger. She wanted to say something to keep her, and she pictured her mother reclining among her teddy bears while she confided about not going to school, about not having any friends, about fingerprints washed down the drain. But no words came. The cicadas kept scrambling the words she tried to line up in sequence.

Her mother kissed her face and touched Lisa's open textbook, "All done?"

"I did it in study hall," she muttered, thinking for an excited moment that her mother was going to catch her.

But her mother's hand didn't open the blank notebook. "Good for you," she said wearily. "Well, I'm all in, goodnight."

The door softly closed.

Lisa tried to recall the descending footfalls. Had she imagined her mother's visit? She opened and closed her notebook, stumbled to the bathroom for a Band-Aid, and kicked over the wastebasket, spilling red-stained tissues across the carpet. It crossed her mind that her mother had nearly tripped over that basket.

She dozed in her chair. Near midnight she awoke to a jaunty "Cucaracha"—her cell ring-tone to announce a text: "prty in GP, u wnt 2 cum?"

The guy. Must be him, the guy who talked about a party in Grand Prairie. He'd said that they could maybe hitch together, inasmuch as he had no car and she no license. Alert now—something to do—she texted back: "now? whr 2 meet?"

It took only a minute to strap on her sandals, and another to climb out her window and down the fire escape.

Hours later, Lisa came awake, unsure where she was. Her head throbbed, she felt sore. She was lying on a mattress in a dark room beside a snoring hulk she didn't recognize. There was a wet smear between her legs. She felt an urge to flee, but saw that she was naked. She paused, her heart beating in her mouth, to fish around for her T-shirt and jeans. With her sandals and handbag in her hands, she ran down a flight of stairs she couldn't recall having climbed, stepped over comatose figures strewn across a shag carpet, made it out the front door, and ran for it. On a curb under a street lamp she strapped on her sandals, tried to call a taxi—and so discovered her cell-phone was no longer in her purse. Her wallet was there, but the cash was gone. Lost, knowing only that she must be somewhere in Grand Prairie, she got up and started walking toward the distant roar of the interstate.

It took her an hour to reach an interchange where she might hitch a ride. Blisters bulged under her toes, but she kept going, animated by her urge to shower. Limping up the on-ramp to Interstate 20, she felt dizzy, thick-headed. She'd recall later that she thought, as the big rigs rushed by, that she now ought to turn and put out her thumb. But she didn't. She felt too woozy from pills and smoke, too bone-tired. Panting, she trudged up the on-ramp toward the huge ribbon of concrete, toward the streams of red taillights and white headlights, toward the roar of radial tires and hurtling steel. She never saw it coming.

∾

Lisa recovered from her injuries slowly. When Lisa agreed that she was ready, her parents re-enrolled her in high school. They tried to monitor her and coax her into a systematic academic routine. She said she was trying. Yet even before she dispensed with her crutches, she'd already fallen far behind in her homework, and failed all of her mid-term exams.

One morning, after she'd gone to school, her parents climbed the stairs to her room and smelled the unmistakable stench of marijuana. Alarmed, and then angry, they searched her room, read her diary, found her drugs under her mattress, and fished out a soiled pair of male underpants from under her bed.

Enough: Without telling Lisa, they consulted an experienced educational consultant, who recommended a wilderness program and, because they feared she'd run away, an escort.[53]

While Lisa was in the field for eight weeks, her parents toured therapeutic boarding schools the consultant recommended. They confided that they'd been humiliated to learn of Lisa's promiscuous, sneaky, secret life, which they hadn't suspected. In their application for a place for their daughter, they described her misbehaviors and academic and social difficulties.

II

Ever since Lisa turned sixteen, a year ago, she became depressed. We saw this. We got her a psychiatrist, who prescribed pills that Lisa didn't want to take, and wanted her to come to his office for cognitive-behavioral therapy to change her attitude and the way she was thinking. We thought we talked her into trying the medications, but pretty soon she balked, and she refused to go back to see him, because "none of it helps." Unfortunately, we had to agree. With the pills maybe she could concentrate a little better, and maybe she was a little less depressed. But soon after she started the medications and the CBT, she also started to engage in dangerous behaviors and dropped out of school.[54]

In the meantime, Lisa hid her risky behaviors from us. We didn't know about them. Until she got hurt, we didn't guess how much trouble she was getting into. There's an awful joke in all of this, because at that time, when she was really at risk, we weren't worried, and we slept well. Now that she nearly died on the highway, we *do* know where she is, and we know she's safe. But now we cannot sleep. We keep waking in the night to see it coming. We watch it happen, over and over again, in our nightmares. If she were here at home, we'd be afraid to let her out of our sight. Yet we cannot just put our own lives and responsibilities on hold to be with her, quite literally, every minute of the day and night.

Accident. Three months ago while hitch-hiking in the middle of the night, Lisa was hit by a hit-and-run vehicle, maybe a drunk driver. The impact broke an arm and a leg, and she had internal bleeding. She suffered a skull fracture and concussion, and she was unconscious for two days. She cannot recall what happened the day before, or so she says (we're less trusting now, and less gullible). We've had to become detectives, talking to teachers, interviewing grade-school friends, talking to classmates, to learn about our daughter's secret life.

The surgeons keep reminding us how lucky we are. It could have been the end of her. We're so upset with ourselves we can hardly speak of this. We're so grateful her brain is okay—that she woke up pretty much herself, that her spine is intact, and that the scars will heal.

School. While she was still in a fog, after the accident, we talked to her guidance counselor and checked her attendance. She'd stopped going to class last January. Who knew? In the morning, we'd drop her off at the front door, and she just ran out the back. Why? She says she'd decided she could learn "all she needed to know" in Trinity Park. There, the police tell us, she hung around with homeless adults, whose lean-tos and tatty tents are pitched in the trees along the river; and other dropouts, who all use drugs. So Lisa was using them, too, as we now know. An officer traced her to all-night parties in Dallas and Grand Prairie, where he said there was heavy use of drugs and alcohol, busy bedrooms, and no supervising parents. We're now pretty sure she often sneaked out of our home to attend these parties until the wee hours of the morning. We believe she was trying to hitchhike home when she was nearly killed.

Drugs. After the accident, we read her notes and her diary—something we'd never done, because we were respectful of her privacy (gosh, how naïve we were!). Under her mattress we found a freezer baggie with pills the police call "downers," and there were a few of the Ritalin pills her psychiatrist had prescribed.

Run-Away Plan. In her room we found a few notes from a young man we never heard of, who wrote a lot of raunchy stuff about what he'd done and wanted to do to our daughter. He suggested they run away to New Orleans to "live on the street." She told us he was "just a guy." But he sounded serious. He mentioned it was *her* idea to make money by playing the harmonica (him) and singing (her) in the subway, which was how they thought they'd pay for food, clothes, and shelter. Neither has a skill. So they would have starved. Then, who knows? Sell sex?

We cringe to think about this "plan." Beyond sticking out a thumb, there *was* no plan. Clearly, they don't even know there's no subway in New Orleans. We wake up in the night in a sweat about this, too, thinking what might have happened if they'd hitchhiked away. We might never have seen Lisa again.

Diary. Lisa left her diary unlocked under her lamp, as if for us to read it. After the accident, we did. We were shocked at all the very unhappy things she said, and about wishing to find "another way out," so she could "end it all." She never said anything like this to us. She didn't look to us like a young person contemplating suicide.

Low Self-Esteem. Clearly she felt down. On reflection, we think her biggest problem, over the years, might be low self-esteem. We think this might have started with her learning differences. She always hid her faults. She must've been ashamed. She didn't ask teachers for help. So presumably this was why she didn't like going to school. Yet again, she camouflaged her depression, if that was what it was, under a seemingly cheerful demeanor. At home, we often thought she just looked like a shy, pretty girl who was happy to stay home doing her homework and listening to her music. As to that, we've listened to some of her CDs, recently. Wow! All that ugly talk about cutting yourself, about how life is hopeless, about suicide! That music was a downer, too.

Manipulation. Lisa can persuade you that black is white. She can make it sound logical for her to cut classes, because she "doesn't need to know that stuff." When she got caught smoking pot last year, she made it sound perfectly innocent, a one-time try-it thing, and assured us she'd never purchased drugs for herself or carried them around—as if this were a critical distinction. She was so convincing. This was "just something kids do." She insisted a "friend" had just given her half a joint to try. So, she sure fooled us. She lied to us, again and again. It's worrisome to us how good a liar she is, how convincing she can be, how lacking in remorse. Of course, her grade school friends knew, and were no longer willing to hang around with her. They tell us that she's been smoking marijuana and using pills *for years!*

Values. As we've found out all the ways Lisa has been disobedient, has ignored our rules or thrown aside our values, we've become very upset with her. More than this anger that we feel, however, we wonder who this girl really is, who's lived with us all these years? We used to think we knew.

Who Knew?

This intelligent, affectionate parental account has the distanced objectivity of an observer who doesn't know Lisa very well. This isn't recognition. Even after all of their detective work, Lisa's parents have no idea what has caused their daughter's nearly lethal troubles—a congenital learning difference? A psychiatric disorder? A subversive boyfriend? Low self-esteem? Personal sneakiness? Lack of moral values? They suffer over their own blindness, their naïveté, their failure to protect. It has dawned upon them that those paltry artifacts under Lisa's mattress and those confidences in her diaries could easily have surfaced only after none of them would ever matter. They have only just registered what they didn't know. They haven't yet guessed that their own obliviousness will rank high among the sources of their daughter's unhappiness.

It's commonplace for teenagers to elude parental supervision for brief interludes. The opportunities for American teenagers to slip through parents' fingers, to find ready access to drugs and other forms of serious trouble, are but one aspect of a mobile urban and suburban culture. It's also common for parents both to be busy and distracted, and to lose track, and then catch on, often just in time. The timely discovery that a teenager has managed to fly under the family radar may simply provide the occasion for parents to step in firmly, set limits, and reset the radar, as part of normal childrearing.

When, as in Lisa's case, a teenager has been whisked away from danger to a wilderness program, matters usually have gotten far out of hand and cannot be put right without a dramatic intervention. Parents mark this theme, as Lisa's parents did, with exclamations of "shock" after they learn about a son or daughter's lying, evasions, thefts, and betrayals of family relationships. In these circumstances, anguished mothers and angry fathers have to revise their own recollections, rescind the trust they had too lightly granted, and swallow the news of unsuspected drug use, promiscuity, or debauchery. This shock has become so familiar that now, whenever I hear this leitmotif, I prepare myself to hear a young person's experience of not being seen. And so I knew, weeks before Lisa arrived at the ranch, that in her own time she'd explain how she'd become *invisible* to the adults in her life, and how *lost* she'd felt.[55]

III

For teenagers struggling with a profound immaturity, a conventional outpatient treatment failure is not uncommon. Quite properly, worried parents almost always try an outpatient approach before deciding, if these attempts fail, to send a troubled teenager to a wilderness program or therapeutic school.

Prior to her roadside accident, Lisa's parents noticed her grumpiness and collapsed mood. They dragged her to visit a Dallas psychiatrist for a consultation. They explained to him that the onset of her unhappiness seemed to coincide with a sixteenth birthday party they'd given her as a present—a lavish celebration to which they'd encouraged her to invite all her friends. Only a few taciturn teenagers arrived, and they all left early. Lisa's parents felt badly about this. Lisa looked deflated, and they wondered, in retrospect, whether this had been the onset of her "low self-esteem."

The psychiatrist listened to their accounts of her symptoms and recent events. He spent an hour with Lisa. After this interview, he announced that she suffered from several DSM-IV "disorders," which explained her symptoms and unhappiness:

- Oppositional-Defiant Disorder (313.81)
  Dysthymic Disorder [chronic low-grade depression] (300.4)
  Attention Deficit Hyperactivity Disorder [ADHD] (314.00)
  Cannabis Abuse (305.20)
- No Diagnosis
- Acne Vulgaris

His logic is not hard to infer.[56] He clustered Lisa's symptoms and misbehaviors into diagnostic syndromes. He subsumed her sneaky behavior under the "oppositional-defiant" rubric. He ruled that daily marijuana smoking met criteria for "substance abuse." He inferred from her truancy and lack of interest in school, as well as her history of early school difficulties, that she probably suffered from defective "attention." In short, he repackaged her symptoms and misbehaviors under these clinical labels.

Yet this assignment of her symptoms didn't alter their nature or lead to an effective remedy. Her troubles were still just descriptive symptoms or signs, behaviors she'd confessed to or misbehaviors her parents reported. The psychiatrist fit them into official syndromes, but couldn't explain them. There were no known *causes* for her troubles. The profile simply rehearsed a firm grasp of what had already become obvious: Lisa was oppositional, she didn't pay attention in class, she smoked cannabis if she could get her hands on it, and she looked unhappy. By giving her symptoms these labels, however, the psychiatrist dignified them, as if these clusters of symptoms, or the very word "disorder," transformed them into clinical entities whose mechanisms were well-defined and whose remedies were well-understood.

Treatment in this case simply meant a prescription for pills that in controlled studies relieved those symptoms somewhat more successfully than sugar-pills did.[57] Accordingly, the psychiatrist prescribed for Lisa an "anti-depressant," hoping it might lift her mood (and so "treat" her Dysthymic Disorder by relieving the symptom by which Dysthymic Disorder is defined). He prescribed a stimulant to relieve her inattention (and so to "treat" her ADHD by relieving the symptom by which ADHD is defined). There was nothing illogical about this approach to symptom relief. Yet in Lisa's case it didn't help. Perhaps if she'd taken it as prescribed, Ritalin might have improved her focus in school. But this could have remedied Lisa's truancy only if the psychiatrist also had a pill to transport her to school and handcuff her to her desk. Similarly, Prozac might have lifted her mood, albeit in this brief trial no one noticed a difference. Even her parents had to agree with Lisa that, relative to the debacle that her life had become, symptom relief wasn't going to be sufficient. In the event, these prescriptions of pills and outpatient "cognitive" therapy with which, in any case, she soon would refuse to cooperate, did not suffice.

What had broken down for Lisa was adolescent development itself. She was failing across the board at all the tasks of adolescence: at school, at home, and socially among her peers. This global failure couldn't be relieved at the synapse. In the state park, at the mall, in unsupervised homes to which Lisa had begun to find her way in the night, there was nothing going on that she cared for a stimulant to bring into sharper focus. In any case, she'd begun to try her own *ad hoc* pharmacological trials. Although she might have welcomed a lift in mood, there was no way that an antidepressant, in the absence of a profound intervention in the rest of her life, would alter her downhill course. Uncooperative as she was, Lisa was right when she told her parents that these attempts at symptom relief were not the help she needed.

A Developmental History

An empathic developmental history isn't an arcane construct. It's the sort of chronology that a traditional therapist reconstructs at the start of psychotherapy. A developmental history is, in effect, a *parental* grasp of a son or daughter's upbringing. Therapists and pediatricians retrieve the detailed sequence from parents (usually there's no other source), which is to say that this information is already available to parents. To recognize their own children in this way, mothers and fathers need only a close relationship, an empathic capacity to imagine the world from a young person's point of view, and an understanding of child development.

IV

Lisa was born to busy parents who put aside their other preoccupations long enough for her conception and delivery. Lisa's mother was warmly attentive in Lisa's first weeks of life, but soon had to put her daughter into the hands of housekeepers. When Lisa was four weeks old, Raquel joined the family, telling Lisa's mother that she needed work for at least a year before she'd return to her own *hijas*, whom she'd been forced by economic circumstances to leave with their *abuela y abuelo*, so as to send home the *remesas* the larger family needed. Raquel started out doing the laundry and cooking and cleaning, to free up Lisa's mother to nurse and rest. But when Lisa's mother got busy again, Raquel stepped in to care for *la gringa pequeña*. Nothing more was said about Raquel's plan to go back to Mexico.

So, it was in the company of Raquel and her smiling *primos*, who were soon doing the household gardening and repairs, that Lisa rolled over, crawled, and then got to her feet. Her mother was pleased and relieved that Lisa's first word was "ma-ma," but her second word was "*leche*." Soon she was calling for "Raquelita," who appeared beside her crib in the middle of the night. When she learned to eat solids, Raquel held her *cuchara* and coaxed her to try *las zanahorias y los frijoles*. From Raquel's *mano* Lisa first experienced *enchiladas con pollo*. When she crawled across a manicured lawn, *tío*-Pepe called from a flowerbed or ladder, "*Hola chica*." And when she was ready to let go, Lisa tottered across the kitchen, laughing with pleasure, to stagger into Raquelita's embrace. When she was older, and could mount *las escaleras*, she climbed to Raquel's *habitación*, high above the laundry, and often slept in Raquel's narrow *camita*.

Lisa's schoolgirl years passed without major incident in this quiet, cheerful, bilingual household—in which her parents became, so to speak, visiting VIPs. Lisa spoke English at school and *español* with the servants at her house. Playing on the floor while Raquel prepared meals or ironed shirts, Lisa learned to *comprender y parlar* while Raquel conjured another world, no more real to Lisa than Oz, where Raquel once lived *con sus padres, que sono muy agradables, y sus dos hijas, que tienen ocho y diez años, "como tú," y sus abuelos,* who cared for Raquel's daughters in a village outside Leon. As a toddler, Lisa had no concept of *remesas* or any way to understand why Raquel might have children in a strange other place she couldn't visit. Yet she sensed Raquel's anguish in her embrace, puzzled by the timbre of Raquel's voice when she called Lisa *"mi otra hija."*

By early grade school, Lisa took Raquel's perpetual tenure for granted, inasmuch as Raquel had simply become the woman who cooked while Lisa did handwriting and spelling assignments on the kitchen table; who nodded and smiled when Lisa brought home gold stars on her spelling tests. Raquel presided over a kitchen and backyard in which the neighborhood kids came over to play. At evening, Raquel put dinner on the table and put Lisa to bed, telling her stories about good little girls who obeyed their *mamacitas* and never forgot to say their prayers.

There was no transition, no anticipation, no goodbye: Raquel simply vanished. Years later, Lisa would only recall that she came home after school to an empty house and lay curled up at the top of the stairs outside Raquel's high bedroom. No doubt this memory was faulty, oversimplified, a reconstructed dramatization of her grief. For there must have been neighbors involved and a call to her mother, who didn't remember that abject scene outside the maid's quarters on the night Raquel was arrested, along with her two cousins, in a Department of Homeland Security raid at a friend's Mexican restaurant, and promptly deported. Her mother did recall, however, that in the year after Raquel's arrest Lisa frequently wet her bed. In the night, she called for "Raquelita." And years later, when Lisa walked in her sleep in the night, her mother would find her in the morning at the top of the stairs, curled up in a ball outside the door to the maid's bedroom. After Raquel's departure, a medley of maids and gardeners swam the Rio Grande to clean, garden, and cook, but they remained shadowy figures in Lisa's memory of the last of her childhood years. She never again let herself care very much about any of them.

Her parents became more central to her emotional life. Sometimes, in the years after Raquel disappeared, Lisa awoke from a nightmare in her mother's embrace. Of course, her mother sometimes wasn't there when she woke alone, screaming. So, even after she became a teenager, Lisa kept under her pillow a tattered consolation: a silk scarf that faintly preserved the fragrance of her mother's perfume. Lisa was thrilled by her father's avid interest, when he came home. When she was little, he'd crawled with her on the rug. Tirelessly he held out a finger for her to toddle across the living room to grasp. He threw a ball with her, when he had time, and from his travels he always brought her a stuffed animal—a lion, a beagle, a giraffe, a bear, a panda, a puffin, an elephant—until, over the years, her daddy stand-ins became an enormous heap on her bed.

To her teachers, Lisa seemed young and fragile. They noticed when she reached sixth grade that Lisa had trouble sitting still and made slow progress in reading. Her teacher sent a note home about Lisa's "squirminess," her primitive handwriting, her reversed E's, F's, b's, and d's, and suggested that her parents sit her down to nightly drills. Lisa's mother took her to a psychologist, whose tests revealed good intelligence but an idiosyncratic spread between Performance and Verbal sub-scores on the IQ tests. She stumbled with confusion when she had to read in front of the class, hearing other students snickering, and she became very self-conscious when called upon. When her mother reported Lisa's squirminess and difficulty working at her desk at school, her pediatrician prescribed Ritalin. However, what her mother called her "learning difference" continued. Lisa was so embarrassed by the stigma that she often "forgot" to go to the nurse for her pill, and so this medication trial never fully confirmed or disconfirmed her need for it.

To her middle school teachers, Lisa looked withdrawn and anxious, a quiet pretty girl who kept her own counsel and hung back from social encounters and school activities. Her classmates began to figure out how to flirt, but Lisa seemed awkward. She was ashamed to tell her parents that she didn't have any friends, that she often sat alone in the cafeteria, and that she'd come to the conclusion she must be stupid. When she came home, she was often grumpy. The servants braced themselves for her homecomings after she started seventh grade. Her outbursts were provoked by small frustrations—when she didn't find her favorite group on MTV, or when her favorite snack wasn't stocked in the refrigerator. On days when there were exams at school, Lisa began to have bellyaches, and, if her parents were away, she stayed home to watch television in her bedroom. Repeated visits to the pediatrician produced a variety of workups, but no effective remedy.

Lisa was so lonely in eighth grade that she rushed to make a bosom pal out of every new arrival in her class. She attached herself by offering sympathy about coming to a new school, offering to help open a locker, find a classroom, or choose the right bus. In these sudden crushes Lisa felt suddenly happy to be of use to another person, to be known and needed. But after a brief honeymoon of phone calls, passed notes, and whispered confidences, the new girl found less clingy friends and pulled away. Soon the ex-friend was giggling (about Lisa?) with popular girls, and Lisa was alone again, crushed. She holed up in her bedroom when she came home, so ashamed that she pretended in front of the cocinera that she was talking and laughing with her lost friend on her dead cell-phone.

This excruciating loneliness continued in ninth grade. Lisa's parents moved to Arlington, half way between Forth Worth and Dallas, where Lisa knew no one. In the new cafeteria in her first weeks she often sat alone. She tried to reinvent herself as a Prep, but she could never say or do the right thing. She overheard a popular girl laughing about how "fake" she was. She began to smoke, because the students who walked out at lunchtime to smoke at the culvert that marked the campus edge were fine about her joining them. None of the girls asked much of her, so long as she wore mascara, dressed in black, and listened to Marilyn Manson, and so met the minimum requirements. Listening to their sardonic mutterings about experiences with guys, Lisa pictured the acts they described. At home, she became aroused by young men gyrating on MTV, and in front of her bedroom mirror she practiced the vacant stare, hip gyrations, and the way the dancers flung their hair on the screen. She suffered, too, not liking her pug nose, thinking that her legs were too short. Yet she couldn't miss the way boys stared at her breasts rather than looking into her face, and although they became glassy-eyed and incoherent, Lisa craved even this peculiar attention. She began to wear revealing blouses, excited by the results of these experiments when senior boys asked for her phone number. She sensed a solution to her problems.

On occasion, however, these successes worried adults. A teacher sent her to the office for violating the dress code. As she waited for the vice-principal's sanction, Lisa met a senior boy who was about to be expelled for fighting. He offered her a ride home. In the back seat of his car, two older teenagers, already along for the ride, persuaded her to join them for an eight-hour detour to an unchaperoned house in the Dallas suburbs, where she met other dropouts and took a lot of unlabeled pills. Soon she couldn't stand upright, and, in part for that reason, perhaps, she experienced intercourse for the first time with a pushy stranger on a mattress on the floor of an empty bedroom.

Lisa's social isolation ended. Soon she figured out how to climb down the fire escape into the night, and, with practice, to creep back up through her own window. The night after her first sex, she sneaked into her mother's bathroom and removed an old-fashioned two-edged blade from an old razor her mother kept on the rim of her tub. She could hardly wait to record in her diary what she'd done in clinical detail—and then to cut herself. She thought her mother might wake up and ask what she was doing, and so she left her door unlocked, so her lacerations were accompanied by the suspense of the remote possibility of her parents' entry.

Soon after she began sneaking out of her bedroom in the night, Lisa began to carry her mother's razor to school, the blade broken in half and carried with the sharp edge embedded in an apple. Sometimes, when her life felt dizzyingly unreal, or sometimes just passing invisibly down a crowded corridor, she casually pulled up the sleeve of her sweater, walking through giggles and shouts and slammed lockers with her lacerations exposed. No one noticed, however, any more than they did in math class when she raised her hand, let her unbuttoned sleeve slip, and asked a trivial question, trying to sound interested in the answer as the teacher, startled to hear anything from her, went on effusively, oblivious to the peek-a-boo glimpse she'd just offered him of her scabbed stigmata.

Lisa paid dearly for the pseudo-kindness she received from randy strangers. Her classmates and their parents, who heard rumors about her behavior, concluded that she was a "bad" girl and blamed her for her poor sexual choices, as if Lisa ever thought she'd had any other kind. In the company of predatory young men, she experienced a physical contact she longed for, but also the anguish of wretched misrecognition. The men who plied her with drugs and bullied her for blowjobs never saw her at all: to them, she was reduced to a devalued, impersonal body part to be fondled or groped, used and discarded. In her acquiescence they misconstrued a reciprocation of their own coarse urgency; in their eyes she saw only a blurred, sordid reflection of their lust and displaced self-contempt. Inevitably, because they were capable of nothing else, they saw a slut, a ho—and failed, of course, to recognize, much less to care, that she was only a lonely little girl.

Lisa's parents were taken aback by her academic collapse in tenth grade. They tried to help her make more of a social success by asking her to invite "all your school friends" over for a party. Despite expensive preparations, few of her classmates came at all, and few stayed for long. Soon after, noting Lisa's wooden unresponsiveness at the breakfast table, her parents took her for a psychiatric consultation in Dallas, whose resulting prescriptions seemed not to do the trick. The attendance office sent notices of her truancy in the fall, but Lisa intercepted and signed the reply cards herself.

At the end of the semester, one of her final grades was an F, and the others were D's and C's. This got her parents' attention, particularly after they also received a personal note from Lisa's assiduous math teacher, who described his worries about Lisa's inattention and offered to let her make up her many missing assignments. Lisa made excuses and lied about that "mean" teacher's remonstrances. She promised she'd take the Ritalin the psychiatrist had prescribed, and catch up. Her worried parents grounded her, and so she came home after school on most days, when her parents were in town. But unfortunately, she didn't stay home at night.

At three a.m. on a Sunday morning a Texas trooper found her crumpled, battered, and abraded body lying on the pavement of an on-ramp to Interstate 20. Her arms and legs had to be splinted and her spine immobilized for transport to Parkland Memorial. In the emergency room, the nurses found five "ecstasy" pills in her jeans, and a tox-screen was positive for alcohol, marijuana, and amphetamines. X-rays revealed cracked ribs, a fractured radius, a compound fracture of her right femur, and a skull fracture. Her belly was rigid, and an abdominal film suggested fluid in the peritoneal space. So, still unconscious, Lisa was hydrated and rushed to surgery.

As the surgeons wheeled Lisa's gurney into the elevator to the operating room, the ER doctor called the number the police supplied from information in Lisa's wallet. Her father answered the phone, apparently confused and slow to accept the news. The ER physician knew it was a shock for a father to wake up to a call from an emergency room. Yet the man's denial seemed more strident than usual, as if he doubted the doctor's truthfulness. It occurred to the physician that perhaps the man had been drinking, because he kept insisting a little irrationally that it had to be some other teenager, not his Lisa. No, he said, he really didn't think he needed to climb two flights of stairs to check, because his wife had kissed her goodnight only a few hours before, around ten. He just *knew* that his daughter was safely in her bed, surrounded by her stuffed animals, sound asleep. He knew it, without having to look.

Part 2
Limits

6   A Need for No

THE SECOND essential parental task is to set limits, which normal children need if they're to grow up to become mature adults.

Why? Why do limits promote psychological development? Or to put the question the other way around, why does a lack of limit-setting result in obnoxious arrogance or selfish self-importance in teenagers?

Selfish from the Start

To answer, we must begin with immaturity—and consider what limits do. We are born without consideration for others, without empathy or altruism. All normal infants and toddlers are self-preoccupied. They want what they want, and they want it now. They don't care about anybody else's wants or needs, or whose turn it might be. In fact, they hardly recognize that their wishes and needs are distinct from those of important others in their lives. It's natural for young children to take others into account only insofar as others offer them what they want and need. At the start of our lives, in a word, we're *self*-ish.

A decade later, however, it's normal for teenagers to have begun to get over this childish narcissism. Normally, teenagers, at least some of the time, approach the challenges of adolescent life in a less selfish way. What does this look like? A mature teenager can be remarkably considerate, some of the time. Moreover, a mature teenager becomes capable of true empathy. This means that he can imagine what it might be like to be a person not at all like himself—a girl (if he's a boy), a parent (if he's a son), a cop, a little brother, someone less economically advantaged or of a different race or religion. He can imagine what it might be like if he himself were also sick, or blind or deaf. He can imagine the future consequences of his present acts or the likely results of inaction. He can fully imagine a goal and deduce the logical steps, called a plan, that would get him to that goal. He can consider important other persons in his life to be separate—and to have a right to different ideas, motives, and wishes than his own. When he considers his choices in an ethical way, he can think abstractly and take into account moral ideals, such as honor. And he can think beyond his own selfish wishes to consider social ideals, such as the good of the family, the team, or the country. He can put others ahead of his own desires. All these things he can do—some of the time.

Not all teenagers develop these unselfish capacities. Maturation is neither automatic nor inevitable, and many men and women reach the age of majority without transcending the narcissistic self-preoccupation and self-importance of toddlers. It isn't that immature teenagers or adults sometimes behave in selfish ways, but rather that they're not capable of thinking or feeling in mature ways. It isn't that sometimes they *don't*, but rather that they *can't*. Why? Because if a teenager fails to achieve these developmental milestones, he can only remain childishly *self*-ish. Informally, we consider him to be a jerk. Clinically, we speak of narcissistic character pathology. The arrogance and obnoxious self-preoccupation aren't an acquired illness, but a hangover from childhood, a failure to get beyond a child's normal self-preoccupation, now-orientation, magical wishful thinking, incapacity for empathy, lack of consideration, manipulative relationships, and moral selfishness.

The Second Parental Task

Limits confront childish narcissism. They challenge that approach to life that can only cry, *Me! Me! Me!* Limits confront the obnoxious insistence that it's got to be *Me first! Only me!* Limits refuse to accept arrogant indifference to others, confronting the childish assertion: *I don't have to care about you!* They resist the child's shameless belief, *I'm entitled! I have to have it now. I shouldn't have to work or wait!* Limits thwart a child's perpetual expectation *that* you'll *work and save to provide what I want—and you'll wait on* me! Limits face down a teenager's grandiose exceptionalism, the very idea that *the rules do not apply to me.*

In short, if teenagers are to become unselfish and considerate, parents need to say "No." It's only the parental "No" that pushes young people to experience the alternative to a perpetual infantile "Yes." Limits teach: *No, you're not always first.* Limits insist: *No, it's not only about you.* They announce: *No, it's* not *all right for you not to care about your little sister.* They protest: *No, you are not entitled, and you will work and wait to earn it, if you want it.* Limits delay gratification: *No, you wait your turn,* or *No, not until it's time,* or *No, not until I'm ready, too.* They put future events into sequence: *No, not until you have done your duty, your chore, your homework,* or *No, not until you do what you said you would do.* Limits draw a line, hold up a standard, and refuse to rescue. Within the capacity of a teenager to work independently, to take care of her own business, to solve her own problems, limits tell a daughter: *No, I won't do it (all) for you.* Limits prick the balloon of presumption by insisting: *No, I'm not your servant,* and *those others are not your lackeys, either.* Limits lift a teenager's eyes from his own preoccupations to a wider social order, and to other people beyond himself, and so help a teenager join that collective village by pointing to social obligations, called *duties,* from which *No, you are not excused,* and for which *No, you will not be paid.* Not least, limits challenge the ultimate narcissistic arrogance: *No, the rules **do** apply to you—**all** of them.*

In short, firmly set limits push normal teenagers to grow up. They challenge and squelch the childish narcissism that *is* the flawed approach of a residual adolescent immaturity. Without those limits, young people fail to become mature adults.

A Culture of Narcissism

Given the importance of limit-setting, one might imagine that all parents would willingly collaborate and support without question teachers, cops, coaches, and other parental figures setting limits. One might expect all parents to learn to say "No" skillfully, without angst or reluctance or anger. Yet this isn't so. If the Victorian Age was a culture of "No," we now live in a culture of "Yes." Films make casual sexual and material self-indulgence a common spectacle, and commercials have for decades urged us to think we deserve to have it all, and why wait? In the privileged precincts of America's cities and suburbs it's possible to meet sixteen-year-old boys to whom no one seems ever to have said "No" about anything. Might he want a credit card, the car keys, a drug, a tutor, a blowjob? Parents in those neighborhoods who try to say "No" get little support from many other parents, who may not even agree that "No" is a legitimate parental prerogative.

This commercial matrix is old news, of course. It's been thirty years since Christopher Lasch summarized the factors responsible for the demise of the Victorian neurosis and the rise of a "culture" of self-indulgence. Lasch suggested that a loss of parental authority (limit-setting) meant a decline in the modern super-ego (conscience). He foresaw that without parental limit-setting creating in young people the inner constraints of conscience, no inner scruple would constrain greed, irresponsibility, licentiousness, and the grandiosity of a modern epidemic of self-indulgence. Without conscience to oppose naked selfishness, Lasch argued, there'd be much less neurotic conflict and much more self-indulgence. Today, as we watch the behavior of Wall Street financial executives and others in our society, we can see that, if anything, Lasch's dramatic prediction of an emerging "culture of narcissism" was understated.

Why Some Parents Are Reluctant to Set Limits

Although limits are fundamental to rearing fine, graceful young people, some parents fail to set them. Given what's at stake, this may seem odd. Why would parents resist setting limits? To find the answer I have simply asked parents who were unwilling or unable to set limits for young patients, or watched them not do so. I've considered my own reluctance over the years with my own children and other parents' teenagers. Some of the reasons have become clear to me. Here are a few of them.

Not Convinced that Limits are Necessary

Some parents remain skeptical about the whole uptight enterprise of adult constraints. They view a parental "No" and disciplinary consequences not only to be unnecessary but also punitive, Gestapo-like tactics to which—having never forgotten the muddy magic of Woodstock—they prefer unconditional love and limitless praise. They recoil from the cruelty of limits. They don't wish to bully; they dislike strident voices in confrontation. They love their teenagers, identify with them, and hate to see them frustrated. When a daughter complains about a soft-spoken "No," compares her father unfavorably to Dick Cheney or her mother to Ann Coulter, and mentions Fox News, these parents back off.

In fact, these parents eschew assertions of authority, and try not to sound bossy. They prefer family consensus, if not a democracy. They ask their teenagers when *they* want to be expected home, whether *they* would like it if their parents monitored homework. They're reluctant to ask, much less expect, that a son will do anything he doesn't really want to do. They're allergic to adolescent rage, and so they try to convince a daughter with logical arguments about her "best interests." They want their teenagers to agree to what they, as parents, think they ought to do. They hope this reasonableness will spare them a debate.

They have their reasons. They experienced rigid, unjust authority themselves. They didn't like it, and they don't wish to inflict that tight-lipped, libido-hating rigidity upon their adolescent children. In college they read Rousseau and believed in that balmy state of nature, a prelapsarian world before "society" put us all in chains. So when it comes down to it, they'd rather keep authoritarian expectations hazy, even covert, and fear that to publish clear rules would be to invite debate, even resistance, and they'd have to enforce those rules. They prefer that the lines of authority remain vague, so that it's not entirely obvious who makes the final decision. They wish adolescent misbehavior would stop, don't get them wrong. But they find it painful to insist.

Actually, when young, this dad may have been a bit of a rake and a scamp, and this mom may have been a bit of a tramp and hellion. They're still sympathetic with adolescent ambivalence about rules. In principle, truth to tell, they're more in favor of fun. They don't think they ought to be hypocrites, either, and so they don't punish defiance or rudeness. They admire grit and spunk, they approve of a girl finding her "voice," even if there turns out to be a lot of profanity when she uses it. They don't press for conformity (e.g., to rules), because they despise sheep-like acquiescence, and look down on a passive lack of imagination. They're romantics, in short. If they had their dreams come true, they'd live forever with their sons and daughters in an amiable climate in which emotional storms are kept away, and one takes shelter to wait out scattered showers. These parents aspire to an egalitarian household of pals.

More Important Things to Do

Other parents are too busy. In theory they believe someone *should* set limits. They'd do it themselves, if they could find the time. They see the logic, even the virtue, to setting limits and they wouldn't argue that it *shouldn't* be done. But they've been warned that inconsistent limits are worse than no limits at all, and so they hate to jump in on impulse with an *ad hoc* enforcement. They let exceptional problems pass, because they don't really have time to set up a whole common law. Of course, they hate to contemplate the consequence of not setting limits in the long run. But they don't like the way it feels when they actually have to do it. Better to let the *au pair* do it.

In fact, their teenagers already resent it when these parents try to say "No." Actually, the kids don't like a number of things about parents' limit-setting. They, too, prefer it to be left to the *au pair*. For a start, they don't like to be kept waiting. They're not receptive to news that *a* and *b* come before *c*. And these parents hate it when the teenagers aren't happy. They recoil from adolescent rage, too, and from accusations that they're hardly ever *there*, so who are *they* to tell *us* what to do? Moreover, arguing about rules, or calling a boy on his misbehavior, ruins the day—and it's a pity to make a mess of a nice day together, when there are so few of them. Given how busy they are, these parents hate to spend quality time having an argument. So discipline, however sensible in principle, doesn't in practice get assigned a high priority.

There are many other problems. These parents are already stretched by the demands of their important careers. They're in a hurry; they have to go. So they have to delegate to others the care of the teenagers. But— let's face it—an *au pair* isn't all that interested in limit-setting. She just wants to keep the peace. In sum, limit-setting is a grand prescription, a good idea, and these parents don't disagree in principle. But when it comes down to it, they approach it with the same theoretical enthusiasm and ambivalent good intentions they bring to flossing their teeth.

Lack of Skills

Some parents simply don't know how. It's not that they think limits are a bad idea. They admire and envy those who make the task look easy. Yet when they have to confront an indignant teenager they are shaken. When they encounter a wily debater, they come away feeling they just walked out of a slick car dealership, having signed on to a deal they should have refused. Faced with a sad or withdrawn daughter, they fear that they should avoid a confrontation that might provoke a suicide. Engaging with an angry, demanding, fast-talking son, they worry they cannot out-argue or out-shout him. So they give up on limits they fear they cannot successfully justify in debate.

Therefore, despite obvious infractions, these worried parents aren't sure what to do. They wonder what other parents do, but don't know who to ask. They're not even sure their own spouses will agree, and they fear that the child-rearing-pundit-du-jour won't back them. Worst of all, they're not sure what helps or harms, why one says this rather than that. They worry about imposing a federal consequence for a municipal mis-demeanor, and wonder how long sentences should be.

Sensing hesitation, a daughter or son salts the parental tail with doubts—as to whether she did or didn't do it, whether he did or didn't mean to do it, whether the rule was stupid to begin with (and so foolish to enforce), whether another parent with a lick of sense would make this huge deal over a minor infraction, whether (as she puts it) all the other kids routinely get away with precisely the same behavior, whether *blah, blah, blah. . . .*

A Vulnerable Child

My wife had to correct my view about an otherwise sensible mother who behaved like a pulling guard for the Chicago Bears, running interference for her arrogant son. If the son didn't do his homework, this mom hired a tutor. If he got caught with marijuana in his prep-school dorm and was expelled, she hired an attorney. If he earned mediocre scores on his first try at the SATs, she got a physician to certify a need for extra time. I thought her excuses for his misbehavior suggested arrogance about the rules, a conviction that her boy was too special to be expected to share the common lot. There may have been some of this, but my wife pointed out that this intelligent mother already had reared an older brother who'd done very well, without needing her downfield blocking before he ever got near the ball. My wife suggested that this wasn't presumptuousness, but rather a parent who'd detected in her son a flaw that made him vulnerable. Like a grizzly, she'd defend this runt against all predators. The result was a spoiled boy; but this wasn't her intent, nor was it a function of her own self-importance.

Limit-setting may not occur, then, to a parent whose fearful secret knowledge (and grief) is that a son has a flaw that leaves him unable to compete. It may happen in the context of a congenital defect (e.g., ADHD, dyslexia, or Asberger's syndrome), or trauma (e.g., divorce or the death of a father), or chronic illness (e.g., diabetes). Limit-setting inevitably means frustration, and for parents of young people who've already had more than their share of frustration and unhappiness, it may seem unbearable to inflict any more.

Shame, Guilt, Remorse, or Fear

Some parents are reluctant to set limits because doing so is a legitimate function of shame or guilt. Some parents have had the personal stuffing shaken out of them. They're ashamed and guilty about marital failure, sorry about what divorce has cost the children. Some recognize their own defects as parents and know they should control their tempers better, come home sooner, drink less, and pay the bills on time.[59] Some are humiliated by past failures to conceive and worry they may not be able to bind an adopted child to themselves without genetic hoops of steel. Some adults are themselves ill or disabled, and sorry about what they've been unable to provide. Widows feel sorry about a daughter's grief, a son's lack of a "father figure." Blaming themselves for a son's learning differences, a daughter's scoliosis, a boy's speech idiosyncrasy, or a girl's congenital heart defect that's required painful surgery, they wince at the idea of holding a son or daughter to account.

So an ashamed, guilty, or sorry parent is likely to cut a teenager more slack than he deserves. How can they upset an upset child any more? How can they hold a teenager to answer when they, themselves, are at fault? When teenagers have much to worry or grieve about or regret, how can a parent cause more anguish by chewing them out or saying "No"? If the kids fail to do chores or forget their manners, why must a parent make a big deal? Given a parent's weaknesses, grief, misbehavior, sins, lack of discipline, and all the owed reparations, how can one call the kids on the carpet? Given all the larger worries, why bother them for small-bore errors? Will teenagers love a flawed parent who tries to say "No"? How can a parent presume?

When parents feel ashamed and guilty, a teenager's threats do not provoke the indignation they deserve. Those threats can immobilize an anxious, remorseful parent. *She won't speak to me again!* Playing upon shame, a daughter may successfully threaten to bring up what a parent feels terrible about hearing. *What do you mean I should come home on time? What do you mean I can't get drunk? What do you mean I'm a slut?* Playing upon parental fears, stroppy teenagers may threaten *not to love you!* They may offer to abandon their parents: *I'll never visit your nursing home.* They may blackmail a parent who already suspects he doesn't deserve much consideration. *You'll never see your grandchildren!* In sum, a disgraced, fearful parent may find it difficult to call a teenager to account and set limits.

Too Special
Not withstanding an alternative explanation above (a "vulnerable" child), some parents think their adolescent sons and daughters are so exceptional that the rules simply don't apply to them. They debate with coaches, teachers, or headmasters, making threats to back claims to an exception or special dispensation. Unable or unwilling to set their own limits, these parents also resist other adult efforts to set limits. Why? Because their children are extensions of their own narcissistic conviction that the rules or laws ought not to apply to themselves.

This adult childishness leads to irony. Parents bring sons or daughters for residential treatment because they won't comply with home curfews; because they fail to take academic deadlines seriously; because these teenagers have been shoplifting or bringing pot home. They visit the campus, however, and let a fifteen-year-old drive a rental car, or permit a high-school sophomore to sip their cocktails at a restaurant, or purchase clothes that violate the school dress code—and then tell a son or daughter: *Don't tell your therapist!* If challenged, these sneaky parents offer the same lame excuses their teenagers try. They attack the "inane" rules, although they've given their word they'd follow them. They argue that other parents don't follow the rules either, as if this made any moral difference. They discover reasons to make an exception, or suggest that their own misreading of the rules made it a "promise." Yet for all their evident self-importance, they refuse to admit that they simply think they're too important, too wealthy, too smart, too special, and that the rules that apply to lesser mortals ought not to apply to them.

Coach Fitz

Parental narcissism is contagious, and teenagers catch it like a virus. They recognize a parent's contempt for rules, and soon they acquire the same symptoms. How do they know? Because when they themselves break the rules and are called on it, their parents defend them. They hire lawyers to get them off, or bully a teacher, principal, coach, or cop who tries to hold them accountable. Some years ago, Michael Lewis described this parental arrogance in the *New York Times Magazine*. He profiled a baseball coach at a Louisiana prep-school who had to contend with resistant parents when he tried to set limits for their sons:

> Two days before . . . the 2004 season, eight players were caught drinking. All but one of them—two team captains, two members of the school's honor committee—lied about it before eventually confessing. After he handed out the obligatory school-sanctioned two-week suspensions to the eight players, Coach Fitz . . . [told them that, as a consequence, he would also make them run.] . . . The first phone call, a few hours later, came from the mother of the third baseman, who said her son had drunk "only one sip of a daiquiri" and shouldn't be made to run.[60]

That is how kids know. This mother tried to spare her son the consequences of his misbehavior. She was right, of course, that Coach Fitz intended her boy to feel pain. But of the connection between that discomfort and her son's growing up she clearly had no idea. Clearly she believed punishment to be a mindless exercise about misbehavior that she was prepared to ignore. She thought penance should fit the crime, sip for sip. The coach had a different idea. When it came to disgraceful disloyalty and dishonorable affronts to the rules, a bunt was the same as a home run. He insisted on making that transgression, and the boys' comeuppance, an indelible memory.

This conflict between a parent and a coach raises a psychological question: What *is* the connection between punishment and character? Is pain *per se* the source of integrity? Is punishment the remedy for misbehavior? Does punishment make a boy virtuous? And if not, why did Coach Fitz want to make misbehaving players suffer? As it happened, the writer, Michael Lewis, had traveled back to his own high school to grope for this deeper logic. In the process, he recalled his own comeuppance from this same coach. In his own experience, however, there'd been no "punishment," not even extra laps. Instead of inflicting physical pain, Lewis wrote, Coach Fitz "changed my life."

To explain, Lewis recalls that he had himself been an arrogant, unserious freshman, who demanded little of himself as a student or athlete. He talked back to teachers, resisted reasonable authority, and went off on a family vacation, failing to show up for practice, the week before the team's opening game. On the field during that game, Coach Fitz publically dressed him down as a slacker. Lewis was mortified, ashamed. He hurt and squirmed because he admired his coach and cared about his team. He was made to feel ashamed to have been selfish and disloyal to those who'd counted on him. This "discomfort" was transformative. Yet that transformation was still hard for Lewis to explain. After that season, Lewis found himself changed. He noticed that others saw the change in him, too: "Not long after that [my] English teacher, who had the misfortune also to experience me as a freshman, held me after class to say that by some happy miracle I was not recognizably the same human being I'd been a year earlier."

Years later, this transformation still seemed mysterious. Other alumni had noticed this change in themselves, too, however, and credited Coach Fitz. They also found it difficult to explain. Yet each of them knew that the change had something to do with that close relationship they once had cherished with a coach who "had something to tell us and us alone." Coach Fitz had punished them when they needed it. But clearly he'd also wanted them to grope for something ineffable. In describing this experience, Lewis uses the verb "teach," and yet there's no tangible fact or skill or lesson to learn. Rather, a personal transformation had come out of suffering. The coach described it as a confrontation with self-indulgence. Lewis writes:

> Coach Fitz [believed that] privilege corrupts. It enabled you
> to do what money could buy instead of what duty demanded.

... [Y]ou developed a conviction, buttressed by your parents' money, that life was meant to be easy . . . that nothing mattered so much that you should suffer for it.

There it was: *duty*. Coach Fitz pushed them to take seriously an abstract, social ethic. When Lewis came back to his high school to revisit his adolescence, he understood that a relationship, and an adult's limit-setting, had helped him to become a man. No longer was he a spoiled boy. He saw that what had changed was his approach to his life—a change he credited to this implacable love. Although he found this transformation hard to describe, he knew where it came from and who'd helped him. On the occasion of his first serious success in the world, Lewis wanted to share that success only with the man who'd changed him:

I never could have explained at the time what he had done for me, but I felt it in my bones all the same. When I came home one day during my senior year and found the letter saying that, somewhat improbably, I had been admitted to Princeton University, I ran right back to school to tell Coach Fitz.

Lewis's difficulty in describing the inner change of maturation is quite usual. Teenagers seem not to notice that inner shift in themselves. They imagine that others have changed, rather than themselves. They feel that the world has shifted, that old friends have become boring or foolish, that parents have unaccountably become reasonable, that academic challenges have become easier. After some intervening years and a trip to Louisiana, however, Lewis could see, in retrospect, the change in himself. He figured out what it was—and could now identify that adolescent transformation: "I *grew up.*"

What Limits Do

If deft limit-setting (within a meaningful relationship) pushes a teenager to grow up, and if growing up is not "learning" in the same sense that one masters a spelling list, then what exactly do limits *do*? If, as Michael Lewis suggests, Coach Fitz's limit-setting made him grow up, how is it that limits accomplished this remarkable transformation? The answer is complex. Not every developmental achievement requires limit-setting, or consequent pain or squirming. Many developmental challenges provoke little resistance. They are intrinsically fun, or they give pleasure. Practicing eating an ice-cream cone, for example, is a new skill for toddlers, but it seems not to be an effort parents have to push small-fry to make. Nor do parents usually need to prod a boy to practice riding a shiny new bicycle, either. It's rare, also, for parents to have to push teenagers to practice driving a car.

But not all milestones on the way to an admirable personality give pleasure. Many of those achievements—e.g., weaning, continence, waiting to eat or speak, sitting still, tidying up a playroom floor, making a bed, completing homework (while others play), and getting to class on time—are not pleasurable. These steps toward civility cost an effort, require restraint and patience, provoke anxiety, and feel like privation. Much of what we mean by gracious behavior—e.g., speaking with courtesy, finishing a chore, putting others first, cleaning up a mess, minding one's manners, following a clock, working now for future ends—require that young people do, for reasons that seem obscure, what does *not* come naturally. From a teenager's point of view, aversion and resistance are reflexive, comprehensible responses. This is to say, to behave like a grown-up requires doing things that teenagers prefer not to do, e.g., think of others first, wait for dinner when one is hungry, plan for a distant goal, restrain an immediate urge so that others may go first. We can parse the sources for a teenager's unease, when disciplined. He feels:

- *A thwarted urge* or wish or want—a "No" that leaves his desire unsatisfied, his impulse suspended, his appetite unsated. *No, wait until dinner!* is a constraint that forces a boy to endure hunger.
- *Frustrated narcissism*—a "No" implies that a girl is not a princess, that it is *No!* rather than *Yes, right now, Your Highness.* That "No" provokes indignation in a child. After all that immediate gratification: *How can they say No to me?*
- *Anxiety*: caused by the above two frustrations, of which parents must determine the proper concentration by gauging how much thwarting a child (at various stages of maturation) can endure without panic. Parents have to push the

envelope, little by little, to enlarge a child's capacity to wait, defer, and stay hungry, etc.

When considering these displeasures, who among us when we were children, given a child's unencumbered choices, would choose to become an admirable, gracious adult? Who, given the choice, would bear the frustration, put up with waiting, or endure the humiliation of "No"?

The trick in parenting, then, is not to leave these choices unencumbered. To encumber them is what limit-setting *is*. That is, we set limits around choices that require a young person to choose to do what is *not* (yet) intrinsically pleasurable, not (yet) a reflexive choice. Teenagers, like younger children, will make these choices willingly and make such choices a part of their permanent repertoire, but only if adults line up disincentives and rewards in such a way to prod them to make grown-up choices themselves. Accordingly, a limit deftly set will cause or prolong an unpleasant feeling only if a teenager insists upon making the boorish choice. On the other hand, a limit deftly set may also line up with positive incentives—of two kinds:

- *Concrete rewards*: a treat for a patient toddler; presents from Santa Claus, who knows if a schoolgirl has "been bad or good"; a gold star on a quiz; and use of the family car for a teenager who drives carefully.
- *Intangible incentives*: sustaining acts of recognition—a teacher's praise, a parent's respect and trust. In the context of warm relationships, teenagers behave well in order to preserve those relationships, which are intrinsically rewarding, so as not to let down an adult who matters.

In these ways, recognition sustains developmental milestones—e.g., a child's decision, given the alternatives and deft limits set for him, to make mature choices.

To set limits well requires adult good judgment, for limits thwart a young person's natural urges, frustrate a normal childish narcissism, and so can leave urges unsatisfied, provoke indignation and narcissistic rage, and arouse associated anxieties. Parents setting limits must keep this dysphoria within bearable bounds, or risk making moral failure inevitable. The level of frustration a parent reasonably can expect a teenager to endure—e.g., *I'll be home in three hours to get dinner ready, so stay out of the cookie jar!*—would undo a six-week-old infant, who cannot be expected to endure three hungry, panicky, purple-faced hours of a parent's failure to reappear. Like other aspects of maturity, the capacity to wait is a muscle that exercise strengthens, as long as parents measure the resulting unhappiness and anxiety appropriately to fit within the capacities of an infant, toddler, schoolgirl, or teenager. The parental task is to find the Goldilocks prescription: *Not too much, not too little, but just the right amount.* Asking too much and provoking panic is *not* what makes a small child grow up, and teenagers need not to be pushed beyond what they can endure, either.

Yet maturation requires healthy doses of frustration. A child so protected and indulged that she never feels frustration becomes spoiled. This being so, a teenager's dysphoria in the face of a set limit isn't the signal to relax that limit, but rather a confirmation of that limit's effectiveness. A measured, limit-induced dysphoria, endured in the context of a close relationship with an adult, motivates a young person to feel around for a more mature approach. This key point bears repeating. Setting limits produces a useful dysphoria, which provokes a ready teenager to grope for a new perspective, a new way to frame challenges, new options. Because he's ready, the teenager can find that new approach. Motivated by set limits and consequent frustration, he can make new sense of a problem he has heretofore failed to solve. Prodded by the constraints of the chrysalis, the caterpillar becomes a butterfly.

Here is the corollary: If we, as parents, cannot endure a son's distress when he's confronted with his misbehavior and given consequences, we cannot help him grow up. If we cannot endure a daughter's whining when reasonable limits frustrate her, we'll fail to help her grow up. We needn't inflict pointless pain. But we must tolerate a teenager's dysphoria long enough to let him find his way to the next stage of maturation. That is to say, if we cannot set limits and make them stick, we cannot be effective parents. We'll spoil our children and leave them to flounder in the face of the responsibilities that await them. We must find a gracious, calm way to confront a teenager's outmoded, childish narcissism. This requires both skill and fortitude. Limit-setting doesn't have to be a fight that leaves parents drained or ashamed. Nonetheless, we have to stand up to noisy debate and, when necessary, endure a teenager's indignation at the very idea that we set limits at all. We must stay the course in the face of a teenager's reluctance to grow up.

Limits Challenge the "Flawed Approach" of Immaturity

Here are a few examples of what graceful parents might say when setting limits. Notice that the word "No" often suits this purpose. Don't be afraid to say it. I urge parents to express a genuine courtesy and respect for their children, and to require equivalent good manners in return. Limit-setting should frustrate that flawed approach we've been talking about: its narcissism, failures of empathy, lack of consideration, puppet relationships, failure to anticipate consequences, lack of future goals and plans, and its concrete and selfish ethic. To illustrate, let's take these elements in turn.

Well-constructed limits challenge self-preoccupied, self-important **narcissism**. Your "No" introduces other creatures who share the planet and ought to be taken into account. Your "No" calls attention to other persons, whose claims should be acknowledged. Limit-setting reminds a teenager of other pronouns in the language aside from *I*, *me*, and *my*:

- "No, you may not wear that—it belongs to her."
- "No, not yet. You'll have to wait—he's ahead of you."
- "No, you may not cut practice and still start—it's unfair to your team-mates."
- "No, you may not eat the whole pie—others must have their share."
- "No, you may not go out tonight. You didn't wash the car, as I asked."

Limits confront a teenager's **lack of consideration** for the feelings of others. Your "No" should nudge an adolescent toward **empathy**:

- "No, you may not hit your sister—you're hurting her!"
- "No, we're not going to make cookies tonight—I'm too tired."
- "No, you may not wear that skimpy top—your teachers will be embarrassed if you show up half-naked, and the boys won't learn any algebra."

- "No, you may not call your little brother a 'fruit.' You're hurting his feelings."
- "No, I will not cooperate with you, because your attitude makes me angry."

Limits can insist upon **separate relationships**. Setting a limit is a puppet's protest. A limit can require a teenager to treat others as separate and equal:

- "No, we're not going to do that—I don't want to."
- "No, you may not do that—I don't agree that it's all right."
- "No, you cannot have that—it belongs to your sister."
- "No, let's do it my way, for once."
- "No, not tonight—your father and I are dining out."

Limits can introduce into an adolescent conversation the concept of **sequence**. They stretch a teenager's perspective on time. When adolescents can think abstractly, limits do more than merely impose an arbitrary ordering of events. They also link past and present in logical or causal chains of events that young people care about. For example: "No, I'm not making any loans tonight. Yesterday you spent your allowance on candy, and so today you don't have sufficient liquidity for a movie ticket. Find something else to do."

In this way, a limit makes the future contingent upon the present and past. Parental limits connect what a teenager chooses (now) to do (or not do) to the **consequences** of those choices. Such contingencies can be shaped to emphasize pleasure or pain.

- "Sure, you can go to a movie tonight *if* by the time your mother serves dinner you have finished all your homework, mowed the lawn, and swept the garage. If you have not taken care of all those chores, don't ask to leave the house tonight. You will have made the answer 'No.'"
- "Let's understand, shall we, that it's all right to use my car. I like letting you use my car. But I expect you to be considerate. If you again bring my car back with the gas tank empty, so that I have to stop on my way to work to refill it, then

you had better buy your girlfriend a pair of track shoes for Valentine's Day, because you're going to be jogging on dates together."

Such constraints broaden the field to include "later." They frustrate a teenager's bid to keep the discussion only to "do with now." Clever parental limits connect future outcomes to all the intervening variables, which includes a teenager's **past, present, and future** choices.

More than this, contingent limits shift the onus from a parental decision to a teenager's **goal** and **plan**. For her to achieve a goal requires her to picture the future and line up the logical steps that can take her from here to there. The answer to a request to go to the cinema becomes a paradigm for the way to prepare homework on time, to save money for a future purchase, and to prepare a college application. Contingent limits challenge teenagers to wait, and to hold in mind the goal and the intervening steps in a plan. Contingent limits don't reward last-minute tantrums. They prompt teenagers to reach for their goals by making plans and taking logical steps, not by wishful thinking. And the parental limit, set as a clear contingency in the proper sequence, is the paradigm for planning. *Sure, we can talk about c, but there can be no c until you accomplish a and b*:

- "No, not yet. I know this is a back road, but it's against the law for you to drive until you're sixteen and have a permit. I don't want you to think for a moment that I will put up with your breaking laws. So yes, I'll teach you to drive when you're sixteen, *if* by then you've learned the traffic laws, and *if* you've passed the written test, and *if* you've acquired a learner's permit."
- "No, midnight is too late for your first nights out. For now, let's make your curfew ten sharp. But here's my deal with you. *If* you keep precisely to that time for a month, I will extend it to ten-thirty. And if you manage that well, over time, we can talk about future extensions. But please understand that ten means ten, not ten past ten. I can't force you to come home on time. I can't make it easy for you to leave your friends. But if you handle this curfew yourself in a

responsible way, you'll earn greater freedom, and I will be glad to give it to you. But let's also be clear that if you are fifteen minutes late, you lose your keys for a week."

- Yes, you may take Lisa to the prom, and I will look forward to helping you out. But I don't wish even to discuss the prom, or any other use of our cars, until your teachers tell me you are showing up for all your classes on time, without fail; that you've turned in all your missing assignments without exception; and that your average in every class is a B or better. If I get confirmation that you've done all those things by Friday the week before prom, you can count on me. I'll help you get to the prom. But if you fail to take care of school, you may not go."

Last, but surely not least, properly set limits address a teenager's **ethical** thinking. Proper limits call for **social and abstract moral reasoning** that transcends concrete selfishness. Such limits encourage a teenager to subordinate his selfish wish to the group's greater interest. Proper limits, set within a relationship, prod teenagers to consider abstract moral ideas such as *trust*, or a *duty* owed to a *relationship*. Deft limits push kids to consider values that lift above muddy self-interest. To prod teenagers to think ethically, parents need only embed such thinking in their limit-setting:

- "No, because you lied. When you lie to me, the answer always will be 'No.'"
- "No, but feel free to ask again—as soon as you find your manners."
- "No, you may not go out tonight—it's not what's best for the family."
- "No, I won't sign that note. I certainly will not sacrifice my integrity to hide your truancy. I certainly will not be dishonest—with you, or with your teachers. And I will be ashamed of you, and will make you wish you had done otherwise, if I ever hear that you were dishonest about it, either."

In sum, well-set limits challenge all the elements of the flawed approach. When teenagers remain immature, deft limit-setting confronts their tantrums, faces down their entitlement, cuts the marionette strings in our relationships, and discourages selfish self-preoccupation. Limit-setting opens a space in a teenager's mind for patience; empathy; consideration; separate relationships; and abstract, social, ethical thinking. Adults who set limits firmly and well prod teenagers to grow up and become self-disciplined, responsible citizens in a civil society.

7   How to Say "No"

Limits can be set well or badly. My suggestions, so far, amount only to a Goldilocks prescription. Now let's get more specific. The moment has come to say what that "just right" might look like. Here I want to propose a general approach to family limit-setting.

Setting good limits takes forethought, patience, and skill. Some parents seem to do this well from intuition, without having to think much about it. But when the issue is serious, I myself have to give it some thought. Many parents rely upon implicit memories of their own parents' sound parenting, or recoil from their own parents' clumsy mistakes. These experiences taught them how and how *not* to set limits. There are other contemporary examples, good or bad, from parents of our sons and daughters' friends. Perennial self-help books offer useful suggestions, even if they often fail to explain why we bother. So before saying just how I think about it, it's worth noting that there are many ways to draw a clear line, not only one right way. Parents have to do it in their own words, in their own voices, and with their own diction.

Some strategies and tactics work better than others, however. There are skills worth acquiring. A discernable difference exists between clever limit-setting and clumsy bullying. So I offer a few suggestions. In doing so, I'll provide a few imaginary dialogues and offer samples of what I might say. However, let's expect that under similar circumstances you'll use your own style. What does *not* work is not setting limits at all.

The Fundamental Rule: Insist upon Basic Courtesy
For some families, adolescent defiance and bad manners may not be a problem. Those lucky few parents may skip past the next discussions, which offer suggestions about laying down two fundamental home rules

and making them stick without having to call the police or banish a teenager to wilderness. For ease of exposition, I will address "you," even though I know many readers don't need this help, haven't made these mistakes, and won't consider these fictions to be apt descriptions of their own families. Please bear with me, for the point isn't to guess your family's precise predicament, but rather to describe a consensus among adults and teenagers living together in a well-ordered household that permits adults to set limits. This consensus is fundamental, because without it, limit-setting becomes impossible. In some families this consensus is already implicit, and there's little need to talk about it. In other families, however, it doesn't exist and needs to be made explicit—and enforced.

I begin with the assumption that these two basic rules have *not* yet been established. They come first, because they are fundamental. There's no point discussing other limits until these two have been established. This being so, these rules are exceptions to the general principle that adults cannot usefully set limits in a shouting match or in the context of threats or intimidation. These limits must be set, even in the midst of family disarray, so as to establish the context of mutual respect and courtesy in which other limits usefully may be set and honored. If parents and teenagers cannot start a talk with mutual respect and courtesy and an acknowledged parental authority, no matter what frustrations or bad feelings may be aroused around set limits, then there's little point in having the rest of the conversation.

In the imaginary family we'll use to illustrate this struggle, this civil consensus hasn't yet been established. In a conversation between a rude, angry son and a mother who wants to take charge as his mother, I urge her to take him on—speaking directly to her as "you," like a stage director offering suggestions to an actress. As this encounter begins, the stroppy teenaged son demands the keys to the family car to take his girl to a movie. You, his mother, ask politely what movie he proposes to take her to see, and he loses his temper, noticing noisily that, unlike most parents, you turn out to be "a complete moron." He then informs you that he has better things to do than "listen to your moralistic crap," and picks up your purse to fish for your keys. Ready for this confrontation, you have removed them. I suggest that you answer: "Okay. No. End of discussion," and walk out of the room.

Of course, he's stubborn, because your "No" is new to him. So he follows you down the hall to the kitchen to launch a second stanza of the same song. He tells you how "that *really* infuriates him," and that until now he held back a slim reserve of hope, but now has to face the sad but inevitable conclusion that "you really are an idiot."

Interrupt him quietly to say:

"I suggest you not now ask for anything you care about, because as of this moment, if you ever again speak to me rudely, with disrespect, as you just did, then the answer is going to be 'No.' From now, if you are rude with me, or shouting, or ugly, or contemptuous, the answer, no matter what the question, is always going to be 'No,' and it will stay 'No.'"

As he shapes an angry retort, you brace yourself and prepare to be determined. If now he is rude, or obnoxious, then the answers to both questions he has raised (about using the car and about leaving the house) will be "No." He doesn't yet believe this, because you have never truly meant it in the past, but you know that he's been warned. It's up to him to choose. If he now insults you, or makes rude demands, or takes an obnoxious insulting tone when he speaks to you, your decision is already made, and will stand.

He snarls:

"Don't preach at me, damn it. I don't have time for that shit, Mom. Kate is waiting, and I'm late. I don't have time to entertain you, or argue with you about how many times they have sex in this movie. So just give me the damned keys, and I'm out of here."

That was his choice. So you say calmly, "I'm afraid you just made your choice." Getting up to leave, you remind yourself what you must do now: stick to your guns. No matter what happens from here on, in this conversation, whether or not he finds his manners, and no matter how feathery the crow he offers to eat, no matter how sweet his apology or seductive his wheedling, you will *not* under any circumstances back down from this first set limit. He made his choice. That part is finished.

You need not interrupt to tell him so. You need not yell about it or rub his nose in it. You simply need to know it, and mean it.

Following you out of the kitchen now, perhaps a little worried that this isn't going the way it usually does, because you're not behaving as you usually do, he changes tactics, deciding to accept what he takes to be your offer to agree that he can have the car and exit visa if he says the "p-word." Irritably, he tries this. "Okay, *please!*" He still has your purse, because the car keys are in your pocket. "*That* was polite, wasn't it? So I can go now, right?"

This is your cue to say:

> "Actually, No. I'm not going to discuss this any further right now. And if you wish to talk with me any more, you will immediately put down my purse, which you have no right to touch without permission; and you will go away for half an hour and search your bedroom for your manners, wherever you left them. It's now four o'clock. Try again after four-thirty, if you like. If you continue to pester me now, you will be working on the use of the car for the next week, and the answer again will be 'No.' So I suggest you cool off and take a time-out."

Again, you turn to other things. You end the conversation. But you meant what you said, and your offer stands: If he comes back in thirty minutes with his manners, you'll talk with him. If he refuses to go, or comes back at you with contempt, then you won't talk with him, but he'll have given up the use of the car for a week.

Be careful and be clear. What you do *not* mean is that you will reconsider his going out tonight. You needn't say so yet. His uncertainty about that option is part of your leverage. Moreover, you needn't say it yet, because he hasn't yet chosen to get himself back into a courteous conversation with you. To jump ahead to a decision he hasn't yet achieved the standing to ask would be to confuse one issue with another. So you keep first things first: no further conversation at all until he accepts a time-out and comes back with his manners. In your own mind, however, you already know that there will be no car ride or movie tonight. What is at stake is more important than a date.

His move: He can choose among various gambits. Let's say that he doesn't go back to his original snarl, that your determination has chastened him, and he accepts the remote possibility that you might have a right to say "Wait," or even "No." He goes to his bedroom to call his girlfriend to explain that you've lost your mind. He returns in thirty minutes muttering, "Sorry," and he asks you: "Okay, *now* can I have the car keys?"

This is the critical moment, i.e., when he shifts to a civil diction. In the past, let us say, you would at this point have melted, let him make nice, and, conceding "that's a little better," would have handed over the keys. Let's say that in the recent past you would have allowed all his ugliness magically to be erased and forgotten. If so, presumably he now expects you to be mollified. But not this time: This time, you realize that if you again pretend that none of that ugly behavior has just happened, or that it wasn't important, and you let it pass, then you will have decided to allow this culture of contempt to continue. You'll have decided it is all right that this nasty scene repeat itself endlessly in future. You'll have decided, worse yet, that it really is all right for your son to behave like a jerk and a bully. For this critical reason, this time this isn't what you do.

Instead, you take his question to signal the arrival of the moment to set the limit you intend to set. To be certain, you say, "No, I have something important to say. Before I answer your question, however, I want you to tell me whether you are calmed down enough to listen, or need some more time in your room." If he says, "I just want the goddamn keys," then you know he isn't ready. Tell him to go away again until he's ready to listen politely to something important you have to say, which you think he had better know. When he can say, "Okay, I'm ready to listen," you ask him to sit down. You sit across the table from him, and you tell him calmly, politely, but with grim determination:

> "We're not going on like this. I realize I'm not helping you to become a fine man if I continue to let you ask for what you want with wretched bad manners, if I put up with tantrums and contemptuous demands. I realize that if I continue to let you behave this way, you become a jerk. If you recall the way you have just spoken to me, you'll see that you are well on your way. And I love you too much to let you become a bully or a twit. From now on, I will not let you get away with ugly, bad

manners—not with me, not with other adults, either. If you behave like this, I'm going to make you wish you had not. If you lose track of your manners, I'm going to make you wish you had kept them close at hand. I'm not taking this trouble because I do *not* love you, but because I do."

If he's stopped listening, send him away. If he's still attentive, you go on to say:

"From now on, the first rule between us is: respect and courtesy. If you wish to ask me something, you ask first whether I have time. You wait until I do, and then you ask for what you want, but only if you are courteous and respectful. Is that understood?"

If he has stopped listening, send him away. If he is still attentive, tell him you are pleased with his good manners, and go on:

"You may ask for what you want, but only if it is clear to both of us, ahead of time, that my answer may be "Yes," but can also be "No"—and that "No" will be all right with you. If the answer cannot be "No" without you throwing a tantrum, then you're not asking a question, only announcing what you demand of me. So if my answer cannot be "No," don't ask the question. I will respect your requests, and find time to talk, but I won't put up with any further disrespect. Do you understand?"

If the answer is "Yes," you ask him to read it back to you, so that you can be sure you explained clearly what you mean, and that he heard it. *If* he can, you add a corollary:

"You can be angry, but not ugly. I will understand if you are frustrated when I have to say 'No,' but, angry or sad, or whatever you feel, I expect you to be courteous. The first rude word you say will guarantee I lose all interest in what you want. The answer to a rude question will *always* be 'No,' and it will stay 'No.' And, just in case you doubt I mean this, I'm going to stick to the 'No' you yourself chose with your rudeness tonight. You may *not* use the car or go out with Kate tonight. But the next time, if you discuss it with me politely, you may ask again. It would be nice to think I will not always have to frustrate you."

And you stick to it. No further discussion, certainly no debate, about tonight's 'No.' If asked, then you simply reiterate that, "On that subject, I have said all I intend to say."

This first limit may be difficult to set. When a teenager has grown accustomed to treating his parents with disrespect, he won't welcome an attempt to change that family culture. The longer this has been going on, the longer it may take to end—by making it clear, again and again, if need be, that you're not kidding and that you won't back down. You should expect this. In setting this key boundary, moms and dads must stick together. Both of you should keep in mind that no limit has actually been set until you have stuck to it in the face of a son's or daughter's not liking it. In fact, the not liking it is the one sure sign that you've done it correctly. For this reason, it's often helpful, when a teenager complains about a set limit, to admit that

"You're not supposed to like it. I'm hoping you will behave better in future, and not force me to say 'No' again soon. That would please me, too. I hope you don't like this. I want the point to be memorable."

This kind of confrontation isn't pleasant for parents, either—and so a word of caution. I have (above) rehearsed a few reasons why you might not have found it easy to set this limit. It may help to stiffen your resolve if you keep in mind that, if you set this limit and then back down from it, you do more harm than if you had not set the limit in the first place. And the stakes are high. Ultimately, with this limit you push a son or daughter to grow up, to become a well-bred, polite person. You are hoping you can help your son to recoil from bullying a woman; that your daughter will refrain from treating a teacher with contempt. Surely, if you let a teenager get away with this wretched behavior you sustain his (correct) belief that, from your point of view, the basic rules of good manners don't apply to him. He'll know, too, because you'll have taught him that your word doesn't warrant his respect.

Anatomy of a Set Limit

Let's pause here to notice the essential elements of a limit. During a boy's shouting you refused to consider his specific question except to say, "Okay, No." Once he became rude you refused to talk about a car, movie, girlfriend, homework, or even your headache. You refused to be distracted or to jump ahead and you kept first things first: his bad manners. You gave no lectures. You did more than talk. You didn't threaten at some amorphous "next" time to bring him up short, to cost him some inconvenience, or make him squirm. You *showed* him. You didn't set a limit in theory and go on with the debate as if you hadn't. You offered a choice for *him* to make. You framed it in such a way that he had to make a choice, and you didn't try to force him to make one or the other choice. He could be rude, or not be rude. There was no third way, which is to say you didn't try to make him do something you couldn't make him do. If he wanted, certainly he could go on behaving like a jerk. You kept the consequences uncomplicated, entirely under your control. You would either listen, or not listen. You didn't give bossy or imperious orders you couldn't enforce, e.g., "You're not leaving this house!" You generalized from this time to all future occasions, and made it clear that, in the future, too, it would be *his* choice (and his chosen consequence, too).

What you did *not* do was equally important. You did not corner him, or remove options, but gave him a choice. You did not spring a punishment on him by surprise, or make up a consequence capriciously. You did not wilt in the heat of his anger, or debate with him what was none of his business, e.g., whether or not you would listen or say "Yes." And finally, you did not lose your dignity, throw an unseemly tantrum, or set a bad example by treating him with an equivalent rudeness or disrespect. Instead of climbing down into the box to yell and throw sand, you invited a teenaged son to step out of the sandbox and behave like an adult.

Put Privileges in Proper Sequence

When a teenager wants something, the object of desire connects him to a parent as a taut fly line connects a trout to an angler. The tension of desire provides leverage for an adult to maneuver a teenager toward maturity.

And so it helps when adults notice what a teenager legitimately wants. In the imaginary conversation above, a boy wanted to use the family car to go out with his girlfriend. In principle, there's nothing wrong with this desire, and in fact we might worry about him if this wish never occurred to him. So let's call this legitimate desire d. But there are other matters that come first, from a mother's point of view, and so you want to use d to guide him toward other adolescent tasks—let's call them a, b, and c—so he can get to d if he cares enough, but only by passing through a, b, and c. In effect, in the above example, you said to him: "I'll be happy to help you get to d, but a, b, and c come first," where a, b, and c were good manners, respect for you, and his agreement from now on with the fundamental family rule you were laying down.

Other examples are easy enough to create. A parent might also say to a teenager, for instance:

> "Sure, it's fine that you want to learn to drive, but you'll have to wait until you're old enough for a driver's permit, and then learn the laws and pass the test—and then I'll enjoy teaching you how to drive."

Or, again:

> "I'll be glad to help you buy a dress for the Senior Prom—nothing I'd rather do. But let's not plan your dress until we know you're going to the Prom. You still have an English essay to write, and it's now late. So I'll cheer from the sidelines, but if you haven't done your paper, you won't need a Prom dress. You'll just need a T-shirt and Levi's to work at your desk on Prom night. School assignments come first."

The parental message is simple. Activities and tasks must be put in sequence. We can come to d as soon as you have accomplished a, b, and c.

A Second Fundamental Rule: "Or Else"

Adults cannot set proper limits for teenagers if they cannot make limits stick. In some families limit-setting breaks down, such as when a parent puts his foot down and a teenager steps over it or around it or on it.

A curfew cannot be set, for example, if a son climbs out of his window after midnight, or a daughter simply fails to come home at all. Fearing insubordination, parents despair of setting limits. If a daughter refuses to cooperate, knuckle under, or care about "groundings" and goes about her business as if parents weren't there, what is a parent to do, short of calling an escort? When a son threatens to defy and resist, some parents fear to stick with their promised consequences or become paralyzed. How can a parent say "No" if he believes his children won't honor his authority? How can he make his set limits stick?

Before answering, I should point out that parental authority over teenaged children's lives has become more precarious in our time. As Lasch states, modern mass culture has eroded parental authority. In many families, both parents work and are busy and absent from home and from the neighborhood during working hours. Adolescent mobility undermines parents' capacity to govern teenagers' lives, even to know where teenagers are, what they're doing, and with whom. Teenagers have access to cell-phones, faxes, and e-mail; to social networking sites; to pornography and other unsuitable sites on the Internet; to television ads and video violence; to interactive and virtual-reality games; to unsupervised homes and bedrooms; to the back seats of cars; to drugs, cash, alcohol, credit, weapons, and ammunition. Instant access, a modern wonder, thwarts adult supervision and undermines adult control. How can parents prevent what they disapprove of (e.g., cigarettes, intercourse, cocaine, alcohol, abortion, pornography) if teenagers already have cell-phones, cash, and wheels? In this modern mass matrix, how can parents make limits stick?[61]

Parental clout, short of psychiatric hospitalization or forced "wilderness" removals from the home environment, relies, for a start, upon parental control over family resources.[62] When parents fear that their teenagers may refuse to accept their limits, they need to take stock calmly of those resources: money, food, transportation, and capital equipment. Parents must know that, if need be, they can and will use their authority over those resources. Teenagers have to know this too, even if parents never have to mention it. To preserve this clout in the context of marital discord or divorce, parents must stick together, to maintain leverage that may help children grow up.[63]

Beyond these material resources, parental authority depends, in the end, upon bonds of love and fidelity to which both parents and teenagers feel a powerful loyalty. For parental limit-setting to have a shaping influence upon character, that bond is essential.[64] By mid-adolescence a son obeys his father not because his father is taller or stronger, or has the family checkbook; and a daughter no longer obeys because her mother can shout louder. Long after teenagers can resist, they usually don't. They still take consequences willingly from adults they respect and love. They obey if they value a parent–child relationship that acts of open insubordination would unravel. This being so, a rupture in adult–adolescent relations weakens a parent's authority.[65]

In sum, then, parental authority derives from control over tangible resources and from parent–child relationships. Put together, parental power stems from a parent's capacity to put an end to material and emotional life on the planet as a teenager knows it. What does this mean? A teenager who defies determined, coordinated parental authority can find herself living suddenly on the dark side of the moon, without friendly chit-chat or resources from Mission Control. It means that material belongings and logistical support can vanish quickly.

Parents can stop the elective use of cars; refuse to provide rides to places a teenager might want to go (except school); withhold an allowance or lunch money; cut off gym membership and cut up credit cards; sell skis and cut up ski passes; remove bicycles, skates, computers, cell-phones, use of the land lines, radios, CD and DVD and mp3 players, iPods, televisions . . . and so on. Music and language lessons can stop. Ball dresses and sports equipage can be locked up. Summer travel can be cancelled. In short, a luxuriant, middle-class lifestyle can be reduced to a boring monotony, which may be what teenagers fear most.

Yet denial of access to wealth isn't the worst consequence of a disrupted adolescent–adult collaboration. Frank insubordination can damage a teenager's relationships with her father and mother. A material moonscape is then merely a metaphor for the impoverishment that may engulf a teenager's emotional life in her family: her loss of a family's loyalty, intimacy, shared history, and future prospects. A girl who doesn't cooperate with reasonable adult expectations, who declares premature independence from parents' rules and sanctions, may be left to come up with her own resources to pay for her own college tuition, or finance her own move into an apartment or dorm. In my family's case, what would ultimately matter to each of my daughters, beyond these merely material considerations, would be her close relationships with both parents and with her sisters, which any serious defiance of her parents' limits and sanctions would have threatened—as they've known, without having to be told, all of their lives. To sail away from home in this way would have risked sailing off the edge of a flat earth into outer darkness. None of them ever wanted to risk pushing too far from shore.

The ultimate source of parental clout, then, is the relationship that welds adults and teenagers to one another in a powerful emotional bond. For teenagers, what ultimately is at stake is that relationship, if it matters to them. This should give parents pause. If a parent's authority with his teenagers ultimately depends upon his emotional bond with them, then that relationship needs continually to be preserved and strengthened. What makes it strong? When all goes well, that bond is reinforced by affectionate parental recognition and the value children put upon the parental sunshine in which they bask.

The converse is also true. If that recognition becomes attenuated because of parental distraction, lack of interest, departure, or drink, then it may come to mean little to a teenaged son or daughter. Without intimacy and mutual recognition, a weakened parent–teenager bond fails to sustain parental authority, and this alienation may make it difficult or impossible for a parent to set limits. This in turn may make it difficult or impossible for a parent to help an adolescent son or daughter grow up straight and strong.

Make It a Choice

Set limits ahead of time. Don't imagine, except in the event of fire, that it's your task to control a teenager's behavior in real time. You cannot always be there when he decides how to behave. Your task, instead, is to shape his choices well in advance, so he has the experience, required for his maturation, of making choices for himself and then facing the known consequences. Your goal isn't to run his life moment to moment, but rather to shape his character so that when you're not there to guide him, he makes good choices.

Let's consider an imaginary example. You've become exasperated by your son's sluggish response to repeated suggestions that he get up on time to dress and eat breakfast before school. Despite your wake-up calls, he usually goes back to sleep. When he arrives at the breakfast table at 7:20 a.m., complaining angrily that you "didn't get me up!" and misses the school bus that passes by your corner at 7:25 a.m. sharp, he demands that you drive him the three miles to school, because of course it must be your fault that he's late. So far, your approach has been: to remind him every five minutes from 6:30 a.m. onward, then to yell up the stairs that you'll feed his eggs to the gerbils, then to chew him out over breakfast until your exasperated husband, who's tired of listening to it, angrily drives your son to school.

These are frustrated attempts to control a son's behavior in real time. Certainly when a son is six or ten years old, it makes sense to supervise morning ablutions, to remind and goad and hug and hustle a little boy to elementary school. But at some point you'll decide that it's time for him to manage his morning tasks himself, and become punctual. This milestone in maturity may require a limit set ahead of time, to shape a son's choices rather than maneuver him, under your control, to behave in particular ways. To illustrate, let's imagine that, having noticed the pattern, you knock on his door on a school night and sit down to say in a friendly way: "I have a bone to pick with you."

Assuming this gets his attention and he asks, "Okay, what?" you say:

> "I dislike the way we start most school days. I start out angry with you, and I don't want to do that anymore. So I'll teach you how to set your alarm clock, if you need help. I'm going to treat you like the young man you're trying to become, and not a little boy. From now on, *you* decide whether to get up on time to eat breakfast with us and catch the bus. As you know, that bus arrives at your corner at 7:25 a.m. You are fifteen years old. From now on, I'm going to stop nagging you. I'm going to let *you* choose when to get up."

He may not be wholly impressed, of course, by the speech. He may not be listening, because he thinks that he knows you too well, and believes you'll never give up the delicious pleasure of nagging him. You might add, nevertheless, just so that he can picture how it's going to be:

> "If you come downstairs before seven o'clock and ask me politely to make you some breakfast while your dad and I

are having coffee, I will fry up some eggs and make some toast while you're in the shower. But if you arrive after seven, you won't have time both to eat and also to catch the bus, so I won't cook you breakfast. You'll have a choice to make. You can skip breakfast and catch the bus; or you can make your own breakfast and walk to school. I won't decide that for you."

If he's attentive, you might go on to explain:

"Your dad and I agree we've been treating you like a baby. We need to start to treat you like the young man you're rapidly becoming. So catch the bus at the corner at 7:25 a.m.—with or without breakfast. That's all up to you. But by not catching it you'll be choosing to walk to school. Your choice."

You should be able to go to bed without debate, inasmuch as you're not telling him what to do, only what *you* will do. There really isn't much to debate. It's not his place to tell you what you will do. Yet despite their protests to the contrary, teenagers sometimes resent being treated like adults. So your son might say, "That's lame! You mean I'm not going to get any breakfast? And you are making me walk to school?"

To which, of course, you reply:

"I'm not going to make you do anything. You decide to get up or not, to eat breakfast or not, to catch the bus or not. I'm talking only about what I'm going to do. I'm *not* going to baby or nag you. Whether you rise and shine, or sleep in, eat or walk, *you* decide."

And, in a friendly way, you might add:

"Your father and I know all about this. We've been getting up to go to work for many years. We do it every weekday to provide for you. We have lots of experience about this, so if you want our advice, just ask. And we love you, and don't see enough of you, so we hope to see you at breakfast."

This sounds okay, but there'll probably have to be a test. Do you really mean it? Does he really have to take care of himself? So, very soon, this imaginary son surely won't set his alarm, or will fail to get up when his alarm goes off, and so he won't get down to breakfast before seven to ask for eggs and toast. Instead, he'll arrive at the breakfast table breathless, throwing his books into his pack just as the bus goes by. His father has already gone. When you shrug and hold him to the anticipated consequences of his choice, he'll throw a tantrum. He may look sad like a small boy and tempt you to relent. He may cry and treat you to strenuous wheedling and make excuses and promises, insisting that it will be just this once, and that he has an important quiz at eight o'clock and cannot afford to be late, and if he has another tardy he'll have detention after school and then be late to basketball practice ... and then he won't get to play in Friday's game ... and so on.

You must never relent in the face of angry, entitled demands or ugly insults, because to do so sends entirely the wrong message. I cannot honestly say that I *never* relent in the face of strenuous wheedling. Yet you and I must remind each other that, after all, those results of his tardiness (botched quiz, detention, missed practice, not playing in a game) are precisely the anxiety-provoking consequences your limit-setting was meant to put into his mind. The squirming was the point; it prods young people to grow up. So if I relent once, I never do twice.

Don't Make It *Your* Problem

Well-set limits offer choices. Even though parents line up incentives to favor a considerate decision, there's a choice. Even when not completely spelled out, those options are present. For example, if a son demands to stay out until three a.m., and his mother answers "No," the consequences may not be spelled out, but there's an obvious choice: to obey or not to obey. In many households, presumably, this option and its consequences needn't be made vocal, and the odds of his making the defiant choice may be long. Yet troubled teenagers in unhappy families demonstrate every day of the week that the defiant alternative is there.

When the odds are closer to even that a boy might make the defiant or crass choice, then it's important to spell out the consequences in anticipation of a teenager making his choice. Why? Because to make threats only *after* he's acted, or as he's about to act against your wishes, is to make his behavior your problem. Rather than his squirming with a conflict—his wish to and his wish not to—your simply punishing him afterward only makes him suffer a consequence he may not have foreseen. You're trying then to control his behavior with threats rather than making him anticipate and think about a choice. Last-minute threats often reduce to questions of power, to a question of whether you have enough force to compel obedience. There's no internal conflict, only an external coercive struggle between *you* and *him*. The experience doesn't create character; it only produces endless parent–child conflict. Whether he comes home tardy or on time has become *your* problem, not his. He'll only resent your hovering over him like a puppeteer, controlling his behavior, and will feel that, to be his own person, he must defy you.

We say that this mistake is to "split his ambivalence"—and it doesn't help a son to make his own moral decisions. In fact, it only makes barbaric misbehavior more palatable. For if we assume that he is, like most young people, conflicted about a moral issue—e.g., his wish to stay out past curfew to carouse with pals vs. his wish to behave in his family like a good citizen and to have his parents' respect and approval, and not feel ashamed of himself and guilty about hurting them, then he has a difficult choice to make. He'll have to give up one or the other. But if, as his father, you come down on one side and insist that *you* now will police his comings and goings and make him come home on time, then he can focus on sneaking out, because you're taking care of the other side of the conflict. He no longer has a moral choice to make, just a father to outmaneuver.[66] The inner conflict has become an external struggle. It no longer takes place in a son's heart and mind, but rather in an enacted morality play—between a son, who wants autonomy, and a father, who wants to reduce a boy to a puppet.

The solution is to set a limit ahead of time and make a boy own his ambivalence (e.g., about coming home on time), rather than taking away half of it. It's to force a boy to deal with conflict in *his* heart and mind, and to stay out of it. In the end, surely, you want to have a son who acknowledges that all the legitimate family (and civic) rules apply to him, and that he's responsible for obeying them. To set a limit that makes an issue of considerate compliance, you want *him* to have to choose between obeying his parents vs. defying them (and so having to face consequences that, we assume, you will mean and make stick). For example, as a father you might say:

"Your mother and I agree that your responsible doing of chores and homework warrant extending your curfew to midnight on Fridays and Saturdays. We are proud of you. But let's be clear, we mean that midnight is now the *latest* you may come home, not the earliest. We expect this to be *your* problem, not ours—that you will care about time and think of your parents, who worry if you're late. Just so we have no misunderstanding, let's also agree that if you're late there will be consequences:

- Minor tardy, 1–15 minutes ➔ grounded the next week-end.
- Serious tardy, 15–30 minutes ➔ grounded *and* lose use of the car (except to and from school) for *two* weeks.
- Felony tardy, > 30 minutes, and you don't call us before nine p.m. to discuss your plans ➔ your weekend curfew will be seven p.m. until further notice."

These choices are clear, and the problem now belongs to the son, not the father. You aren't bullying him *not* to do something he's already decided to do, or arbitrarily punishing him after he's made a mistake. You make him choose his own consequence. By making the limits clear, you prevent them from becoming a matter of debate—"You didn't tell me," or "That's too harsh," or "How about we start *next* week?" If he takes the car keys on this basis, he's agreed to the terms, and the struggle is his. When he makes each of the subordinate choices it takes to get home on time—e.g., whether to be tempted by friends who badger him to stay out, whether to ignore his watch, whether he's distracted by a song on the radio or an erotic dalliance—he now has to resolve all of those decisions like a grown-up or face the (known) consequences.

Put the other way around, you aren't hovering over him to micro-manage him in real time. You're not fighting for control. You're on his side, rooting for him, hoping he'll again earn your respect. You haven't solved his problems for him or stayed up all night to call him on his cell-phone or chase around the neighborhood to herd him home. You haven't even lectured to him about the virtues of punctuality. You just set the terms of his choice ahead of time, and you defined the consequences.

This may not sound too difficult when it comes to a curfew, but what about more serious and immediate risks, like drug use or sexual intercourse? How can a parent let a teenager make his own choices when the consequences of a bad decision are so serious, even lethal? Don't parents have to say, "No, you *won't* drink," or "No, you *won't* have sexual intercourse"—and then prevent a teenager from doing those forbidden things? Isn't it better to threaten, punish, and try to control a son's drug use or a daughter's erotic behavior to eliminate the choice entirely, and reduce the risks to zero?

The answer is "Yes"—with a three-year-old. We cannot expect toddlers to decide about drugs or sex, and, as parents, we don't let them do so, because we don't let them out of our sight. In our culture, however, this level of supervision is rarely available for teenagers, except at great cost. For most parents to insist upon making these decisions would require the imposition of total control over teenaged sons and daughters 24/7, and for most parents this isn't possible, even if it were a good idea.[67] True, other cultures, e.g., Saudi Arabia, might allow one plausibly to prevent a daughter from using alcohol or having intercourse, but only in a police state, where the *mutaween* walk the beat "protecting" people's virtue, and women are confined to wearing *abayas*. When we send teenagers to high school and go to work in the United States, as many of us must do, then they'll have access to drugs and sex, whether we like it or not.

The solution is to protect teenagers as best we can, so they only have choices we trust them to handle wisely, and within that protected family perimeter set limits so they struggle with conflict and become mature. If we do so, teenagers will grow up making choices and taking consequences, and survive their adolescence. Put another way, if we don't "over-parent" them and refrain from taking control of all domains in their lives in which they may legitimately make their own choices, then they may grow up to be able to make their own ethical decisions.[68]

Most boys and girls who've had good relationships with reasonably attentive, constructive parents will want to do the right thing—to make their parents, grandparents, and family friends proud of them, and preserve their own self-respect. But teenagers also have access to drugs and alcohol, which are endemic in our society, and their friends may well be using. Like adults, teens want to be touched and embraced, to feel erotically excited, get close, and feel loved. Like the rest of us, adolescents live in the land of the lotus-eaters, and they're conflicted about Eros. They want to join their friends in Dionysian revels, and they think about sex and long for its pleasures, morning, noon, and night. On the other hand, they also want to be "good"—whatever that means to them and their parents. They hope to do the "right" thing—whatever they think that is. They want to be restrained, to feel self-controlled, and not ashamed or guilty.

So, they are in conflict. To struggle and grow up by resolving this ambivalence in their own ways, according to their own emerging ideals and precarious self-discipline, require that a teenager contain these alternatives. To develop a mature capacity to tolerate ambivalence, and to behave in a gracious, self-disciplined way despite the call of the wild requires that they wrestle with these opposed motives, set into conflict by deftly set limits.

Mean It

Limits mustn't be set on a whim, on the fly, or when you're angry. A limit ought not to be impulsively un-set, either, whether in the heat of a debate or from a failure of nerve, from caving in to extortion or as a round of applause for a moving aria in an adolescent soap opera. It isn't that you should never change your mind. However, the time to listen to a debate is before you set a limit, not during the bathos that often follows a teenager's discovery that sometimes your answer is really going to be "No." Often a firm "No" with inconvenient implications brings out a teenager's eloquence, her capacity for intricate legal logic, and her vision of future good behavior. Whenever you successfully make a misbehaving adolescent squirm, you're going to hear at least one of the following:

- "If you let me go this time, I'll never do that again!"
- "Gosh, I never guessed that when you said it, you were serious, but hey, now that I know, well, next time I'll behave."
- "That is *so* unfair—you let *him* do it twice. So you have to let me get away twice, too. And, in the lovely by and by, I promise I'll do what you ask, but you just have got to let it pass this time."

When you hear the above, lash yourself to the mast and don't be persuaded by the siren song. Once you set a limit, treat it as an oath you've sworn on the future happiness of your grandchildren. Don't unsay it, but insist that your children live graciously for now within the limits you've set. You may express a general willingness to change the terms once a teenager abides by the terms you've defined without complaint, and over time. Don't back off when a teenager balks at accepting them at all. Don't promise to relent on any particular date. The problem must be a teenager's own problem—to demonstrate gracious acceptance over time—and not your burden to figure out when they might satisfactorily do so. Keep before you the firm knowledge that this squirming, that eloquence, and all visions of future good judgment and exemplary behavior are sure signs that your limits are working, and needed. They're not the bells that toll to mark the end of a need for them.

So instead, your answers should be:

- "I should hope you will never do that again! Gracious!"
- "I *am* serious. You finally have got it right. And assuming you behave yourself, there might someday *be* a next time."
- "I have to do *no* such thing. I'm offended to hear you suggest I should let you misbehave. I do not, and I will not; and in future we'll watch what you do—not just listen to what you say. I will be proud of you, believe me, when I *see* it."

This is important enough to say again. The last thing you want a teenager to infer, as they will from any un-setting of limits, is that your solemn word has no lasting meaning. The last lesson you want an adolescent to learn is that whining or bluster or insults can reopen the gates of Eden, and let him back into the garden of childhood. So plug your ears to all blandishments. There *will* be a next time, but wait for it. As for now, think before you set a consequence, but set that limit in concrete, and mean it.

Accept Dysphoria

Limits frustrate. This is the point! When you confront a boy about bad manners or lack of consideration, the whole idea is to put him on the spot and make him squirm. When you set a limit, you mean to make a girl uneasy or ashamed, to leave her feeling anxious, if that's how she feels when her bad manners are confronted. Your limits confront her narcissistic entitlement, call out her lack of empathy, and challenge her assumption that you're forever her puppet. Your limits make an issue of her selfishness. You needn't feel badly about bringing up her faults, be reluctant to note her misbehavior, or shrink from chewing her out. Let her be uneasy! Don't rush to end her dysphoria. If your relationship has substance to it, there'll be no lasting breach. And keep in mind that you're doing what she needs, even if it isn't what she wants. You're pushing her to grow up. This is what you owe her, as her parent, and you must expect that, if you're good at it, she will suffer a little. In fact, if she doesn't squirm when you enforce a limit, you probably haven't done it properly.

However, as you set limits, use empathy. Let teenagers know that you understand perfectly well they don't like to be told "No," that they don't like consequences: Why should they? There's no harm in letting them know that you know they wish it were otherwise: of course they do! But don't make nice, either. Try not to make a fetish of your guilt about having to set a limit and enforce it. It's all right to say that a teenager needs a lesson "to become a fine (wo)man." And if you need reassurance in the face of a teenager's squirming, anger, threats, indignation, or hurt feelings, then remind yourself that setting limits is what loving parents do for sons and daughters—and it is for you also to endure those unhappy feelings, so that a son or daughter can become a fine adult, rather than a spoiled, unattractive, and dysfunctional person. Your squeamishness, if it prevents you from helping a son or daughter to grow up, is no kindness.

Hang Together

Limits cannot be set effectively unless adults stick together. This sounds obvious, but sticking together can be hard to do. In children, the ancient stratagem of divide and conquer seems to be hardwired. No one has to teach a teenager to say one thing to dad about mom ("I'm too hungry to do algebra in school, because Mom won't cook me any breakfast!"), and something else to mom about dad ("He thinks you're pretty uptight about this bus deal!"), to persuade one parent to undo a limit set by the other ("Heck, get in—we'll stop for a muffin, and I'll drop you off at school with a note . . ."). We've called this tactic *splitting*. When teenagers split adults (parents vs. teacher, or coach vs. parents), one adult tries to hold fast to a limit that the other adult gets talked into opposing or undoing. To get suckered into this is a foolish thing for an adult to do, although it's always a little tempting. One adult gets the satisfaction of becoming, however briefly, a teenager's favorite, who is "nice." The other adult, of course, gets to be the goat.

Marital discord and divorce make splitting likely. Divorce is a common obstacle to child-rearing in divided and blended families, and limit-setting becomes nearly impossible. Judy Wallerstein, who's written definitive studies of divorce, has considered the complexities involved but in the end she contends that, for this reason among others, the children of divorced parents are often at risk for delayed maturation.[69] Her follow-up studies demonstrate that more than any other indicator the quality of parental collaboration among ex-spouses predicts the children's developmental outcome. As she would say, parents may need to split up, but the less "split" they become as parents, the better the children will do.

How to prevent splitting? In principle, the answer is simple: stick together by talking and listening to one another, and make determined efforts to treat one another with respect, at least on the subject of the children. Willing collaboration has no substitute. If one parent is annoyed, she must tell the other (politely) why; if one is exasperated, he must listen to the other's reply. If this doesn't happen, splitting can only make one parent contemptuous of the other, a needless hostility that often evaporates when one parent checks his perceptions with the other ("Oh, *that's* what you meant about not cooking him breakfast—he made it sound like you were trying to starve him").

One adult's basic trust in the other helps, as does empathy. This may be obvious, but it's nonetheless difficult. The anger and hurt feelings that so often persist after a divorce can dissolve empathy. Parents get split even in intact marriages, where they sleep every night in the same bed. Transient annoyances make compassionate talk less likely; each parent fears the other's blame and his or her own anger. So, splitting becomes more likely when other stresses have already frayed a couple's patience with one another or opened a rift. In this context, a son's complaint about his mother's unreasonable criticism resonates with his father's own grievances.

Even in intact marriages, daughters and sons can spot this seismic fault in adult unity with uncanny acuity. It takes little adolescent discernment to find the line of schism when parents are openly fighting or divorce has supervened to open a gap in empathy. Against a teenager's clever splitting, a divided house cannot stand. Resenting a rule or limit, a teenager will worm her way into the division. The relenting parent, flattered by a daughter's admiration for his superior *savoir faire*, consoled by her (temporary) offer to take his side, joins her in a campaign against the other parent's apparently unreasonable ("stupid" or "mean" or "small-minded") constraint. In this tug-of-war, limits get lost, and maturation comes to a halt. In the long run, the children always pay the price.

Splitting doesn't only happen inside the perimeter of the family. It occurs when a narcissistic parent, hearing an angry son's warped account, flies into a protective snit and sides with him against a teacher's legitimate limit-setting.[70] It happens when narcissistic parents, enraged by a coach's confrontation with a son's narcissism, withhold contributions for the new gymnasium unless the headmaster fires the coach. Or when an arrogant parent hires a lawyer to undo a boy's speeding ticket on a technicality. In all these cases it would clearly be better in the long run for the teenagers involved if a calm parent simply made a polite phone call to confirm the justice of the set limit. Or if a sensible parent joined with her ex-spouse, or the teacher, coach, or trooper, to make it abundantly clear to an adolescent son or daughter that *all* the rules apply to them. Parents do better to show up with sons and daughters to speak directly to teachers, coaches, or judges, demonstrating how adults take responsibility for their own behavior. In these ways, parents help rather than hinder the rearing of responsible students, athletes, and citizens.

Firm up the Boundaries

Parental limit-setting requires boundaries and hierarchy. For a start, parents cannot exercise authority within the family without a "vertical" distinction—a generational boundary—that distinguishes responsible adults from teenagers, who must be expected to accept adult decisions with reasonable grace. Parents must sustain this generational boundary by making clear what decisions are adult and which ones properly are delegated to teenagers to make for themselves. As children grow up, parents properly relinquish those choices that young people demonstrate sufficient maturity to make, a delegation that starts with toddlers ("Cornflakes or Wheaties this morning?"), broadens through college ("What have you decided to major in?"), and expands until young adults become financially and emotionally independent. This widening scope notwithstanding, parents must also make clear which decisions they don't relinquish.

For example,

"I like hearing you sing, but sure, you can decide to drop out of choir. Let's be clear, however, that loitering at the mall is not an alternative to choir, nor is doing 'nothing' an option, either. Video games aren't a legitimate substitute and neither is text messaging. So if you drop choir, that'll be fine, so long as you pick up a sport or another organized after-school activity, or get a job."

In effect, this parent is saying, "*This* choice is yours to make, but not *that* one." When parents distinguish between consultation and decision-making, they preserve the authority to say "No" when necessary. When it comes to parents' decisions, it may be important to ask children what they think, depending on how old they are, and to listen to how they might feel. Yet when it comes to adult decisions, children don't get a vote. A family is not a democracy.

Generational boundaries become a problem when they get blurred or vanish. In intact families, parents sometimes fudge a boundary out of ignorance or a misguided wish to be pals instead of parents. Generational boundaries become a problem, too, when the parental alliance weakens through divorce, illness, adoption, addiction, or death—and so a child or teenager rises to quasi-adult status and participates (or thinks he ought to participate) in decisions that aren't for children to make. Economic stress or social strain—e.g., immigration, war, violent crime, or a natural catastrophe—can also undermine adult authority. For example, an immigrant father's inability to make a living in the manner he used to routinely diminishes his family authority, particularly relative to an adolescent son or daughter who quickly learns a new country's customs and patois. When a spouse dies, the lonely, stressed widow/er may too easily permit a son/daughter to become the "man/lady of the house." Such premature promotions of teenagers undermine adult authority and risk that adolescents may become too big for their britches. Then, without an adult able to set limits, he may fail to have a proper childhood experience of limit-setting, and so fail to outgrow a childish grandiosity.

Pick Your Battles

Parents cannot set every needed limit at once. Adults have to choose which problem to address first. This can be difficult, for adolescence normally evokes all the prior conflicts of childhood from infancy on. When a troubled, immature teenager begins to fail at all the tasks of adolescence, many limits seem to need to be set simultaneously and immediately—about diction, dress, homework, punctuality, manners, chores, music, Internet access, video games, consideration for others, use of the car, drug use, and erotic boundaries. To set them all at once is a set up for failure (yours and hers, too) and for frustration (yours and hers, too). Generally, when a teenager has fallen behind in development, it's prudent to set a few limits at a time.

Which ones first? I've suggested two fundamental rules, which seem to come first: mutual respect and basic acceptance of adult authority. These are the *sine qua non* bases for any other limit-setting. Once these rules have become a consensus in the family, there are many ways to proceed. You might take up whatever comes up next, as psychotherapists do, trusting that a teenager unerringly will present the next problem that should be addressed. This is what parenting often looks like: adults and teenagers going about their usual routines until an issue surfaces that must be dealt with. When maturation has been delayed, however, and a teenager's whole approach to life remains childish, and problems emerge in every venue (school, family, and social relations), it may be best for parents to think developmentally and start with first things first: trust, autonomy, initiative, industry, and identity.[71]

When (in a therapeutic school, for example) we deal with global breakdown in teenagers who no longer can safely live at home, we begin with basic trust and go on to a fundamental acceptance of rules. We cannot proceed further until we can agree on this much. We begin in this order because we cannot deal with other problems, which haven't yet presented themselves within our new relationships. We choose trust and trustworthiness because trust (or mistrust) becomes the basis for all the recognition and limit-setting that will follow. We look at lying, sneaking, cheating, half-truths, manipulation, stealing, vandalism, and cutting—all the various actions and words that prevent us from believing what a boy says or trusting what a girl will do. We insist upon our talking directly and honestly with one another and demand that we—student and staff—mean what we say. We make sure that adults live up to trustworthy expectations, as parents also must do. And so we set the stage for mutual recognition. If we are to get to effective limit-setting, we need to create relationships that matter to both parties. Once we have examined matters of trust and honest mutual recognition, we can then go on to whatever comes up next.

Choose Where and When

Misbehavior must be addressed and limits set promptly, not after a problem has become ancient history. Promptly doesn't always mean this very second. To set some limits it may make sense to choose a place and a time to get rid of distractions. For a start, take the teenager aside to talk privately, if it's possible. You may wish to point out that you don't want him to be humiliated in public. Take the boy into his own bedroom and shut the door—out of consideration and respect, which is usually appreciated. At the start, at least, there may be no need to shame him, and this usually will prove to be true if there still exists sufficient affection and respect between you and him for you to expect that he'll want not to disappoint you. If I know a teenager will take my blunt words to heart, I don't need to say them in public.

On the other hand, there are times when it becomes necessary to dress down a teenager in public. I've done it, and no doubt will do it again, but only when I want deliberately to cause shame, to create a crisis for an arrogant, defiant teenager who isn't sufficiently chastened by a considerate word to the wise. I do so when there's too little inner capacity for regret, guilt, or reason. But a public shaming is never my first approach.

Fit the Consequence to Its Occasion

What penalty is right? When is a punishment "enough?" No doubt parents ought to aim for the Goldilocks prescription. But what does *just right* look like? The metric should be: a desired effect on a teenager's emotional life. I aim to make sure a sanction causes sufficient inconvenience, boredom, or humiliation to make its point. Too little sanction fails to cause suitable frustration, and too much sanction, or one that goes on and on, tends to thwart the purpose of limit-setting, which is to bring about an internal change.

Teenagers need finite, uncomfortable consequences, which soon come to an end, and don't last longer than a child's capacity to focus or to remember. If a consequence goes on and on, even a teenager will forget why he's been grounded or has lost his allowance income. There's little point in punishing a teenager if all she can think about is the gross injustice of the sanction, or if she forgets how she chose it. This is why exasperated adults ought never give a vague, interminable punishment for a modest infraction. If a parent tells a teenager, "Okay, that's it!—you can never, ever, ever use the car again!" or "Now you've done it, you're grounded for a decade!" then he'll have to undo the limit he's set because he suffers from guilt or shame about the extremity of the punishment; or because it's become more inconvenient for him (e.g., having to drive a teenager to school and pick her up) than for his daughter; or because he realizes, with exasperation, that the point has long been forgotten. Moreover, parents need to be cautious that their routine consequences are not so extreme that they discourage a son or daughter from admitting a mistake or confessing to a misdemeanor.

In sum, a consequence ought to be apt. There's a poetic justice in the cleverest consequences, a sense of fit between crime and punishment. A boy who misuses the family car, for example, may properly lose its use. A girl who comes home late may properly be required for a time to come home early. A boy who comes late to school may be asked to "stay after." These consequences enjoy a natural logic that is not lost on teenagers, who see that it makes sense for a boy who fails to come in out of the rain to get wet and cold.

A General Approach to Limit-Setting

Let me repeat: a parent who cannot or will not set limits is powerless to help sons and daughters grow up. Moreover, if we parents leave this fundamental parental task to others (teachers, coaches, bosses, detectives, spouses, attorneys, ex-friends, prison guards), those other adults aren't likely to be gentle with the obnoxious, incompetent, irresponsible, and childish adults our children become. Surely, if we love our children, it's better that we ourselves prod them to grow up.

There's no sense in not setting limits. Going too easy on our children isn't really going easy on them. So limit-setting ought to be one important aspect of what we do to rear our children, because we love them. We ought not to view these constraints as avoidable disruption in a cozy palship, but rather as fundamental parental tasks. Moreover, we do best to frame limits in active, purposeful diction, because limit-setting should be proactive not reactive, direct and clear, not indirect and vague, and thoughtful rather than carelessly offhand or angrily impulsive. Taken together, these various suggestions sum up a general approach to limit-setting:

- *Insist upon Basic Courtesy*
- *If Necessary, End "Life As You Know It"*
- *Make It a Choice—Ahead of Time, Not in Real Time*
- *Don't Make It Your Problem*
- *Mean It*
- *Accept Dysphoria*
- *Hang Together*
- *Firm up the Boundaries*
- *Pick Your Battles*
- *Choose Where and When*
- *Fit the Consequence to Its Occasion*

The first is the prerequisite for all the others. Parents must follow this one, too; for all the rest have no point if we've not adopted a dignified, respectful, truthful approach to limit-setting. Given their complexity, limits ought not to be set in adult rage, or when an adult is distracted or intoxicated. It isn't only our children who need to be well-behaved and mature.

Taken together, these precepts are meant to create a culture (in the family or classroom, on the field, or in a courtroom) in which both adults and children can be heard and taken seriously. They define a "parental" leadership appropriate to the family and suited to other venues. As a leader's paradigm, on any team, they promote grown-up behavior in teenagers, students, nurses, ball players, and soldiers. The corollary is: if parents have *not* yet achieved that mutually respectful culture at home, they ought to start there. If parents have lost it, they ought to do whatever they can to find it, recreate it, repair it, and then defend it.[72] At stake is the creation of mature adults and a civil society.

8   Spoiled and Beaten: Frank and Gail

I N PREVIOUS chapters I implied that if limits are set badly or not at all then pathological *narcissism* occurs. Neither the next-door neighbors nor we have any trouble making the connection between lax parental discipline and adolescent misbehavior. When a child who hasn't been constrained by adult limits turns into a presumptuous, dishonest, obnoxious, and irresponsible teenager, we infer that his parents applied few limits or failed to take them seriously. When we're tactful, we call such teenagers *indulged*, *entitled*, and *childish*. Yet we know these aren't passing problems, and we discern that such teenagers have been durably harmed. When we're less tactful, we say they're *screwed up*, and we know they're damaged goods. We say they've been *spoiled*.

CASE I: AN INDULGED BOY

Years ago, a boy provoked my exasperation—as did his parents, for they found it all but impossible to stick to a "No," even on those rare occasions when they managed to say the word at all. They couldn't hold *any* line. As with most parental errors, there were reasons for this wobbliness. From their neighbors' vantage, however, they weren't valid excuses, only explanations. But before we turn to why this happened, let's remind ourselves briefly what an indulged, undisciplined boy looks and sounds like.

I'm aware that in choosing Frank as the subject of this study, I could have picked a more nearly normal teenager, whose narcissism might more closely have resembled a reader's normal or nearly normal adolescent son or daughter. Yet to demonstrate the sub-optimal taste of a pie when there's less sugar than the recipe calls for, it's more impressive to leave out the sugar completely. The resulting defect isn't subtle, and the lesson is obvious. Frank's symptoms and misbehaviors were noisy and florid.

By the time his parents applied to enroll him in a therapeutic boarding school, his defects were hard to miss. They described him this way:

> Our son has been rough on us. His current behavior patterns include verbal abuse, disrespect, devious actions, lies, lack of academic motivation, not obeying rules, and an unwillingness to accept responsibility for his actions. Frank also has become very manipulative to get his way. He expresses anger by yelling, talking back to both of us, hitting a wall, or throwing things. When told to do something he will ignore the command and do whatever he wants. It's felt like he wanted to control his own life and not answer to anyone else, especially us, his parents.
>
> Last summer—all within a three-week period—he turned sixteen and obtained his driver's license and found a new girlfriend. From that point things have gone rapidly downhill. He was picked up by an Ohio State Trooper for reckless driving on the way to her house. In court he was so rude that the judge revoked his license for six months. Then he drove his car anyway, without a license. He could not handle what was happening and became depressed. He became obsessed and possessive about his girlfriend. He hid behind a tree in her father's garden, trying to catch her cheating on him, so kids at school started calling him "Sneaky Snake," which he didn't think was very funny, and so he got into fistfights.
>
> His jealousy made her break up with him. He still felt she belonged to him, though. He was willing to sacrifice everything—family, friends, school, and his personal reputation—to somehow win her back. Because of all of this, doing schoolwork has become the furthest thing from his mind. So now he is failing all his courses. He is so preoccupied with his rivalry he does not seem to care, although we tell him he will never get into a good college if he does not do his homework.
>
> We know all this makes Frank sound bad. But he's basically a nice person when he's not angry. When he was little, he

seemed to care about others. However, he will now do almost anything to be accepted by peers, who no longer seem to like Frank very much. This causes him to do show-offy things that get him into trouble. He makes bad decisions.

Diagnostically, the broad sweep of Frank's misbehaviors and repetitive failures is reminiscent of Lisa's similarly global troubles. Now seventeen, Frank is floundering at home, in high school, and socially among his age-mates. This is adolescent immaturity.[73] His tantrums would be amusing slapstick, except that he risks doing grievous harm to someone either by assaulting them in a jealous rage or driving wildly. This kind of defiant, impetuous childishness becomes unfunny in a young man with car keys. Frank demonstrates a reckless arrogance and self-preoccupation. He lacks consideration or empathy for others; he has no college or career plans; he is indifferent to consequences of his impulsive actions; he relies on bullying "puppet" relationships with his girlfriend and his parents; and he has selfish, primitive ethics that concern only what Frank wants now, without abstract scruple, sense of honor, integrity, or concern for the good of his family.

Where does Frank's immaturity come from? It's not difficult to see. For a start, Frank's unhappy parents have reared him on the wrong theory. They want help from a therapeutic school, but they really don't understand the problem they're having such a hard time solving. They believe that Frank's misbehavior results from *bad decisions*—as if he didn't think logically; from *jealousy*—as if his feelings were natural and comprehensible emotions, and so all of us must forgive his wretched behavior, because all of us would be jealous, too; from a *disability*—as if Frank couldn't be expected to behave; and from an admirable, normal boyish wish to *control his own life*. They don't like his behavior, but they also don't see that they can do anything about his unfortunate motivations. Their theory doesn't lead them to action, but their account indicates the very source of the problem. They tell us that despite Frank's "verbal abuse, disrespect, devious actions, lies, lack of academic motivation, not obeying rules, and an unwillingness to accept responsibility for his actions," even after Frank had been "yelling, talking back to both of us, hitting a wall or throwing things," even after he "was picked up by the police for reckless driving," and even after he'd been "so rude that the youth court judge in Cincinnati revoked his license," this presumptuous, entitled, irresponsible, devious, reckless, jealous, and pugnacious young man "drove his car anyway." This final phrase, in four words, tells us the problem: a lack of parental limit-setting. How do we know ? Because in the wake of this minor's behavior, he still possesses a set of keys to a car! Clearly, no one has ever said "No" to this obnoxious boy, and meant it. Frank had been spoiled.

The lack of limit-setting provided the obstacle to Frank's development and makes sense of his childish grandiosity. Some of the reasons for this lack of limit-setting were apparent in a report to Juvenile Court prepared by a psychologist, who met with Frank after his second arrest and interviewed his parents prior to his second appearance before an indignant judge. The psychologist wrote:

> Frank's parents, Dan and Betty, were married for nine years before Frank's birth. Prior to this only child's arrival, his parents endured six miscarriages—some far along in gestation, one a stillbirth at term. Frank was a much-prized baby, whose birth cost his parents multiple gynecological work-ups, surgeries, and medications. During this long vigil, Betty was prescribed medication that helped but did not relieve her chronic anxiety and intractable depression. During this wait, she kept a journal noting imagined developmental achievements of her "lost" babies. Dan blames himself for the couple's failure to conceive and for all the spontaneous abortions his wife endured. He waited on her in bed, hand and foot, during the last months of Frank's gestation.
>
> Frank's birth came only ten days prematurely, but that it was early at all seemed to complicate the couple's triumphant day with a traumatic angst about whether the baby would live, or be damaged, or suffer. Betty could not bear to let the nurses put Frank back into the nursery. She never slept at all in the six days they spent in the hospital, prior to taking him home. In the following months Betty was up and down all night, Dan recalls, checking to make sure Frank was still breathing. The homecoming was difficult. Breast-feeding went badly. Frank turned red-faced when he could not get enough, and, thinking she was starving him, she felt upstaged when Frank avidly

gobbled down the bottled formula the pediatrician finally prescribed.

Frank resisted toilet-training. He continued to have fecal accidents at school and in bed at night until he was six. His mother often kept him home so that he would not be embarrassed about wearing diapers. In kindergarten his teacher insisted that he be toilet-trained if he were going to come to school, a condition Betty resented, because she thought the teacher ought to be willing to change Frank's diapers. The family managed to get him toilet-trained, but only after repeated tantrums. Frank preferred to poop in his diaper and to have his mother change him, rather than get himself to the toilet.

His tantrums were not only about toilet-training, however. Frank threw tantrums whenever he was told "No." His parents did not consider this a problem when he was young, because Betty relented whenever he became "upset"—and just let him have his way. Frank became interested in the playground, but he did not like having to do schoolwork. He resisted even the most rudimentary tasks sent home to do. He got into power struggles with teachers who held him to the line, and so Dan remonstrated with them, because Frank seemed to have learning difficulties. At home, his mother did not insist he do his homework "unless he felt like it," reasoning that otherwise Frank would hate school. In class his teachers disliked his defiance and tantrums, and probably disliked *him*, his mother feels. Following his outbursts in second, third, fourth, and fifth grades, teachers often sent him home. When he was suspended, his mother held private parties for the two of them, because she felt badly about his troubles and wanted to console him, so that he would stop feeling so angry.

Learning did not come easily. School psychologists noted that Frank made little effort. They doubted any actual neurological disability. Nevertheless, a psychiatrist prescribed Ritalin, and Frank's mother refilled prescriptions for years, although Ritalin made no difference in Frank's school performance—always C's and D's. Teased for his short stature, Frank got into fights. One teacher thought other kids found his tantrums so entertaining that they provoked his best performances. Because of Frank's mediocre schoolwork, Dan and Betty hired tutors in fifth, sixth, and seventh grades, but the tutors complained that Frank put out no effort and expected them to do his homework for him. After enduring his tantrums for a short time, his tutors quit. In eighth grade Frank was expelled from study hall after the monitor caught him surfing the Internet for pornography.

During his early teens Frank began openly to defy his parents. His mother says she nagged and begged, but admits that her nagging had no lasting effect on Frank, except that he became inured to her wheedling and tears. When Betty refused Frank's demands, he warned her that he would run away or never talk to her again, and she caved. His rages and threats provoked her to bargain with him. She paid Frank in cash for "good" behavior in high school and continued to pay, out of anxiety, even when his behavior was "bad."

Frank's father, on the contrary, became angry about Frank's bad grades and rude manners. Dan's rages with his son were so violent that on occasion he hit his son or knocked over furniture. This did not remedy Frank's defiance or bad manners or help him do his homework, but when Frank was old enough, he threatened to turn Dan in to Child Protective Services. Soon, fearing his own temper, Dan left the discipline entirely to Betty—although he did not care for the way she did (or did not do) it.

Despite backing away, Dan could not stay entirely out of it. He could not help but overhear his wife's struggles with Frank. One evening when Frank was sixteen, Dan came home from work late, intoxicated after watching a football game at a bar. As he came in, he overheard his son's insults directed at "my wife," and he "lost it"—shoving and punching Frank, and yelling at Betty when she tried to stop him. Afterwards, ashamed about his loss of control, he bought his wife a new washer and dryer. He left notes begging his wife and son for their forgiveness. Betty was quick enough to grant it, but Frank muttered about calling the authorities, and, a week later, Frank arrived home from school to find a Corvette convertible waiting for him in the driveway.

Here are extrinsic obstacles to Frank's maturation: a sentimental, depressed mother, who couldn't bear that the breeze visit her son's cheek rudely; and a father whose temper disabled him with shame. Neither parent could make a "No" stick. Both parents were reduced to bribing Frank, who believed, quite rightly, that no parental rule applied to him, that no dictum would last, and that his own ugly behavior would have no painful consequences, and would even be rewarded.

The problem in Frank's development wasn't just a failure to comply or to learn good manners. A lack of parental constraint had a deeper consequence: that Frank could not achieve empathy, or think selflessly, or exercise consideration for others. He couldn't conduct separate relationships. He couldn't be persuaded to make a goal or follow a step-wise plan. And he couldn't take seriously an abstract or social ethic, even after he was convicted and fined (and his parents paid the fine). What was missing was not a fact or homily, a trick or technique, but an aspect of character—a mature approach to life's challenges.

Moreover, the limit-setting Frank failed to receive in childhood, over the years became in adolescence an unpaid debt that others now would have to make good: his teachers, girlfriends, parents of girlfriends, cops, judges, and jailors. Frank's arrogance, the residue of his mother's sentimental making-nice and his father's lack of control over his temper, have been inflicted upon Frank's neighbors, i.e., the rest of us. For spoiled children, generally speaking, become narcissistic adults, who become a social burden. We all pay the price in police and court costs for arrests, in ER expenses for battered spouses, and in a troubled next generation of children, who will attend school with our grandchildren. At the extreme, when parents fail to create self-discipline and a working conscience in young people, such as Frank, the ultimate social cost may be a very expensive locked cell.

CASE II: A CHASTISED GIRL

There also can be too much of a good thing, however. When limits are overdone, adults (parents, teachers, coaches, pastors, judges) may make one (or both) of two errors: zealous over-control or punitive excess. Parents who over-do limits may smother teenagers with anxious protection or enrage them with attempts at sadistic control. Just as anxious parents may restrain a toddler from trying to learn to tie her own shoes, controlling parents may prevent a teenager from making reasonable choices for herself, and so keep her from making the small errors that ultimately lead to self-discipline. Lacking an inner compass, micro-managed teenagers run wild as soon as there's a lapse in external supervision. Over-controlling tends to "split the ambivalence," to push a defiant teenager to do what otherwise she might have restrained herself from doing.

These case notes from my hospital practice in Fort Worth, years ago, may serve to illustrate.

A fifteen-year-old girl from Weatherford, Texas was so furious with all adults, and surely with all older men, that she refused to talk at all to the ER doctor. Her mother came with her in the ambulance, arriving in the emergency room in the company of the police officers who'd broken down her barricaded bedroom to extract this biting, kicking teenager. They pried her fingers loose from an empty aspirin bottle, but she refused to tell them whether she'd taken any. She'd say nothing to anyone, but just glared—at her mother, at the cop, at the doctor in blue scrubs—no matter the question, no matter who asked.

The ER doc got the cop and the nurses to hold her, and he put a nasogastric tube down her nose into her stomach, poured down charcoal slurry to absorb a lethal overdose of pills, whatever she might have taken, and then gave her an emetic to make her throw up. She wasn't very happy with the world by the time I got there. She refused to talk with me, either. The receptionist reported that there was a teenaged boy at the front desk, looking worried, asking for her—did I want him to come in to visit his girlfriend?

"Not yet. But ask him to wait. I want to talk with him"

I took the girl's mother aside, who told me her daughter, the eldest of three, had been struggling and fighting noisily with her father for six months about her wish to date a boy she'd met in geometry class. On strict religious grounds, her father had refused to countenance a date. Upset about what he heard every night on TV and what he read about in the newspaper, he was determined not to permit his daughters to date until they were "done" with high school. He fought against all her attempts to be attractive, limiting the kinds of clothing she could purchase, forbidding her to wear jewelry or makeup or perfume. He was outraged when she showed up for breakfast wearing a tank top he thought too tight around her breasts or a skirt he thought too short. He announced to anyone who'd listen that he'd be damned if his daughter would "become a floozy." He, personally, was going to make sure that she did not.

The irony, her mother said, was that Gail had been a "pretty good girl" all through the years of a strict upbringing. She used the "f-word" in her father's presence during one of their arguments, however, and he "chastised" her with a belt and buckle. When Gail came home late from school, her father ordered her from then on to come home directly and to remain closeted in her bedroom doing school assignments until he arrived home.

At school, her romance only flowered, however. When her father came to bring her a lunch bag she'd left at home, he saw her holding hands with a boy in the corridor. Thereafter, Gail's father took time off from work (he was self-employed) to pick her up from school himself and to deliver her home. After that, their arguments and her chastisement became a regular thing, her mother said. Recently, Gail stopped speaking to him or looking at him at all.

This all seemed very sad to this weary-looking mother, who recalled that "they used to be close when Gail was little." Her father loved taking her fishing or for rides into the woods in his Dodge rig. However, her puberty had been "real hard on him," the mother said, and soon he became obsessed with her dress and behavior and worried at night about those "filthy boys" at the high school. In the past year, Gail's grades had gone from A's and B's to D's and F's. Her husband yelled at Gail about that, too.

The household, Gail's mother said, had become "so

tense you could cut the air with a chain saw." Despite resistance, her husband insisted Gail come to church with the family every Sunday, where she sat in stony silence. Her father "sometimes listens in while she talks on the phone with her girlfriends about her homework," but she doubted even this had stopped the forbidden romance. Her husband had tried to prevent Gail from talking with a boy on the phone, but she and her girlfriends worked out signals, and lately, her mother said, over her exhausted husband's snoring in the early hours, she sometimes heard the back door open and close.

On the day Gail came to the ER, her father waited for her in front of the high school, as usual, but she didn't emerge. He was late and supposed to get back to his work. So he rushed angrily into the school to look for her. Finding her gone, he roamed the nearby mall to quiz other teenagers about where Gail might be. One girlfriend said she might be at the cinema. That upset him all the more. He bought a ticket, found her sitting beside a boy in a back row, and he dragged her home, where, her mother said, he chastised her again with his belt "real good." She had listened to "a lot of screaming and cussing," and then Gail ran into her bedroom and barricaded the door, refusing to answer from inside, despite her father's pounding and calling to her. Even after the police arrived, she would not speak to anyone.

Most psychiatrists and ER staff will recognize what followed: the hospital bed with its sides up, an empty aspirin bottle on the nursing station counter, a pouting teenager, and the messy overdose drill—nasogastric lavage, induced emesis, the call for psychiatric consultation. Many of these details were repeated so many times in the years I practiced hospital psychiatry that many cases blur together in memory. Yet for two reasons Gail's case stuck in my mind. This was one:

The nurse called me back to the examining room, where Gail stood bare-foot in a white gown, her expression sullen, eyes averted. The ER doc gave me an angry look, and the nurse turned Gail around, so that when she cracked open the back of the girl's gown I could see that Gail's slim buttocks, lower back and thighs were striped crimson—horizontal lacerations, some raw, others scabbed, half-healed. I gave the other doc a look and nodded to signify: Yes, I would admit her involuntarily to the adolescent unit and not let her go home. There would be a report to Child Protective Services, and yes, this was child abused.

There was more history to gather. Gail's mother was so upset at her husband's obsession that she was willing to admit that her daughter had been "chastised" not once, but many times. The daughter's relationship with her father, she said, had come utterly unraveled.

But that wasn't all. What would stick with me over the years was not just a girl's beaten behind, but also her fierce independence and squandered courage: her determination, whatever the cost, however determined her father's opposition, to tie her own shoes.

The ER doc came by the small consulting room later, where I was trying to interview Gail. She'd just begun to talk to me. I really didn't want to be interrupted, but he insisted on coming in to throw the lab reports on the desk. "You might want to look these over." He waited for me to look, so I thumbed through the slips. When I looked up, he was leaving. To her, he said in a kind way, "You take care, 'hear.'" To me he said, "that doesn't really surprise me, once I thought about it, you know what I mean?" He went out.

Gail was just staring at the wall. Except for the tox screen, which was positive for acetylsalicylic acid (aspirin), her blood chemistries were normal. Her CBC was fine, too. Her urinalysis showed an elevation in hCG (human chorionic gonadotrophin).

This was the other reason I remembered her. She would become the exemplar of a radical breakdown of the parent–child relationship—a jealous father's attempt to bully a teenager into behavioral compliance, to control her in real time by shadowing her, and preventing her by force. She was too old for this approach, which does not work very well in American suburbia, surely not for high school sophomores. She became, in my mind, the exemplar of stubborn adolescent grit, of a girl's determined declaration of independence, however disastrously ill-timed. There it was in black and white on the lab slip: she would show him! In brief, she had been lectured, hectored, herded, browbeaten, bullied, and abused, and there was nothing left of a close relationship that once might have permitted him to set limits his daughter would have accepted.

She was, of course, pregnant.

Part 3
Both at Once

9 Parenting

Try, try, try to separate them, it's an illusion. . . .
You can't have one without the other.[74]
—lyrics by Sammy Cahn and Jimmy Van Heusen

U P TO this point we've treated recognition as separate from limit-setting. This hasn't seemed particularly odd. Conceptually, they can be distinguished. In theory, each is a distinctive aspect of parenting.

In fact, the two parental tasks seem to originate from opposite poles. To *recognize* is to notice in what ways a child is distinctive, unlike all others. To recognize a person is to understand her immediate emotions and point of view, to light up her inner life, illuminating what she thinks and feels. To recognize is to encourage a young person to express her personal thoughts and emotions, to encourage her to take them seriously and make sense of them in the context of her life and life history. Recognition, in this sense, is what a conventional psychotherapy offers: the experience of being respectfully understood. As if from the other direction, parental *limit-setting* pushes a young person to conform, to join the group, to share in the collective norm. Limit-setting squelches the individual, puts down rebellion, and suppresses personal desire in favor of group cohesion and shared interests. Limit-setting directs an individual to obey the rules set for members of a group. Limits constrain the self, and prod a young person to think of others, to subordinate personal wishes or impulses. In short, the experiences of recognition and limit-setting seem contrary to one another. The first seems to celebrate the role of the self, the second the importance of the other. To be recognized is to be encouraged to enjoy the freedom of one's own heart and mind. To endure limits is to be constrained, to have to face the fact that in polite society one's natural inclinations must be everywhere "in chains."[75]

Yet these contrary vectors join in one parental enterprise—and, however uncomfortably, they must share one personality. For this reason, recognition and limit-setting are the *yin* and *yang* of one protracted parental effort to transform a newborn human animal into a socialized, civil adult. Along the way, children experience both poles of conflict—in weaning, in toilet-training, in socialization to school routines and rules, in weekly schedules and nightly curfews. In adolescence, a precarious reconciliation of contrary motives—e.g., the desire to be oneself vs. the wish to join the group, or the desire to be sexy vs. the desire to be respected—is a large part of what growing up means. Put another way, maturation is the process in which these contrary vectors become integrated, so that they serve dual roles in the framework of an adult character. From a parent's point of view, this reconciliation requires both recognition *and* limit-setting. Skillful parents make use of both one and the other in the construction of character, just as a deft driver needs both throttle and brake. Neither one is sufficient for the journey.

If a parent only recognizes and fails to set limits, an adolescent remains self-absorbed, selfish, and childish: *spoiled*. If a parent fails to recognize, a teenager feels invisible, disoriented, unsure of herself: *lost*. The absence of recognition has another consequence as well: the lack of the sort of close adult–child relationships that recognition creates and sustains. This lack reduces the constructive impact of limit-setting upon the building of character. In fact, this absence reduces limit-setting to grim experiences of punishment. Without a relationship, and the collaborative, affectionate motives that come with it, a teenager will comply only because of the presence of force and the imminence of punishment. When that external supervision flags or vanishes, a teenager lacking an effective conscience will defy those rules, prohibitions, or laws without scruple. In other words, only in tandem can recognition and limit-setting produce an adult who conforms with essential social constraints in a gracious way because he *wants* to.

To lack *both* recognition and limit-setting is worse than missing only one. Without recognition or limits, a childish teenager feels both lost and un-moored, invisible and feral. Without either throttle or break, teenagers lack confident ambition and graceful self-restraint. The result is an empty, unhappy, immoral adult.

Set Limits within a Relationship

Recognition and limit-setting are reciprocal, but the dual effect is a synergy, even if the resulting personality is inevitably in conflict.[76] A parent's recognition sweetens the gall of frustration parents also must create. It provides a framework in which "No" makes sense, even if that "No" inevitably will be resented. In some examples (above), a parent did both at once: set a limit in the context of recognition. This is to say that a skillful parent may say "No," when "No" needs to be said, and yet not leave a teenager feeling misunderstood, unappreciated, or unloved. Recognition can make a constraint seem just, well-deserved, and acceptable, even if unwelcome.

Without that constructive relationship, limit-setting isn't readily accepted or adopted into character structure. Without a relationship, we can coerce or intimidate, but cannot properly parent a teenager, for an adult cannot parent a stranger. I've tried. Happenstance sometimes forces a teacher, cop, judge, parent, or clinician to set a limit for a teenager he doesn't know. But the result is meager, the encounter unpleasant and, in my experience, this encounter rarely produces a shift in maturation. If I confront a defiant young stranger, I only provoke a contemptuous reply: "Whatever, dude." I usually join in his mind that large cohort of adults who are *jerks*. My point will be ignored.

The basis for limit-setting, then, is a relationship in which we as adults take the trouble to show up, look and listen, and reflect an adult's honest appraisal of what we learn. This is bread-and-butter recognition:

- "I read your essay. I made a few comments in the margin— misspellings, a few small things. But I liked what you said about camping at Mirror Lake—that's great."
- "That skirt looks good on you. It would go great with your blue blouse with the flower pattern, don't you think?"
- "Sorry to be so busy these days—I've missed you. So, you want a raise in your allowance? I tell you what. Let me check with my accountant about cash flow, and maybe we can talk about it over breakfast on Sunday. Would that be all right?"

If you make time and take the trouble for close encounters when you are *not* setting limits, that relationship becomes the proper context for saying "No" when you have to. A teenager will care what you think. Moreover, when you have to set a limit, try also to recognize. Do both at once. Before you say "No" or impose a sanction, allude to this relationship and recognize what that relationship has become for both of you. It's also easier for a teenager to endure inevitable frustration when you set a limit if you make it clear that you recognize how she feels.

> "After all our talks, I trust you know how I feel about you and the faith I have in your good judgment. You also know what I think about teenagers drinking. So sure, I know you want to go. And I don't want to hurt your feelings. But I cannot let you go to Sally's party when her parents aren't home. I care way too much about you to take that risk, even if I know it makes you grumpy with me when I have to say 'No.'"

The emotional capital in your joint account becomes valuable when you set a limit on which you invest some of it.

> "Yes, you may go to the game with Paul, honey, even though it's a school night, but only if you promise to be home by nine. Some kids will go to get something to eat, but I'm *not* giving you permission to do that. Let's understand one another. I don't want you to go at all if you cannot be home by nine, and you'll upset and disappoint me if you let me down."

If that capital is on deposit and if she somehow fails to come in on time, the rupture she's caused in that relationship will be more painful to her than the grounding you impose as a penalty. You have made it clear that, as a part of her choice, your relationship is on the line. So, when she comes home, you might say,

> "Darling, don't you dare tell me Paul's silly excuse or any shaggy dog story. You're grounded for the weekend. This tardiness might otherwise not seem like all that big a deal to you, but I must tell you it's kind of a big deal to me. And it will be

a long cold day in hell before I forget that you failed to honor your word to me."

Grounding is an inconvenience, a frustration to a teenager, and so can be a useful sanction. But if your relationship matters and she values your regard, then her betrayal of *you* and your legitimate upset about it, will bring memorable remorse. It's the enduring memory of that remorse, that shamed squirming within your relationship, that creates character.

To repeat: you shouldn't worry about making a teenager feel legitimately ashamed or guilty. We've been so busy for the past century undoing excessive Victorian repression that we've lost track of the logic of limit-setting. As modern parents, we don't wish to make our children guilty or ashamed about their natural sexual feelings, or about their legitimate bids for autonomy. But when a teenager breaks her promise to us or behaves like a selfish jerk, she *ought* to feel shame, and we needn't be reluctant to make her squirm about it. As I indicated, this experience of shame or guilt is part of what personality structure *is*. When a graceful adult considers breaking her word or letting down those who count on her, potential shame is what prevents her from taking the careless or easy way.

Keep in Mind the Big Picture

The limits we choose for teenagers ought to be set within a developmental perspective. Normal adolescents begin to be able to appreciate time-past and time-future. Immature teenagers still have only a tenuous grasp upon their own (or their family's or nation's) history. For still-childish teenagers, present actions are still only precariously connected in causal logic to a patchy, amorphous, magical future. This being so, as adults help teenagers to paint in one corner of the painting, they should also hold up the panorama of the whole, so that young people, too, can begin to see the big picture.

As you'll see in the following example, a parent recognizes where a teenager stands in terms of responsibility and corresponding allowance. This parent anticipates where progress will lead in the coming year:

"Well. . . . No, not yet. I'm not yet ready to increase your allowance this summer. But in the fall you'll be a sophomore, carrying greater academic responsibility, and next school year you'll be buying some of your own clothes on your own budget. As you handle these responsibilities well, I'll gladly rethink your share of the family income. So let's say we discuss this again in October."

This implicit and explicit recognition places this teenager in this larger picture. Recognition conceptualizes a son's present achievements and defines the current choices, which influence future prospects. Early on, teenagers have trouble connecting the present with recent history or the immediate future, and so it helps them to gain this perspective if parents model the way adults think along the dimension of time.

Not all reminders will be welcome, of course:

"Yes, I get it. You want to go out both nights this weekend and you have ambitious plans. But let's review the history. Your last report card had three C's—and we told you that until you did better we had to simplify your social life. You promise now you *will* do all your homework, and say you *are* doing so— and, gosh, we hope you're right. But that was not our deal. No promises—we said we would look at results. So you must show us on your report card, and if you earn A's and B's, we'll then let you plan for both weekend nights yourself. For now, however, my darling, it's still just one."

To a teenager this may just sound like "No." But, however frustrated he may be in having to wait, he may also feel encouraged by your optimism that he can and *will* earn more adult privileges as soon as he shoulders those more grown-up responsibilities.

Similarly, keep the big picture in mind when you punish misbehavior. When taking note of a teenager's wrongdoing, it's well to recall, as an aside, that this isn't what you expect, because you can remember when she's done better. Her past virtue and her successful past self-discipline are also aspects of the big picture. In this, I don't suggest that you make nice, but rather that you maintain the broad perspective that adolescents may have trouble holding on to. Make that larger perspective implicit in what you say. And when you set a limit for a daughter who's misbehaved, try not to forget her virtues or your pride in them. If it is not strictly true, do not say: "You *always* . . . !" or "You *never* . . . !" Much better to hold in mind past virtues, along with recent failures, so that there remains scope for self-respect:

- "I'm always proud when you keep your word, but when you forget promises and duck responsibilities, as you blew off your homework last term, and brought home three C's, then I'm disappointed and upset with you."
- "No. Not until you *consistently* pitch in. I know *sometimes* you do, but too often you leaf through a magazine while I put dinner on the table; or you fail to do your chores, like cleaning your bathroom this week, until I have to nag you; and then you have the gall to get mad because I nag you. I know we have to be patient. But I sure look forward to your growing up enough to be ashamed of yourself when you fail to pull your own weight. I expect you to help, and also to do your homework, without my having to hassle you. Until you can do this consistently, the answer is going to stay: No."

Hold up the social dimensions of the big picture, too. A teenager may not instantly see your reasons or accept your logic. You need not persuade a son to like limits you set. Yet if you place limits in a social context—family, school, town, country—it tells your son that *you* consider this dimension to be important when you make moral decisions; that *you* know fairness matters, even if your son is slow to agree; and that *you* take others into account, just as you insist he must learn to do:

"You're old enough to get a learner's permit, and yes, we'll help you learn to drive, just as we helped your older sister. We'll cooperate with you, as we did with her, always assuming that you pull *your* weight, too, that you do your best at school and that you're careful not to let the use of a car distract you. Is that a deal?"

It's useful to mention this dimension even when you refuse to conform to contemporary norms, when you set boundaries that are less lax than what other families might expect. You needn't agree with other parents, or they with you. You needn't follow the neighborhood consensus. Yet when you take the views of your community into consideration, you set a civic example you want a teenager to follow:

> "Your mother and I recognize that some local parents let their kids stay out until three a.m. on a Saturday night. Others seem to agree with us that this isn't wise. So not all parents share our view. It's too bad if this is awkward with some of your friends. Nevertheless, after thinking it through, after listening to you, we still hold firm that your curfew must be 12:30 a.m. sharp."

Finally, the big picture includes an ethical panorama, which stretches beyond a childish teenager's narrow, concrete preoccupation with what he now wants. Normal teenagers are on the cusp of discovering social ethical considerations and abstract moral ideals, which soon may prove to be exciting: justice, honor, the good of the team, the needs of a nation. We want a son to take those ideals seriously. So, for a start, it helps for parents to set limits while recognizing explicitly that a son's ethical or unethical behavior has a bearing upon his relationships with his parents and siblings:

> "You may have a party—while we're here. From your remarks, however, I think you may have considered throwing a party while we're not here. We think it irresponsible to let you do that. We will not allow it. So FYI, if you *ever* consider throwing a party here without our permission while we're away, you'll learn the hard way how much it matters that we trust you. If we cannot trust you, your social life will take place on a diminished, barren planet. Believe us, you will not like the sad, lonely result."

Or, again:

> "You know, hurting another young person's feelings is so unkind. If I ever learned that you'd tormented some sad girl

or boy, I'd put your car on blocks for a year. That wouldn't be the worst of it, either. The worst of it, I think, would be that I'd be ashamed of you."

Ethics aren't only about relationships, social orders, or duties to collective groups of other persons. In the end, principle must come into moral behavior. Principles become abstract, as well as social and personal, as young people come to be adults. This is to say that a teenager must come to feel dysphoric about his misbehavior, and be troubled within, because he's violated a principle, not only because he's ashamed to have been caught publicly by parents, teachers, friends, or acquaintances who didn't like his actions. When the relationship with a parent is deep and meaningful, teenagers identify with parents' moral actions, not merely with moral lectures. This being so, your respect (and your contempt) for certain kinds of behavior ought to be explicit:

- "No, my son—because it's against the law."
- "No. That would be dishonorable. It wouldn't matter whether or not I got caught cheating on my income taxes—I'd know."

Your ethical principles become compelling to teenagers when you act upon them, not merely when you talk about what's right. Your children will identify with what they recognize in your behavior, not merely in your lectures. For this reason, it's wise not to preach what you don't practice. Assuming you say what you mean, on the other hand, making your moral thinking explicit as you set limits gives them added heft. For a teenager who violates your rules must also face up to those ethical implications. Research demonstrates that young people catch on to mature ethical concepts sooner if they hear those ideals described in peer conversations and see them made manifest in the actions of respected others.[77]

- "No. I don't want to go to re-up for Iraq, but the platoon needs me."
- "No, I gave my word. It's a matter of honor that I do what I said I'd do."

Naturally, there's no use in your making this ethical point for teenagers if it is mere rhetoric. The deeper context, in which a teenager's choices gain perspective, is always the history of your own actions, as adults, which speak louder than words.

Stay Adult

Preserve generational boundaries. When you set limits, bring to bear an adult's panoramic grasp of social and ethical context and future consequences. Refuse to be split from other important adults. All these are aspects of an adult perspective, which you must bring to the parental tasks of recognition and limit-setting. To grow up, young people need adult recognition, not just the childish mirroring of another child. For this reason, they don't need childishness from adults, and they don't profit from the experience of adults joining them, as co-conspirators, in their misbehavior. They don't need the courtship of an adult who's pathetically dependent upon adolescent favor.

No matter how angry you still are about your own parents, how grumpy about an estranged spouse, or how lonely, you mustn't help your teenaged children evade rules or outwit the other parent, scorn their teachers, or undo structures and constraints that other adults struggle to put in place. You must never rescue a teenager from taking responsibility for her actions. None of these suggestions is easy. For this reason it's obvious that only adult adults can parent well. Given how hard these tasks are, adults need each other's support.

More than this, it takes grown-ups to provide models for emulation. An adult example is what teenagers need, not the spectacle of unstable pseudo-adults behaving like teenagers. If you're a parent, teacher, coach, or therapist, a U.S. senator or president, behave like an adult: take responsibility, put kids' needs before your own, and provide what young people need even when it isn't what they want, or what you feel like doing. Keep your dignity. Sons and daughters don't need to see you sneaking about, lying, not working, sleeping around, breaking laws (e.g., about casual drug use), or refusing to face consequences. Nor do they need to see adults having tantrums, getting soused, or lying around feeling sorry for themselves. They need parents to behave like responsible adults because they need models with which to identify, to see what it means to grow up. Said again, they need recognition and limit-setting, sustained over time, set within a maturational, historical, and ethical panorama. Only grown-ups can do this.

Humor, Paradox, and Surprise

I've learned the hard way, of course, that when teenagers get into serious trouble it can be hard to laugh. Yet I urge you to hang onto your sense of humor, if you can. During an exchange of insults this requires valor. But afterward, when there's time to back away and see a teenager wriggling, it's possible to see how funny, even endearing, that struggle can be. Certainly, the best professionals can laugh, and *do*, and so end up having a good time with teenagers, even those who are struggling, upset, and troubled. This may sound implausible to a parent whose teenager is in trouble. Most of the time, however, adolescence isn't fatal, and its plasticity makes even an implausible recovery possible. More often than not, adolescence turns out to be a moving, auspicious comedy, whose outcome, despite all the angst, turns out to be lively and lovely.

Humor can also be useful. Years ago, when I practiced in hospitals, every once in a while I had to admit a stroppy teenager at three a.m. after an overdose or other suicidal gesture. I'd meet with her briefly in the isolation room off the nursing station, where the nurses could keep us in view—a tiny room with a cot and two uncomfortable chairs. Well, she might announce, she couldn't possibly sleep until she'd watched television for an hour. I'd say sorry but that wasn't in the cards. I might explain that there was a television on the unit the other kids watched during the evening, and she could, too, as soon as she had a bed on the unit. Well, then she had to have a phone to call her ex-boyfriend in Topeka. Surely I couldn't expect her to sleep until she'd confided in him. "Sorry," I'd have to say. Well, then she had to have a Valium. "Sorry," I'd say, "I think you've had enough pills for tonight." Could she have a snack? Sure, when the nurses finished their paperwork. The nurse would poke her head in to say they needed a urine sample and her signature, and my delighted patient would announce cleverly that she would neither pee nor sign until she got permission to watch television. If not, she had it in mind that I might like to perform an anatomically improbable act until hell froze over.

So I'd say: "Well, a girl has to do these things when she's ready—no rushing her!" This would produce a fishy look. "Well, goodnight," I'd say and get up, fishing for my keys.

"Wait," she'd say. "When can I watch television?"

"After you're assigned a bed on the unit, you can watch television with the other kids, if you wish to, when they're all allowed to watch television." I'd pull on my coat. "'Night."

"Hey!" she'd glower. "I'm not peeing, and I'm not signing anything."

"I heard you," I said. "That's why you'll sleep here tonight, I guess; can't put you on the unit until the admission tasks are done. But take your time."

"When do I get a bed on the unit?"

"When you're ready to help the nurses finish your admission," I'd say. "And that, of course, is up to you. Far be it for me to think I can tell a girl when she's going to pee. And I know it's difficult to check into a hospital, so pee at your own pace." And then I'd be gone.

This is paradox, a manipulative irony. I was urging this girl to do what she threatened to do—or not do. I wasn't entirely serious, of course. In truth I didn't want her to take her sweet time. I wanted her to help the nurses finish her admission, and I wanted to go to bed, and I didn't want to have an argument with someone I hardly knew. Yet our talk struck me as amusing, rather than enraging. For it was an irony that avoided a control battle ("You will," "*I won't*," "You will," "I *won't!*") that I couldn't win. It achieved surprise, which is often effective in getting a scrappy teenager's attention. It threw her off-stride, inasmuch as I seemed to urge what she least expected me to want her to do, and instead of the fight she was trying to provoke, I seemed to be on her side in a friendly way. As I went to bed I was certain that, when I checked on her later in the morning, her signature would be on her belongings list and her urine sample would be in the laboratory. I would find her in the dining room having breakfast with the other kids.

Omit Unnecessary Words

This example suggests another useful matter of style: the less said the better. Of course, this isn't always appropriate, or even possible. Many of my examples in this book don't follow this precept. Yet it's often a good idea, particularly when setting limits in the context of recognition, not to go on and on, to say it only once, and use short sentences (for example: "No rush!" or "Take your time.").

Here's another example (and I'm only joking a little). If you want a teenager to pay attention, try *not* explaining. Refuse a rude request—e.g., "Can I go to the movies tonight with Paul or are you just going to be a dippy kill-joy?"—with only the word: "No!" Usually, in my experience, this laconic answer provokes a demand for an explanation. So, if I want a teenager to listen, I might put off any reply until I hear a clamor for an explanation as to *why* I said "No." I stall. I ask whether she really wants to hear an answer, or just wants to be a dippy impolite teenager. I make it plain (by my tone and expression) that I'm teasing. I ask again whether she *really* wants to hear my intricate explanation or just wants to try to push me around. Debate with me all night? Throw a tantrum? I say: If it's just going to be a tantrum or insults, why would I bother explaining? She could save me a lot of time and trouble by cutting straight to the tantrum.

"No, no," she says; she *really* wants to hear all my intricate logic.

"Okay," I say, "but I *never* debate with a girl who's going to be rude."

"Okay," she responds, she won't be rude.

"Well, then I don't mind telling you why—but not until after lunch" (or whatever).

It's my hope we're both playing by now. The point is, however, that by the time I get to my explanation, I no longer need to struggle to get her to listen. In the end, we might even have a useful talk—about why the answer had to be "No."

Recognize Resistance and Its Reasons

When parents set limits, it helps to recognize (anticipate) an unhappy reaction before it comes. I don't mean that you should make nice or propitiate the adolescent volcano-gods with apologies or abject wheedling. I mean that you might anticipate that when you say "No," or set a condition upon a teenager's getting what she wants, or delay her satisfaction, that she'll have some feelings about these frustrations. You might usefully acknowledge that she's entitled to have those feelings, that you've no right to tell her that she cannot have those feelings, because, whatever you say, she *will* have feelings. While you anticipate those feelings, you might add that you think you have a right, too—to expect her to express those feelings in a reasonably respectful way. For example, before you begin to set a limit, you might say:

- "I don't miss your sense of urgency about this. I know you get impatient and anxious when you have to wait for something you want badly, but ..."
- "I realize that you'd rather just make up your own mind. It has angered you, in the past, when you felt that you didn't have a choice. So I realize that you may be tempted to debate or fight with me, but ..."
- "I don't like to hurt your feelings by saying 'No,' because then you get mad, and it's ugly, and your tantrums are hard on both of us, but ..."
- "I'm not sure you really are asking me. Sometimes, I know, you think the answer can only be 'Yes.' You feel so upset about a 'No' that you think you have the right to punish me with an ugly display of your unhappiness, which we both regret. But even though I know you have trouble containing yourself when I have to say 'No,' ..."

When a teenager grows up enough to be ready, you can lobby for the mature reaction you would very much prefer:

> "I don't miss your sense of urgency about this. I know you get impatient and anxious when you have to wait for something you want badly, but I think you're old enough now to contain your impatience, and to remember your manners, and keep your dignity. I'll be proud of you when you can. Either way, however, my decision has to be: ..."

Parental anticipation may not forestall an argument, but on occasion you may be surprised. I recall a large, volatile, paranoid adult patient who once demanded that I let him move into and live in one of the offices in an outpatient clinic I directed. Anticipating a tantrum when I told him "No," as I knew I had to, I stalled. The next week, when I'd gathered my thoughts, I told him I'd been dreading the prospect of hurting his feelings, even though I knew it wasn't my fault entirely, and I didn't want to, because I really did not have a choice about my answer. I'd stalled the week before, I said, because I worried that my refusal would hurt and enrage him, and, despite our friendly relationship, he wouldn't be able to restrain himself from making ugly threats. I told him I thought this would be too bad, inasmuch as we'd started working together in such an auspicious way. When I ended this short speech, he sat back with a deep sigh, and quietly he murmured: "Thank you."

The point of this story is that anticipation is an act of recognition that may help a young person put up with frustration, even when frustration cannot be avoided. This is, after all, the story of our lives: that we can put up with the slings and arrows of our fortune so long as we feel someone understands how outrageous it is, and cares about us. It's a helpful form of recognition when we give a teenager some control over his inevitable pain. Even on a locked hospital unit a deft staff member can give some measure of control to patients who are, in large part, rendered helpless—even if it's only the choice of entrée or dessert.

My father, a children's dentist, solemnly told every frightened small-fry who ever sat in his chair that if she felt any pain, she could lift her index finger, and he'd stop drilling. Given that power (and his gentle hands), little children rarely had to lift that finger. But I've remembered this, and so, when I have bad news or have to confront a teenager about his behavior or tell a teenager "No," I offer that small measure of control by saying: "I have some thoughts about your request—are you ready to hear them?" If I get a nod, I say: "You may not like all of what I have to say—are you sure you want to hear it now?"

As was my father's experience, I can hardly recall when the answer to that gentle question was ever "No." In this anticipation there's a genuine consideration, which a young man or woman usually appreciates, even though I hint that (s)he "may not like all of what I have to say." The truth is that we forgive another person for hurting us, if we know they mean to treat us with courtesy and respect. This is the consequence of accurate, affectionate recognition—to communicate that affection and respect.

Avoid Tactical Errors

A few common mistakes deserve special mention. These are failed tactics, which I suggest that you avoid. They've been tried, and you might as well not waste your time conducting these experiments again.

Hollow Threats

If, rather than offering clear choices, you try to bend a teenager to your will and force him to behave in a particular way right now by making empty threats, and particularly if you make those same hollow threats over and over, you'll become the boy who shouted "Wolf!" Soon your repeated dire predictions will lose any persuasive power, if they ever had any. The nth time you tell a teenager, "If you do *this*, you're grounded for a year!" or "Okay, I'll let that one pass, but now this really is your last chance," and don't carry through, you might just as well shout, "Wolf!"

The gambit that only delays the moment of truth by one "last" chance, reminds me of Sergio Leone's "spaghetti" western *The Good, the Bad, and the Ugly*, in which Eli Wallach enters a house and, finding a bath, strips and climbs in. A scar-faced gunman, seeking revenge upon Wallach and having pursued him for half the movie, catches him half-submerged in bubble-bath. The scar-faced man pulls his gun and launches into a long-winded diatribe—about how long he's been tracking Wallach, how enraged he's become, how long he's waited for vengeance, and how much he is going to . . . and five shots ring out! The desperado goes down, and Wallach stands up in the tub, holding his soapy pistol. Gazing down at the dead man, Wallach says: "When you have to shoot, *shoot*! Don't talk."

And here is the corollary. Resist scattering ultimatums or making repetitive extreme threats that no sane parent would carry out, such as:

- "This is your penultimate, very-nearly-semi-final last chance!"
- "You are now grounded *forever*!"
- "If you do that, pack your bags—I'm dropping you off at a truck stop!"
- "I'll *never* speak to you again!"

If you do, you'll lose all credibility. Such expressions of exasperation tend to occur when a parent takes it upon himself to control a teenager's behavior with threats, rather than setting a limit properly. This is a losing gambit—avoid it.

Cringing, Wheedling, Abject Apologies

These have no place in limit-setting. They reveal a lack of determination, a wish not to be a grown-up, a request that a teenager stand in for the adult. It's fatuous to ask a miscreant to applaud the justice of the consequence, or agree ahead of time not to be upset. To ask a teenager to like a constraint, to agree to a delay or applaud a sanction, is to ask too much. In fact, to ask these questions at all is to reverse roles with a child, and is irrational as well, for teenagers who can raise themselves and pass judgment on adult limit-setting don't need limits set. Cringing and wheedling make it obvious to teenagers that a parent is behaving like a child. This is rarely impressive or reassuring, and, instead, arouses contempt. So, however sorry, ashamed, guilty, or uncertain you may be, and even have a right to be, don't cringe, wheedle, or apologize. These are forms of self-indulgence.

Getting Distracted

Don't get thrown off course. A clever teenager will disorient your limit-setting with smoke and mirrors, throwing up distractions or decoys. Watch out for invitations to debate the justice of your cause, to shift the topic from his misbehavior to your ignorance, to turn the discussion upon your supposed incompetence, or to decry your naiveté about how the world really works in this modern adolescent era, about which you cannot possibly know a thing. Watch out for attempts to shift the blame to others—friends, other parents, an unattractive teacher, an unknown bad person. Watch out for shaggy-dog stories in which the plot thread keeps getting lost—a spectral other person who put the car keys into a satchel that yet another boy must have inadvertently loaded into the back seat of another somebody's pickup truck. . . .

All of this nonsense can boggle you, and make you lose the point you want to make. Moreover, as we've seen, teenagers are good at splitting—i.e., describing the behavior of another student or teacher or coach in such a way that you become distracted by your annoyance or even enraged over the injustice, malice, or idiocy of what that other student, teacher, or coach told your innocent son or daughter—and so you forget all about what you started to take your own teenager on about. These are red herrings. Insist that you'll only discuss *his* behavior, *his* decisions, *his* choices—and no one else's. Never accept that your utterly innocent off-spring has been duped or led astray, even if there might be some truth to it. As my mother said to me so often that I can still hear it:

> "Don't you *ever* tell me that somebody talked you into it, or 'made' you do it, or that you were just 'following,' or were 'misled,' or that someone said something that confused you, because I'll *never* accept that anyone else is responsible for what you do, other than you."[78]

Missing the Victory

Don't fail to notice when a teenager gives up the fight. At times, parents can become so embroiled in a struggle that they fail to register a capitulation. For example, upset about a sixteen-year-old daughter who refused to go to class and threatened to drop out of school without graduating, her parents woke up in the night, debated with her, looked into alternative schools, and considered a tutor. Finally, with exasperation (I thought), the girl announced: "Oh hell, let's stop arguing. I'll just go back and finish high school." However, her parents, still worried over her threats and churned up with angst, kept bringing up other possibilities: home-schooling, boarding school, a break. What they needed to say immediately was: "Sounds like you've made up your mind—good plan!" They could reasonably have added, "We'll help you any way you think we usefully can." Then everybody should have gone back to bed. Enough said!

As a corollary and to make a larger point: Don't fail to notice when a teenager grows up. You may think this error unlikely. After all, growing up is what we all think we hope will happen. However, after a protracted developmental delay it's possible to lose track of the goal. After so many struggles, parents can misinterpret a sign of new maturity as just another variation upon an old sneaky theme. For instance, a seventeen-year-old girl, who for years had exasperated her mother with her indifference about her school assignments and with her hedonistic self-indulgence (sneaking out to parties, illicit drug use, promiscuity), announced that she wanted to sign up for two extra community college courses, to finish high school "by June." Meanwhile, she wanted to apply to University of Montana right away, in December, so she could "start college in September, next year, and major in English," so as to "get to work on a novel" that she anticipated she "could finish before I get my BA." Her mother persisted in arguing with her, e.g., that "Maybe you can't get in to the courses you need," or "Maybe you won't get into UM, and you shouldn't assume you are going to be accepted," and, anyway, "What do you know about writing novels? Maybe you should just start with short stories."

In this case, her mother missed the point: that her daughter's approach had changed. Heretofore, the girl had blown off high school, omitted to make plans for college, and lived always in the present. When asked about the future, she'd always breezily announced: "I dunno. When the time comes, I'll just get a job and an apartment." So the proper response to her daughter's new announcement should have been an act of recognition, something like:

> "Wow! What exciting goals! I'm so glad you've found something you want to learn to do. And the way you've anticipated what you need to do, it begins to sound like a plan."

Never mind that her plan was a sketch. Sure, there'd be facts to fill in. Never mind that not all the pieces may fall into place. No worries that she might create another version of her plan next month. The point was that she'd begun to imagine a future that would be different from now, to fix upon plausible goals connected to the present by a sequence of logical steps. The point was not to argue over details, or discourage this kind of dreaming, but rather to notice that she was trying to grow up.

Nothing But . . .

Here I don't mean that you ought to tell all the truth you know. I don't mean wives should discuss a husband's failings in bed with a twelve-year-old or fathers discuss their affairs with a daughter, just because it's the truth. There ought to be proper boundaries, and a clear line between what is and is not a son or a daughter's business to know. But *if* you say it, then it must be the truth. Even if not the whole truth, it must be nothing but—so help you. For when it comes to trust between parents and teenagers, one lie will undo a hundred truths. After one lie, it takes a thousand truths to restore what was so quickly lost. This is as true for us as parents as it is for our children.

Don't misunderstand this categorical warning. You may change your mind. I don't suggest that you can never make an error, never say by mistake what turns out to be false, although you thought it was true. So long as you mean to be truthful and never knowingly lie to them, you'll be all right. But make no mistake, teenagers can tell the difference. We adults must not imagine that we can put one over on them for long. They're likely to figure it out. Teenagers recall to me every day how their parents lied to them, and even childish teenagers, who tell lies themselves, don't admire mendacity in adults. Fully mature teenagers, having begun to understand abstract ideals such as integrity, trust, loyalty, justice, and honor, prove even less tolerant of parental lies.

So if you think a topic is out of bounds, refuse to discuss it. You needn't ever say anything you don't want to say. But avoid lies, if you hope to keep a teenager's respect.

A General Approach to Both at Once

Taken together, these suggestions sum up a general approach to accomplishing both parental tasks at once: recognition *and* limit-setting, in tandem.

- *Set Limits within a Relationship*
- *Keep in Mind the Big Picture*
- *Stay Adult*
- *Carefully Use Humor, Paradox, and Surprise*
- *Omit Unnecessary Words*
- *Recognize Resistance and its Reasons*
- *Avoid Tactical Errors*
- *Nothing But . . .*

Putting It All Together—a Review

This book, so far, has been about parents who rear children in families. In the final chapter, I broaden the topic to include what I call "clinical parenting," which takes place within institutions and involves surrogate parents. In these pages so far, however, a discussion of real parents in their own real (non-metaphorical) families has circled around a few key ideas. Before moving on, it may be useful to review these six themes.

The first: a teenager's need for recognition and limit-setting to prod him to take the next step in maturation. In a few case reports, I have described teenagers who for various reasons have lacked one or the other (or both) of these critical experiences, and so have remained disastrously immature.

The second theme: the importance of setting limits in the context of recognition. In those same clinical cases I have shown how endless understanding in the absence of limit-setting tends to produce a spoiled teenager; and that firm limit-setting in the absence of affectionate, respectful recognition (or worse, in the context of *mis*recognition), produces an angry, resentful teenager, who blows off the intended contribution to character.

The third theme: useful recognition and limit-setting only take place within a relationship. Anything that disrupts key adult–child relationships, that prevents a teenager from experiencing the recognition and limit-setting she needs, can become an obstacle to maturation. Adults who want to help a troubled teenager grow up must remove obstacles to constructive parent–teenager relationships, if this can be done, or replace a flawed or missing parental relationship with another adult–adolescent relationship, so as to provide critical experiences of recognition and limit-setting before it's too late to do so.

The fourth theme: parenting is a task that must change at each developmental stage. Recognition has to take a different shape, and requires a distinctive diction, at thirteen months and at thirteen years. Similarly, limits ought to be set differently at each stage.

The fifth theme, implicit throughout all these chapters: maturity, at each stage, is not a series of lesson learned, or skills that can be taught, but rather an *approach*—a way to make cognitive and emotional sense of the world. Maturity is a matter of cognitive and emotional style, a peculiar composite of thinking, feeling, and relating. This approach changes as a child or teenager makes progress along various developmental lines, whose milestones, at each stage of life, add up to a composite structure that we call *character*.

In a way, we all know this. Yet, in another sense, we don't. We perennially seem to forget that children are not small adults; that adolescence is a distinctive stage, which entails a particular approach to life different from the way that younger children and adults make sense of their peculiar challenges and opportunities. Throughout these pages I've suggested—in a formulation that's neither my own nor new—that relative immaturity in adolescence results from a delay in the arrival of that typical adolescent approach to thinking, feeling, and relating. The remedy for adolescent immaturity, and all the troubles immaturity brings, simply is to grow up.

Finally, the sixth theme: to propel normal character development onward, or to repair an immature personality, requires that recognition and limit-setting must be well-timed and sustained. Recognition and social constraints are not brief interventions, the parental exercises of an hour or a day, but rather the prolonged context in which a young human being grows. They are the watered soil and sunlight in which the seeds of personality germinate in infancy and come slowly to full adult maturity. Clinically, when supplies of water and sunlight have been disrupted, and normal growth has been blocked in the first two decades, then a timely restoration of recognition and limit-setting, if sustained, can restore developmental momentum.

However, restoration of recognition and limit-setting may rescue a stunted adolescent personality, or do so in part, only so long as there's a still-active growth process. Once childhood and adolescent growth curves flatten onto the adult plateau, the efficacy of these restorative efforts appears to diminish. The apt metaphor may be the espalier, a tree grown from seed to climb a trellis, which shapes the growing branches into an admired horticultural configuration. This character-shaping happens as the tree develops, but only so long as there's growth and plasticity left. The gardener's watering, pruning, fertilizing, staking, and tying appear to shape the tree usefully, but only so long as growth gives scope for an impact, only so long as there persists some of that "force" that "through the green fuse drives the flower."[79] This caveat may explain why a vigorous therapy may have a substantial effect only during childhood and adolescence, and not in adult life. This may be why it takes a sustained period of recognition and limit-setting to restore developmental momentum in "stuck" teenagers, or why the abbreviated, episodic encounters that constitute a modern parent's "quality time" may not be sufficient to rear a child to adult civility.

Recognition and limit-setting need to be the context for a child's upbringing, not an occasional epiphany. It may not be enough for a father to visit a son once a year for an hour, no matter how cleverly he recognizes the changed boy he finds, or how vigorous his limit-setting might be during that one hour. What does it mean for a young child of three, nine, or eighteen months, or three years, that his parents both go back to work full-time and leave him to others? If radical breaks occur in his experience of recognition, or in the setting of limits, does this thwart development? No doubt the answers are not simple. But if the metaphor of the espalier is apt there may be only a limited opportunity to shape character. Just as a tree can be shaped only so long as "the green fuse" pushes upward toward sunlight, so that window of opportunity may remain open only so long as neuropsychological development pushes onward. Certainly, you cannot espalier a fully grown tree, because it's too late. If a pine seedling is grown fully in a dim basement, the result will be a permanently stunted tree, whose character cannot be changed once the growth span ends, even if the misshapen tree is later carried out into the sunshine and rain.

∿

Many aspects of human character are shaped within relationships. Some are not. Constitutional or temperamental traits appear to be innate, the result of genetic or congenital factors that depend little upon experience.[80] Some colors in the weave of personality are dyed in the wool. Yet many other aspects of character rely upon recognition and limit-setting, and these don't develop properly without apt experience. They are shaped for good (or ill) by parental relationships in which recognition and limit-setting do (or do not) take place. Expressing this truth in an elaborate metaphor, the ancient Greeks personified a pantheon who influenced human destiny and provided paradigms for mortal lives. We don't anymore believe that each day Helios's chariot pulls the sun across the sky or that Zeus expresses a patriarch's indignation with his thunderbolts. Instead, we now say that the gods rendered in mythic form a Greek's experience of giant parental adults who inhabited his ancient world, providing recognition and setting limits, and so influenced man's destiny and provided a mirror for mortal lives.

In modern psychology, parents (and other parental adults) provide this pantheon, and children and adolescents identify with the models they know. Their pantheon isn't a mythic social order placed on Mt. Olympus. The immortal lives don't unfold among the clouds. Rather, they inhabit our minds. Our lives begin among reflections of our parents' acts of recognition, which provide the inner sunlight in which we first see ourselves bathed in warm colors of self-esteem (or not). Parents throw the thunderbolts of adverse judgments and set limits in response to our misbehavior or hubris and, in the long run, provide the inner restraining voice of conscience. It startles us, years later, to hear their words coming from our own mouths.

This may be the takeaway lesson: as parents, we may wish to comport ourselves for immortal roles on our children's inner Mt. Olympus. Our acts of recognition, the manner and warmth of our affectionate understanding of them, will survive as inner sources of self-esteem if done well, or, if done badly, lasting inner sources of shame and self-contempt. Our limits, the style in which we set them, the very tone of the "No's" we say to them, will survive in our children as the enduring voices of sturdy conscience, or, if set badly or not at all, as a lifelong lack of self-restraint. In the end, this is what parenting is about: the character of children. We may wish to keep in mind, as we shape them, that ours will be the voices, the very diction, our children will hear all of their lives, and continue to hear long after we've gone.

10 Clinical Parenting

U P TO this point, we have considered recognition and limit-setting to be home remedies and parental tasks, accomplished within the perimeter of the family or with ancillary help from outpatient therapists. For some troubled teenagers, however, recognition and limit-setting cannot be provided at home even with outpatient consultation—for reasons we will now consider. For some, lethal risk-taking renders inadequate the containment and supervision available at home. For others, the limit-setting that can be provided at home or in outpatient therapies is too limited, and just not adequate to the task. In these cases, a restoration of developmental momentum will require residential containment and surrogate parenting. Here I will suggest to you that these are the essential features of the best "alternative" adolescent programs in the nation: a combination of robust limit-setting and perceptive clinical recognition, sustained over time.

In conceptualizing treatment for immaturity, we usefully distinguish between

(a) clinical obstacles to maturation (e.g., neuropsychological eccentricities, psychological trauma, addiction, divorce), which disrupt academic progress and delay psychosocial development, and need to be removed;
and

(b) immaturity itself, i.e., a teenager's still-childish approach to academic and interpersonal challenges of adolescence—the result of an obstruction.[81]

To address obstacles may require sophisticated diagnosis and clinical interventions that only experts provide (e.g., medication, psychotherapy, or specialized academic help). To address immaturity, itself, when it has become socially entrenched and academically intractable, or when a son or daughter no longer safely can live at home, may require professional recognition and industrial-strength limit-setting—a combination I call *clinical parenting.*

Why Outpatient Treatment (for Immaturity) May Fail

For some immature teenagers, outpatient intervention may suffice.[82] Competent clinicians seeing teenagers in conventional weekly psychotherapy, supplemented (or not) by medication, may mitigate or eliminate developmental obstacles. All may go well, if parents become engaged and a young patient cooperates. That is, if a troubled son or daughter is compliant with home rules, responsible about school, motivated to repair frayed family relationships, and willing to collaborate with a respected therapist, then a skillful outpatient clinician may address both (a) and (b) above. To list these necessary conditions, however, is to hint at the awkward truth—that outpatient therapy for troubled teenagers is most likely to be effective when it is least necessary. When strenuous intervention is most necessary, the outpatient level of care may simply fail.

Such treatment failures become more likely when those conditions that make outpatient treatment auspicious cannot be met, i.e., when an uncooperative teenager refuses to attend or participate in school, or will not follow parental rules or behave well in the unsupervised company of disreputable peers. A drastic out-of-home placement may become the only viable option when a troubled teenager's dysfunctional, defiant, sneaky, or hostile approach to helpful adults—at home, in the classroom, and in a therapist's office—makes home life chaotic, academic progress implausible, social relations hazardous, and outpatient therapy ineffective. When a young person's academic, family, and social problems are complicated by illicit drugs, sexual promiscuity, defiance of legitimate authority, dangerous friendships, solitary self-injury, serious nutritional disturbances, or other high-risk misbehavior that outpatient intervention fails to curtail, then parents have to consider an out-of-home placement.

Put another way, some teenagers cannot be treated at home, because outpatient interventions have intrinsic limitations when a young patient is elusive or dishonest. It is possible to treat a psychological trauma with psychotherapy or to mitigate an attentional deficit with pharmacology on an outpatient basis, for example, but only if a teenager shows up in the doctor's office on time and participates honestly. Even under these propitious circumstances, however, outpatient interventions only address (a). To also address (b) requires both recognition and limit-setting—and sometimes only the one is possible. That is, a competent therapist may succeed in creating a friendly relationship with a wary teenager, assuming he can be coaxed to show up and join in. However, when the therapist attempts to set limits, or even just to help parents enforce their own reasonable consequences for misbehavior, a stroppy teenager may become angry and resistant, fail to show, complain to parents that he no longer likes his therapist, tell them he is not cooperating (and so they are wasting their money), and refuse to go on or demand a change in venue. Some parents cannot set limits themselves even with help; they crumble before a daughter's renewed hostility or fail to hold the line in the face of a son's scary tantrums. To obviate these complications or (supposedly) to preserve a precarious alliance, some therapists give up on setting limits. Others refuse to talk to parents at all, so as to create a rigid "confidentiality" that also happens to insulate the therapy from reality. When such a therapist locks himself in his office with his sly patient, his cozy interviews are walled off from parental reports of continuing jerk behavior, truancy, drug use, or promiscuity. Such a therapist relies upon an unreliable narrator for the news, and so his "treatment" takes place in the dark. Even a brilliant therapist cannot overcome this limitation in outpatient therapy with an elusive patient. Such therapy can offer neither accurate recognition nor effective limit-setting, and so cannot promote maturity. A sneaky teenager reduces conventional outpatient psychotherapy to Blind Man's Bluff.

Moreover, even when a young outpatient cooperates, his therapist has to compete for his attention with other influential rhetoric. Other persuasive voices assure an American teenager that he is entitled to have what he wants when he wants it, or that she deserves to have what she wants just for showing up—and *now!* Commercial ads tell entitled teenagers that they ought not to have to work or to wait, to save or pay for a purchase anytime soon. An oppositional teenager in possession of a set of car keys can drive away in the company of friends who encourage his defiance and offer alternative psychopharmacology. There is an imbalance in face-time and access: the therapist gets fifty minutes a week while the commercial siren songs play 24/7. Friends can be in touch all night and day on social websites and hand-held gadgets. Relative to these media, a therapist gets little airtime.[83]

In sum, an outpatient therapist operates at a disadvantage. She may advise engaged parents and treat cooperative teenagers. But when parents do *not* help, or get shut out of the therapeutic process, when a teenager is sneaky or obstinate, then—lacking accurate intelligence and effective sanctions, left in the dark, unable to secure an insurance company's authorization for inpatient containment—an outpatient therapist cannot provide the clinical parenting a troubled, flailing teenager needs. If also a psychiatrist, the therapist may supplement or replace psychotherapy with pills. In some cases, however, none of these outpatient gambits proves effective.

Why Public High Schools Also May Fail to Foster Maturity

Inasmuch as we are talking about immature high school students, who have not kept up with peers in psychological maturation while living at home, we ought also to ask: Why don't local high schools successfully prod them to grow up? Surely it is unfair to indict schools for failing at tasks for which they were never designed nor adequately funded.[84] Yet teenagers spend most of their time outside home at school or in extracurricular school activities. Empathic teachers try to provide the parenting that some students obviously need. And reformers, pointing to failures in public education, call for changes (e.g., smaller class size) that might enhance surrogate parenting. It makes sense to ask the question.

Moreover, the public high school possesses much of what clinical parenting requires. School occupies the core hours of the adolescent day. It proffers academic and interpersonal rewards and sanctions. It provides an educated staff well-suited for mentoring relationships in which recognition and limit-setting might well take place. One prolific author, Douglas Heath, has described high schools' rich potential to be potent influences upon psychological maturation. Too often, however, he saw the high school as a missed opportunity. Much conventional teaching and scholarship about teaching falls short in his view, due to a failure to appreciate that maturation, not course content mastery, should be *the* pedagogical priority:

> [W]e have failed to understand and assess and thus have underestimated schools' potential maturing effects—on which to build a firm foundation for a vision of human excellence. Teachers devote 95 percent of their time to rearranging their liberal arts courses rather than learning how to teach students to fulfill their liberal educative potentials. Researchers use tests to assess schooling's effects that are not specifically designed to measure teachers' gifts or guided by any comprehensive model of schools' potential maturing effects.[85]

For all of this potential, thirty percent of American teenagers who start high school fail to graduate. This startling statistic suggests that the contemporary high school, as designed and operated, fails to provide experiences of recognition—and so fails to create close relationships that can hold marginal students to graduation or prod them to become confident, curious students.[86]

Given what we know about recognition and limit-setting, and about the typical public high school, we may infer why this is so. For a start, a typical American high school has too many students (i.e., too few teachers relative to their numbers) to make close relationships a priority. A swamped teacher can focus only upon her best students, who reward her by learning, and upon the worst, who refuse to learn and disrupt her classroom. For this reason, the great mass of students in the middle of the bell curve must feel invisible. Some might argue that the student/teacher ratio ought not be important, that "teaching" ought to influence the many as readily as the few. But good data show otherwise, and every private school if it can marshal the requisite resources reduces the ratio.

It is not only the numbers, however. The architecture and the structure of a typical school day should be designed to foster recognition and limit-setting, if maturity were the priority. Rather than an industrial plant with featureless corridors and segregated lunch facilities, a relationship-oriented architecture would provide nooks for conversation and lunch cafés with small tables and comfy chairs, where a teacher and a few of his students could talk over a cup of soup. The day would not be organized as an assembly line, where teachers have but a fleeting moment, as students move by in batches, like toasters, to install an algebraic nut or to tighten a grammatical bolt. A typical teacher has about ninety seconds to give to each one of his 150 students. This is too little time to learn a student's history or to know his parents. A teacher this busy has time only to glance at a student's work, and not enough to recognize a teenager's idiosyncrasies or suffering. An English teacher assigning a 500-word essay will have to grade *War and Peace*. A math teacher has time to check homework sets, but no time to learn what a boy worries about at night or what a girl hopes her life might become.[87]

Alternative Programs

If neither outpatient interventions nor the "parenting" available in a public high school can provide the recognition and limit-setting an immature teenager needs, if parents cannot intervene effectively or provide sufficient supervision, then an acting-out teenager may not be able to be helped at home. Some obstacles (e.g., furtive eating disorders or suicidal depressions) may not be remedied without expert care and a secure facility. Moreover, a teenager's impulsiveness, defiance, sneakiness, violence, or drug use may overwhelm a family's ability to contain and protect, disrupt siblings' lives, and prevent parents from fulfilling other duties.[88] Even when a very troubled teenager tries to cooperate, the repetitive failures that an immature approach makes inevitable may not be remediable at home.

Once this decision point arrives, two paths diverge. If residential treatment is *not* available, because parents can't afford alternative private care and insurance companies refuse to pay for it (as they usually do), then parents simply have to muddle through as best they can with ineffective outpatient therapies and the heartache of a struggling teenager's unhappiness and costly failures. If immaturity leads to criminal misbehavior, then forces beyond the family may intervene. The court may order a delinquent sent to a state-run residential facility (jail, prison, boot-camp, or drug rehab for adjudicated youth), where the adult staff (guards, rehab counselors) provide a tough brand of surrogate parenting. Unfortunately, these facilities usually provide only a grim, stereotyped recognition and harsh, confrontational limit-setting. Too often, public programs for adjudicated youth and state penal institutions are not effective at changing the downward trajectory. Too often they do more harm than good. Their outcomes, even relative to modest success metrics (e.g., short-term rates of sobriety or recidivism), are unimpressive. In these facilities, moreover, a recent multi-center survey documents a scandalous incidence of sexual assault and physical violence.[89] Moreover, when wayward youth meet hardened young criminals in these facilities, delinquency spreads by contagion.[90]

For parents who *can* afford private care, however, there has come to be a divergent second path—a diverse offering of "alternative" (non-medical) private treatment programs. Despite the enormity of the expense for this usually unreimbursed care, adolescent programs have sprung up like mushrooms in the absence of effective, available medical help for these destructive adolescent problems. In the first decade after its founding in 1999, the National Association of Therapeutic Schools and Programs (NATSAP) grew to nearly two hundred members: behavioral programs, wilderness treks, inspirational adventures, leadership schools, home placements, faith-based residential group homes, residential rehab centers, boys' or girls' homes, residential treatment centers (RTCs) and therapeutic boarding schools. The free market rushed to fill the clinical void created by "managed" care.

There was always a problem of access, however. These programs are scattered across the nation, even overseas, and located in less populous areas far from urban-suburban hub cities. They are various in admission criteria, length of stay and cost, and they are diverse in type, theory, practice, and staff training. Parents have usually needed guidance from experienced educational consultants, who have made it their business to travel, visit, and know the range of available programs so as to help parents find their way around. These experts help parents to locate, visit and gain admission to programs with requisite skills and experience to help a particular teenager, given the specific mix of neuropsychological, family, academic, and social difficulties. Their consultations provide a valuable service to parents who are busy with other responsibilities and other children, and to outpatient clinicians who have no time to visit programs that are dispersed over great distances. When a teenager's need for residential placement presents as an emergency, and parents (and outpatient clinicians) need to take decisive action quickly and a teenager is not disposed to cooperate, experienced educational consultants become indispensable.

Despite all of these practical problems, including geographical distances and challenging topography, and the clinical need to match the problem with the program, thousands of parents have enrolled a distinctive, *non*-adjudicated cohort of immature teenagers to remote residential programs.[91] Compared to state-run facilities for adjudicated youth, in which staffing, theory, and ambience have been quasi-military or penal, NATSAP's alternative private programs provide a very different kind of remedy for a vastly different clientele. They operate on distinctive clinical premises and aspire to (and routinely produce) very different outcomes.[92]

The best of these private programs have become mainstream: subject to state licensure and site visits; committed to national clinical norms and ethical standards; accredited by regional academic associations (often the same ones that accredit public high schools); and inspected by national commissions that apply universal clinical standards, e.g., the Joint Commission for Accreditation of Health Care Organizations (JCAHO), the same organization that accredits the nation's best hospitals. In the most clinically sophisticated programs, parent surrogates are experienced, professionally trained clinicians (psychiatrists, psychologists, social workers, MA-level therapists, and addiction counselors) and certified teachers. Although some remain "alternative" in ambience, most NATSAP programs share in common a general approach to adolescent problems that is understanding rather than punitive; oriented to the outdoors rather than to locked hospital units; interpersonal and academic rather than narrowly biological or pharmacological; and family-oriented rather than military or penal. The best do not aspire merely to symptom-relief, but mitigate obstacles and restore vigorous normal psychological development. Rather than striving to cure a disease or treat a "disorder," the best programs help parents to call a sustained time-out from disrupted urban-suburban lives and help childish teenagers grow up. The general aim is to prod immature teenagers to become considerate sons and daughters, motivated students, empathic friends, and responsible citizens.

Wilderness

More than a decade ago I first learned about a teenager who had been transported in the night to a "wilderness" program a thousand miles from home. His parents, who had come to our ranch to talk about their son (let's call him Sam), explained that they were provoked to take this radical step when, over more than a year, Sam had become more reckless, more obnoxious, more rageful, more recalcitrant, and more often stoned. They were unable to put a stop to it all, despite medical and psychiatric consultations, outpatient weekly therapy, and lots of pills. Knowing little about "wilderness," I was skeptical. Why the need for a sudden snatch from home? The remote terrain? The back-pack? The cold beans? Was "wilderness" (referred to as a noun, in common usage, as in "he was sent to wilderness") a treatment or a punishment? An exile for a prodigal son, or banishment for a promiscuous daughter? Whatever it was intended to accomplish, I wondered, did "wilderness" have anything to do with legitimate psychiatry?

Shortly afterward, Sam emerged from the high desert and arrived at the ranch. I had many occasions in the weeks that followed to ask him about it. He startled me, for the first but by no means for the last time, with what appeared to be a radical shift in his attitude. He'd hiked for miles carrying his few paltry belongings in a pack on his back, he explained cheerfully, and helped to carry the group's common food and equipage. In the evening, he'd cooked rice and beans over a fire he'd "busted" for himself and made a shelter for the night. Was he resentful? Had he felt abused? He admitted that at first he was angry with his parents for sending him away from his well-equipped bedroom, electronic gadgets, car, and "friends," but also admitted he had been failing in school, using drugs, and "going nowhere." He had come to like the field staff and to admire the psychologist who'd been his wilderness therapist. Moreover, now that he had thought it all over, he was sorry he'd been "a jerk" to his parents. He regretted all the ugly things he'd said to his mother. He was sorry about all the shouting. And now? He radiated optimism and confidence. He was proud of the record he'd set in wilderness for the most fires "busted" with a bow drill he'd carved for himself. He was proud he'd made Air Phase—quite a distinction. In the future, he hoped to go back and join the field staff in wilderness, to "help kids" as he'd been helped.

His attitude adjustment was remarkable, but also a little precarious. Some weeks later, when a pretty girl lost interest, he regressed. He re-tested his parents' resolve, complained of the unfairness of their making him come to a therapeutic school and not "giving me a chance to prove myself at home." He missed "friends" and drugs. And so I wondered whether Sam's remarkable shift had been a sham. Yet after his parents expressed affectionate pride in him and told him they were simply unwilling to let him come home until he completed this second step—and when they reminded him that they were in this, too, and would come soon to visit and to talk things over in person as soon as he got to work—he settled down again. Soon I saw a return of his initial confidence, self-respect, and self-discipline. In the following months, he demonstrated unmistakably that his change of heart in wilderness, albeit ambivalent at first, had been an accurate foreshadowing of the poised, mature young man he soon became. When he graduated and went on to college, this mature approach had become a stable aspect of his personality.

Over the years, I repeatedly have seen this pattern: a remarkable shift in a teenager's attitude in wilderness, which impresses and pleases parents, albeit they often cannot explain just what happened, or why it did. Then there is a regression that, if parents stand firm, soon ends. Over subsequent months, students assimilate this new approach into a distinctive, productive young-adult version of themselves.[93] I have seen this so many times, that I've become impressed, too, although initially I had no way to make sense of this transformation either.

Yet, doing what I do for a living, I wondered about it. What was it about "wilderness" that brought about this remarkable, if initially precarious, transformation? Two common explanations, which parents and consultants heard from field staff, were often repeated in my hearing. One of the popular theories relies upon a romantic faith in the power of the natural world to inspire virtue and instill common sense—a Wordsworthian belief that a traduced, warped city life can be redeemed by the awe-inspiring beauty of spacious skies and purple mountain majesty, once a jaded young person got removed from suburban Sodom and urban Gomorrah. A second, related theory also relies upon the salutary influence of the natural world, but emphasizes nature's capacity to punish fools, to bring a careless urban teenager up short—e.g., with a sodden, sleepless night as a "natural consequence" of her failure to anticipate a storm and take the trouble, no matter how trail-weary she was, to build a shelter.

Neither theory holds as much water as a good sleeping bag. I was dubious, albeit I could see that, from a field staff point of view, these explanations for adolescent misery served a useful purpose. They spared staff and therapists the enmity of grumpy teenagers, who arrived feeling put out with all adults. The theory of natural lessons implied that it was not *they*, the adult wilderness staff, who brought suffering, but a teenager's own "bad decisions," which had resulted, for example, in a sopping wet sleeping bag. This formulation framed a teenager's misery as a "bad choice," and so situated field staff in roles as competent pals, who, if treated with respect, might teach a boy or girl to bust a fire, to build a waterproof lean-to, and lay out a down bag to dry in the morning sunshine. Natural consequences made the therapist a wise mentor to guide a tenderfoot in an exploration of other bad choices—not just the one that resulted in a cold night, but also those that resulted in failing grades, domestic squabbles, social rejections, public intoxication, low self-esteem, and an exile from home. The metaphor situated therapy as a reflective re-evaluation of past obliviousness, an anticipation of better choices that might make the future different, less damp, and less wretched, than the recent past. It exculpated staff, keeping them apart from adolescent ire, for even an exasperated teenager knew better than to blame an adult for making it rain.

On the other hand, this theory—about the invisible hand of nature—didn't truly make sense of a teenager's predicament. It suggested that a teenager's own "bad choices" were entirely to blame for his predicament, as if no one else were involved, apart from the impersonal forces of the natural world. In time, I began to think there was something (or someone?) missing from this explanation. Moreover, it occurred to me that Sam already had experienced plenty of natural consequences. When he failed to turn in his algebra, had he not received an F? When he failed to make his bed at home, had he not endured his mother's shrill remonstrances? How come a consequence was natural—and transformative—only when it happened out of doors, near to an ineffable sunset? How come the epiphany had not happened in an urban therapist's comfy, dry consulting room during a conversation about Sam's F's and unmade beds?

When the question got framed this way, the answer became obvious, although I only saw it after I had encountered a long line of damp, scruffy teenagers emerging with their smiling parents from forty days in the wilderness. Wait, I thought, *these* were the adults who paid for the airline tickets; *these* adults had decided, at long last, that enough was enough; and *these* people had written the check to pay the educational consultant, who suggested immediate transport to wilderness? When I remembered the parents, it all became clear. A wilderness trek was not merely an urban teenager's first encounter with a thunderstorm, not just a natural lesson about coming in out of the rain. It was not merely a journey down a forest trail with Chingachgook, who could teach a city-dweller to rub sticks together. It wasn't even a "lesson," natural or otherwise, because what ailed Sam was not to be remedied by learning. His problem was stuck development, and none of the many lectures his exasperated parents already had delivered, nor any of the insights his therapist offered, nor any of the blackboard lessons about how to "solve for x" were going to make Sam grow up. His problem, I had (by then) begun to learn, was going to require limit-setting within a meaningful relationship. And so, there it was. Sam had needed to grow up. In the worst way, he had needed a limit set. He had needed that constraint to be enormous enough in its impact to jolt him from the fatuous dream in which he had become marooned. He needed a limit set within a close relationship, so that it would matter to him, as nothing else would matter. And that was precisely what he got.

It did not happen in the leafy forest or high desert, however. It happened instead within the closest of all his relationships. It had taken a while to sink in—many hours, once all the drugs were gone and he was free from distractions, so that he could think and feel, as he hiked down the trail. It took a patient staff to help him. It required new teenager friends to keep him honest about a predicament that was very much like their own. He needed a therapist to help him to face this new knowledge, which he struggled to wrap his mind around. But it did not begin in the field, this novel understanding, although that was where it fully dawned on him. It began when two men entered his bedroom, identified themselves, and walked him down the stairs and out the front door, and no one stepped in to prevent them from taking him away. He caught another glimpse of it from the airliner, watching the dark continent pass slowly under his window. And then, night after night, he had felt it, like an ache in his belly, as he stared up into that infinite sky. For what impressed him in the solitude of his sleeping bag was not the proximity of so many stars, but the singular absence of his beloved family. This fact finally jerked him out of the self-absorbed somnambulism that had become his life. They weren't kidding!—*that* was over. Alone in the wilderness, far from home, he got the message.

His parents had just said: "**NO!**"

∾

What a skilled wilderness therapist choreographs, with help from field staff, is not merely individual therapy during walks in the woods, or group therapy around the campfire, but also an intensive family therapy, carried on at a distance. At the start, the therapist sizes up an arriving camper to gauge how ready he is to face his own role in his exile; how prepared he is to endure emotional hardships as well as blisters; how inclined to whine, to blame others, and to pressure his parents to "just take me home!" When the therapist gets back to cell-phone range, he calls parents to prepare them for the work ahead.[94]

In these early days the therapist listens to both accounts of recent history. In the discrepancies he discovers a son's dishonesty, a daughter's secrets. He finds out how badly a son or daughter misreads parents' motives. He learns how grossly parents have failed to recognize, or have *mis*recognized, their child. He discovers parents' weaknesses: a disabling worry that a beloved son will never forgive them; a wish to rescue, to exculpate, to minimize a daughter's egregious malfeasance; their doubts about their own judgment, their fears they have gone too far, their impulse to pack up and go home and forget this travail. The therapist keeps in touch with the educational consultant, who, thus informed, helps shore up parents' flagging confidence or sagged determination. Working at both ends, the therapist prepares both the camper and the parents for the rituals of recognition."[95]

Physical separation helps to make this preparation possible. Teenagers whisked away to wilderness become frantic to talk to their parents, so as to quickly undo parental limit-setting, to argue and debate, to explain and excuse, to obfuscate and rationalize. Sometimes they are (rightly) confident that if they can just get on the phone they can work the old magic and put unendurable pressure on vulnerable, worried, weary parents. This being so, it is helpful for the therapist to keep the two camps apart, so as to make a slippery teenager squirm and to protect parental resolve. Writing letters, rather than talking on the phone, helps by slowing down the early exchange. The therapist, who can see all the missives before they are delivered, can help a young camper to think about what (s)he writes. He can help parents to calm down, and to think carefully, before they reply.

Those first letters can be revealing. The correspondence often begins with poker-faced queries about the possibility of a case of mistaken identity. A teenager wants to figure out what his parents know, but, even more important, he wants to figure out what they *don't* know. He asks in all innocence whether it could be that the escort service got the wrong address or the wrong miscreant (surely others deserved this *much* more than I do?). Could there have been some semantic ambiguity (something I said that you misconstrued)?

When coached parents answer calmly (no, actually, no mistake—although of course we wish there had been some misunderstanding), there may be an eruption of volcanic rage and scorn (*this* is your pathetic gambit?), righteous indignation (how *dare* you?), accusations (*your* stupidity, *your* fault), protests of innocence (who, *me*?), and revelations of heretofore inadequately expressed respect and fealty to the family (*awesome* parents, exemplary siblings) a new acknowledgment of obliviousness (gosh, if I had only *known* you meant it), silly excuses (the dog ate the car keys, the cat dragged in that baggie of who knew what that must have belonged to that stranger at the party who left it in the back seat of the car). There may be propitiation (I'll make it up to you, I'll stay home Saturday nights and play Parcheesi with my little sister), or an epiphany (gosh, I had no idea you were *this* upset), or crafty negotiations (if you bring me home *now*, I'll do *x*) and a few new year's resolutions (if you bring me home now, I'll never again do *y* or *z*), expressions of optimism (now that I get it, all will be well), and, if parents hold the line, threats (if you *don't*, and I mean *now*, you'll never even *hear* about your grandchildren).

When these efforts to circumvent what the family has come to do peter out, the therapist takes the cue to bring back to camp the parents' carefully composed *Impact Letter*, which begins with an act of recognition:

> You seem not to recall what you did to get yourself sent to wilderness. You seem to imagine that all this might have been

avoided. You blame us, and you do not take responsibility for the impact of your behavior upon your brothers and sisters, your aunts, uncles, grandparents, and neighbors, much less upon the few reputable friends you still have. So let us remind you.

Parents then enumerate the disgraceful history of academic carelessness, failing grades, pathetic excuses, family fracas, broken promises, bald-faced lies, disregarded oaths, personal betrayals, irresponsibility, lack of cooperation, sneaky or criminal acts, sexual indecencies, and inebriated indignities. The recipient must read this letter aloud to the others gathered around the campfire.

This letter brings the parents' point of view into the group and into individual therapy. Inasmuch as parents are not present to debate or offer exoneration, or even to provoke a child's threats or obfuscation, the young recipient has to digest it all with his therapist, field staff, and peers—a rumination that may take weeks. However, there is no ducking that indictment. To digest it is what comes next, what is expected. No further promotion or privileges will be granted until that self-examination takes place. Moreover, there is no easy escape—no car keys, no pals to run off with, no iPod or marijuana to distract or anesthetize. A boy cannot hide from others that *he* has problems, not only his parents. A girl cannot hide from others her wretched, sneaky behavior, which may arouse sympathy (for her parents) among other campers and staff. After this, it becomes obvious to a son or daughter and to everyone else that the road home will be painful and without shortcuts.

This rumination, however long it takes, culminates in a second ritual of recognition, a second ordeal. After the parents' letter is read, the camper is expected to get honest with the group, to tell the truth about the past, *all* of it. The defined task is to put an end to secrets, to come clean, first in camp, then with parents. In sending a son or daughter the list of particulars, parents reveal most of what they know—and so give away what they do *not* know. For this reason, a teenager's draft reply gets a lot of attention from the therapist and from the group—and must be added to, and revised. There is much to discuss as a son contemplates how real he should be with his parents, as a daughter imagines what her parents are going to say when they find out what she is going to have to tell them. In the end, this formal account, an attempt to confess to all of it, gets drafted, edited, and sent home as a *Letter of Accountability*.

This exchange of candor changes relationships. The process can be painful, but may bring relief. A boy has to contemplate the damage he did to a beloved little sister or brother, or live with a disgrace he brought upon himself in his grandparents' eyes. A daughter suffers the shame of a revelation she never intended to have to share with her father, or feels a new remorse that comes from hurting a mother who did not deserve that anguish. Parents find this exchange excruciating, too. The accountability letter forces them to revise their own histories, and brings them into painful proximity to the unsuspected truth of their own behavior and experience. Parents may discover that in blissful ignorance they partied through a son's nearly lethal overdose. They may find out that, while they slept peacefully in their warm beds, their nearly comatose little girl was raped behind a dumpster.

And so, when the wilderness therapist departs for town to drop that weighty missive into a mailbox, a daughter can walk more lightly in her boots, relieved of the burden of a secret she had carried for too long. A son now can sleep soundly under the stars.[96] For a time, after that letter arrives at home, as it often happens, parents have trouble sleeping at all. Yet from that anguishing knowledge there may come relief eventually. For the truth can set a family free and bring parents closer to an alienated son or daughter. An accurate understanding provides a basis for a revived relationship, a restoration of parenting. Mutual recognition can become a turning point in a family's journey.

Residential Therapeutic School[97]

If a recalcitrant teenager's temporary exile to wilderness is an abrupt departure from civilization, a respite from the complexities, temptations, and distractions of mass culture, his enrollment in a therapeutic school is the opposite: a re-entry into a complex social order. He must make himself at home, starting from scratch, in an intimate society whose structures, rules, procedures, customs, and incentives are the challenge. This is, of course, the point. For if wilderness strips away the complexities of life at home and sets limits for a teenager who was failing at all the tasks of adolescence, the next logical step is surely not an immediate return to all the temptations, distractions, unsupervised beds, and ubiquitous drugs of the permissive culture he already has demonstrated only weeks before that he couldn't handle. A brief excursion in the wilds cannot create a durable carapace of mature personality that can stand up to the toxic chemistry of modern society.

For this reason, teenagers successfully completing wilderness are often enrolled in therapeutic schools. There they face most of the healthy normative challenges of adolescence, but not without supervision to prevent a prompt regression. The school's goal is that students master academic learning, engage in teamwork and athletic competition, that they make durable friends and fall in love, but not return to all the old mistakes, resume the old arrogance, take up with the same pals, and return to the fecklessness that became the occasion for that sudden exile.

This is the risk: regression.[98] Even after a very successful wilderness experience, a teenager's gains may evaporate in the context where the original breakdown occurred. Regression to slovenly academic habits, drug use, automotive irresponsibility, promiscuity, and defiance of family rules can happen rapidly, if parents are too quick to regard that breakdown as over and done, leaving all a teenager's dysfunction "fixed" in wilderness and no longer needing sustained parental attention. Here it may be useful to pause to clarify this term with an instructive example from a simpler stage of life. When all goes well, parents successfully coax a toddler to use the toilet and to remain dry at night. This milestone can be sustained so long as the family preserves the key relationships and structures (e.g., daily schedule) on which continence was founded. However, a toddler's dry bed may be vulnerable if his routine gets disrupted (e.g., by a sibling's birth) or if he loses a key relationship (e.g., his mother departs for the hospital).[99] Abruptly, that developmental step forward may be reversed—and we now call that pathological step backward "enuresis" (bedwetting). After a wilderness success, a teenagers loss of academic discipline or achieved planfulness or sobriety, would be a regression, too.

To minimize such steps backward, a residential school provides structure and clinical parenting. It challenges adolescents academically, and makes school the central spectacle in students' lives, because learning is the proper job for teenagers. It offers robust athletics; artistic, musical, and social extracurricular activities; and so provides ample scope for real accomplishments that create a new sense of purpose and a legitimate source of self-esteem. However, an exemplary therapeutic school also provides adequate supervision to protect a still-immature adolescent, whose good judgment cannot yet be relied upon. To promote character development, therapeutic schools set firm, clear limits.

The best therapeutic schools look very much like conventional high schools or prep schools, offering:

- a challenging academic curriculum, i.e., all the courses needed for college admission, taught in small classes at a demanding standard, so as to prepare bright students for challenging colleges;
- a required fitness program, which may include intramural sports and teams (e.g., soccer, basketball, cross-country) that compete with other schools;
- co-ed group activities, which encourage leadership and provide social practice, e.g., drama productions, jazz club, student government, a prom;
- vigorous weekend activities—e.g., hiking, fishing, biking, camping, downhill and cross-country skiing, and rock-climbing, which may be off-campus excursions.

This is to say, the experience should feel as normal as possible. Students ought to be encouraged to take pride—to feel about their school in the end much the same pride students in conventional prep schools feel. A visitor should not too easily discern that the structure of a therapeutic boarding school is any different or more intricate or confining than a conventional school, either in terms of what is provided or what is forbidden. The school ought not to look or feel like a hospital or penal colony.

Yet a competent therapeutic boarding school *is* much more intricate and structured—so as to focus upon clinical parenting. Inasmuch as the point is to promote character development in relatively immature teenagers, good therapeutic schools build in for every student an intensive, sustained experience of recognition. To this end, they provide regularly the expressive encounters we call (individual, group, and family) therapies. Even the school's architecture, its schedules, its procedures and rules, promote relationships—in the classroom, on playing fields, in the dorm, and in the dining hall. For accurate, influential recognition does not occur without close relationships. For the same reason, good therapeutic schools attend closely to limit-setting. Where there are rules, codes, prescribed good manners, and dire prohibitions, staff must be trained not to take a casual approach to supervising and enforcing them. Unlike some conventional prep schools, which tolerate drugs and alcohol use on campus so long as it remains covert, a therapeutic school's faculty may not take a "see no evil" approach to discipline. In sum, a therapeutic school must be appraised primarily on the basis of its capacity to deliver recognition and firm limits.

To discern the effective structures upon which recognition and limit-setting depend may require a closer look. In the therapeutic school I know best, for example, an arriving student joins nine other students to form a *team*, a durable group that functions a little like a family. As in a family, the team is the central context for both recognition and limit-setting. To encourage intimacy, the team enjoys an exclusive membership, all girls or all boys. It shapes its own culture, makes and remembers its own history, and keeps its own secrets. Members belong to other groups, of course. They attend co-ed classes during the week, whose membership is assigned on the basis of academic need. They attend co-ed weekend activities, whose participants are selected on the basis of earned privileges. They may hang out with friends from other teams during the evenings. Yet all the team's members inevitably will feel, in the end, that the team was the beating heart of the entire school experience, for each student sleeps in a team bedroom with team-mates, eats with them at every meal at a common table, does her chores (e.g., kitchen clean) with them, and goes on outings reserved exclusively for them. Her team meets for group therapy four days each week, where squabbles, progress, and discipline get discussed, and team-mates talk with one another about their quotidian experiences, painful memories, private business, troubles about parents, worries about boys, addictive longings, erotic thoughts and experiences, struggles with trauma, and current sadness, anxiety, or joy. In sum, her team-mates get to know her very well, and they look out for her. Except when asleep, she is rarely beyond shouting distance from staff who remember her story, recognize her family, and know about her troubles.

Like a family, a team has its own permanent staff: a therapist, two (weekday and weekend) team-leaders, who function like watchful parents, and an academic advisor (a teacher). All students on the team share the same therapist, who conducts team groups, meets with students every week for individual therapy, and talks regularly with their parents (on the phone or in person during visits). The therapist presides over team staff meetings, so as to direct each student's treatment plan and to monitor her progress and the course of her campus life. In short, a team is built for recognition, but also for setting boundaries and constraints. Team staff determine a student's privileges, and, under the therapist's affectionate eye, the team monitors each student's campus life and behavior beyond the precincts of the team's own encounters. In this peculiar pseudo-family, all "parents" are attentive, firmly in charge, well-informed, and engaged in close relationships with all the members of the team and with one another.

Beyond these intimate groups, a first-rate therapeutic school provides campus-wide opportunities for recognition and universally applicable standards for decorum. Students meet with staff in community and dorm meetings, where they can talk about common concerns. In quarterly awards ceremonies, the community recognizes exemplary students and staff. Awards are given by clinical supervisors (best program performance), team leaders (various virtues), teachers ("best" and "most improved" academic performance), student council (for traits that students admire), and by students (honored staff). Team and individual sports (skiing, weightlifting, hiking, fishing) provide opportunities to excel, to learn, and to be recognized as competent and fit. A therapeutic school provides broad, universal structures for firm limit-setting, too. Beyond the team, limits are also built into a student's experience from start to finish. A student's enrollment is rarely left up to a student to choose—and so a son's or daughter's very presence on campus constitutes an early limit set by parents. On arrival, a student begins with few options and fewer privileges, but gradually earns both. In the school I know well, *clans* define a student's program status. These are created categories of privilege and responsibility that mark a student's progress (in effect, beginning, middle and end) through the program. Clans reify program privileges, but also program limits—and although these markers are not visible to any casual visitor, every student knows who has earned which clan status. In a healthy therapeutic community, these earned prerogatives command respect—as do the other rules and published norms that regulate social decorum. In the school I know well, clan promotions are announced in the dining hall and greeted with an ovation. In addition to these broad set limits, the daily and weekly chores are assigned, checked, and rated. There are sanctions for students who fail to carry out their assigned duties. Academic grades (both acts of recognition and set limits) are announced each week in groups. In general, behavior and performance are widely discussed on campus—as matters of civic and personal virtue. In team, dorm, and community meetings, students talk about what they think and how they feel about the rules—and about those who violate community norms.

For all this attention to discipline, the ideal school is not preoccupied with sanctions or conformity. For it is hateful to live in a community whose adults are reduced to cops, where too much is made about policing rules and punishing miscreants, or where teenaged citizens think misbehavior a victory or an achievement. It is ugly for adults and teenagers to become polarized over rules, so that young people admire, or even think it acceptable, for other young people to misbehave. Certainly this does not have to be. Rules should be discussed and debated, and taken seriously as the basis for communal lives, but they should not be the dominant leitmotif for community life. Students participate in making rules, and are not expected only to accept them as given on stone tablets.

This should be true for mature teenagers within a civil society, just as it should be so in families in which children are given a voice. In a therapeutic school, these are particularly important family issues insofar as parental authority has broken down at home, or has been defied or subverted in the past. A restoration of legitimate adult authority is often one critical family therapy goal. Curfews, dress code, tattoos, choices of friends, use of drugs and alcohol, and acceptable academic standards—all must be debated and agreed upon as shared expectations, prior to visits home and in anticipation of graduation.

∽

By their very nature, therapeutic schools must control their perimeters; this is surely true to some extent of any school and any family. But boundaries may be the more critical in a therapeutic school, whose students usually have experienced and may have participated in boundary breakdowns at home. Therapeutic schools control who comes to the campus; staff conduct searches to exclude contraband; limits are enforced on phone calls, letters, and packages; and weapons are outlawed. In the school I know best we also proscribe or closely control distracting technologies (i.e., television, DVD and CD players, iPods, cell-phones), ban student vehicles, and put limits on the amounts of clothing or other belongings that students bring to campus. These limits—on gadgets, drugs, weapons, erotic display, and sexual behavior—reflect a priority placed upon immediate human relationships, including adult–adolescent friendship.

In a school whose students arrive after having failed to discipline themselves properly, campus-wide limits protect the opportunity for young people to develop capacities for mutual recognition, interpersonal honesty, and respect, friendship, and love—without rushing past these hurdles to use drugs, distract themselves from thoughts and feelings, or engage in self-indulgent sexual intercourse. We discovered the hard way long ago that for immature teenagers this opportunity must be protected from virtual distractions, noise, and twitter. These defended boundaries preserve a calm, safe space (on campus and in students' minds) for sustained thinking, articulate expression, frank conversation, and respectful affection. As part of a complex structure of incentives, finally, a therapeutic school limits options (e.g., weekend activities) on the basis of earned clan status. The school sets priorities, as parents do—e.g., that academic assignments and clean-up chores come first, and watching a movie comes later.

Similarly, in the school I know well, where students are as gorgeous and as sexy, and care for one another as helplessly and wantonly, as teenagers anywhere, we place explicit limits on erotic touching and sexual expression. These limits may have to be more restrictive than in other kinds of school. The message must be: until students manage to subordinate childish narcissism to respectful consideration, until they have achieved empathy and personal forbearance, adult sexual license isn't warranted. Put the other way around, when students are truly able to approach all the other serious responsibilities in their lives with a reliable maturity, it will be time to send them home (or on to college). There will still be plenty of time after graduation for those most adult of all prerogatives. The issue has little to do with any wish to deprive students of affection or to discourage erotic pleasure. It's a matter of first things first.

The problems that bring young people to a therapeutic boarding school must take priority. Immature teenagers have not as yet earned a right to indulge in sexual relationships for which they are as yet unready, unwilling, and unable to take adult responsibility.

∾

It remains to say what parents can usefully contribute while a son or daughter is enrolled in a wilderness program or therapeutic boarding school. In a phrase, they should join the adult treatment team. Parents ought to do so, once they have chosen to send a child to a particular program, not just to help therapist and staff, but to help sons and daughters grow up by providing what *all* teenagers need from parents: firm limits and adult teamwork. There can be no effective clinical parenting without delegated parental authority and unwavering collaboration from moms and dads. Parents help a program succeed by getting behind it, endorsing its aims and methods, seconding its authority, and backing up a teenager's work by joining in it. All suggestions in previous chapters about how to recognize and set limits—and how not to—are relevant here.

In particular, parents ought to avoid splitting the family from the school, just as they are wise to avoid domestic divisions between mom and dad. When a son demands to come home, parents must sustain his participation, encourage him to get down to work, and commit themselves to show up and to join in to help. When a daughter complains that the kitchen feeds her worms, or that a teacher unjustly graded her homework, or that her therapist was "mean," parents help when they reply: "Gosh, it sounds like *you* have a problem, and we're very interested to hear how you're going to handle it?" It doesn't help for parents to ingratiate themselves by promising to chew out the chef, argue with a teacher, or undermine a school rule. It's a teenager's task in growing up to learn to choose from the salad bar, negotiate with teachers, and accept campus discipline. These aren't parental tasks. If something a son or daughter reports sounds worrisome, then parents have every right to ask the therapist or team-leader to make sense of it. But parents ought to do so adult-to-adult, starting with basic trust and continuing with courtesy and humility, and not imagine it is their job to manage the kitchen, grade the homework, or rescue a daughter from the consequences of her own behavior.

The most helpful parents in my experience concentrate first upon their own failings. The most impressive assume they may have something to learn. Not paralyzed with remorse, they recognize that they may have made mistakes. Neither obsequious nor propitiating, they recognize that if they aren't the (only) problem, nevertheless they are a big part of the solution. They use the time and respite a program can provide to reconsider how they approached a parental task, and try to figure out how, in future, to approach that task more effectively. They try to make sense of the past, so that in future they can deal more effectively with their own feelings. To do so, wise parents often find a trusted therapist to talk to: about their own past experiences as children, about their own relationships (e.g., marriage or divorce), and about their own child-rearing. They avoid the folly of sending a troubled son or daughter to a therapeutic program only to try to badger the program staff to handle that teenager the same way as they themselves have done. Sons and daughters, I should add, recognize and admire parental self-scrutiny, curiosity, and willingness to learn from mistakes. They are likely to emulate these virtues.

Cultural Norms

There isn't only one way to parent teenagers. From one historical era to another, from one culture to another, from one family to another, parenting and parents differ. In *fin de siècle* Vienna, attitudes, mores, prohibitions, and sanctions about sexual feelings, thoughts, and behaviors were generally more rigidly prohibitive than those that inform bourgeois recognition and limit-setting in contemporary Los Angeles or London. There is no one right way. Yet the style and content of parenting is no matter for indifference. Parenting has consequences—whether neurotic or narcissistic, happy or unhappy, successful or unsuccessful, attractive or unattractive—in children's future adult lives. Our parenting will reverberate in the rearing of our grandchildren.

Yet the style and shape of the parenting our children and grandchildren experience is never wholly in our own hands. It takes a village, we say—and a state and a nation, I might add. This is to say, it's never solely up to parents or the nuclear family, but also a matter of culture and sociology. We have some choice about the way our sons and daughters are reared, but we cannot trade in our neighbors, go back to Freud's Vienna, or move our families to a remote village in the Amazon rainforest. This being so, if our children must grow up among our neighbors, we might usefully consider what political sea change it would require to restore to ourselves some of the parental prerogatives that wilderness programs and therapeutic boarding schools have come to insist upon—so as to protect teenaged children for as long as they need protection, to recognize them accurately, and prod them to become mature adults. It may be worth asking how easy or difficult it might be for us to protect them from drugs, cigarettes, thugs, casual sex, and the distracting cacophony of modern life. If we had it in us to rear our children differently and more effectively, how might we do so?

I raise these political questions because they may be worth pondering in an era in which perceptive, worried parents, acting individually and at great expense, enroll thousands of their sons and daughters in programs that are in effect alternative child-rearing cultures. Their search for surrogate parenting, for a safe remote society to which they may send troubled sons and daughters temporarily, raises questions that can only be answered much closer to home. It would seem that modern culture maroons some teenagers in a childish narcissism. It would appear that some teenagers are having trouble growing up there. Why should this be so?

Certainly there are many relevant factors. The list surely includes the impact of a generation of women's educational, economic, and professional successes, which have been associated, it seems to me, with a failure (of men more than women) to fully accommodate parental responsibilities within established institutions (e.g., hospitals, law firms, and corporate offices). The list must also include the impact of divorce and family blending; the special developmental problems of adopted children; the ubiquity of drugs and alcohol; the brutal influence of criminal gangs; and the contagion of rampant narcissism. Rather than thinking of ways to export our way of life overseas, we might more usefully ask ourselves whether *this* is the culture in which we want to rear our own children. After all, they *are* our future.

This question seems the more poignant at a time when many friends wish out loud for greater maturity among randy politicians, doping athletes, selfish bankers, self-important CEOs, and sociopathic corporations, whose narcissism puts at risk the world our grandchildren will inherit. Our public debates over education, energy, taxes, health care, and foreign policy sometimes seem to be dominated by strident people who lack consideration or empathy for those unlike themselves; who propose no fully imagined goals or step-wise plans; who demonstrate little concern for the consequences of their words or actions. Among them, is an ugly intolerance for those different than they, a willingness to bully, and a conviction that we ought to be allowed to do anything we can get away with doing. These now-familiar markers of adolescent immaturity are the hallmarks of adult pathology, of course—for the one if never redressed merely turns into the other.[100]

So we come full circle, back to the dual tasks and societal goals of parenting. Inasmuch as moms and dads do their best to respect a young person's inner life, but discipline a son or daughter to conform within reason to societal norms, it's inevitable that children will grow up to be conflicted—as, no doubt, we ourselves are. There is no way around this. To become mature adults, young people must become able to restrain themselves, and so our parenting cannot only be all about "Yes." And yet to enjoy work and play, to be imaginative and creative, to participate joyfully in erotic relationships—as we hope our children will become able to—young people also must be permitted to take pleasure in their minds and bodies. So our parenting cannot only be all about "No," either. We don't admire the shamelessness now common in our culture, and yet we really don't wish to return to the shame-inducing rigidities of the Victorian past. For these reasons, I've suggested that our parenting should aim for recognition *and* limit-setting, which is to say that, as parents, we ought to aspire to produce mature, *civilized* adults.

Notes

1   I make this statement without bothering to defend it here. To do so would merely repeat the case I've already made for disrupted psychological development and for persistent adolescent and young adult childishness in *An Unchanged Mind: The Problem of Immaturity in Adolescence* (New York: Lantern Books, 2008).

2   I rely for this portentous implication about the life's work of George Vaillant, M.D., who for most of a distinguished professional lifetime directed *The Harvard Grant Study* and other prospective studies of the psychology, psychiatry, and life outcomes of adolescent men. See *Aging Well: Surprising Guideposts to a Happier Life from the Landmark Harvard Study of Adult Development* (New York: Little Brown & Co, 2002). For an accessible discussion of these remarkable studies and an exegesis of Vaillant's conclusion that "happiness" over a lifetime is a function of "maturity" (of defenses), see also: Joshua Wolf Shenk (2009) "What Makes Us Happy," *The Atlantic*, 303(5):36–53.

3   *The American Heritage Dictionary of the English Language* (Boston: Houghton Mifflin, 1992), p. 1509.

4   Snow White, *Grimm's Fairy Tales* (London: Ernest Nister, 1898).

5   Psychological immaturity also presents in adolescence as a global breakdown, a series of repetitive failures in all venues of adolescent life—at school, home, and among social peers. This debacle is associated with various signs and symptoms and a variety of misbehaviors that are attempts at self-distraction and self-consolation (e.g., drug intoxication, compulsive playing with video-games, obsessional use of pornography, self-injury).

6   This is the emptiness to which those with narcissistic character disorders are doomed, i.e., the fate of those who never grow up; for there's nothing behind the mask but another mask. They cannot let anyone "look behind the mask," because, as Gertrude Stein said about Oakland, "There is no there there."

7   Martin Buber's phrase is also the title of his book (1923) *I and Thou*, Walter Kaufmann transl. (New York: Touchstone, 1996). I am indebted to my friend Julian Svedosh for the nudge to look at Buber's profound rendering of the experience of self and other.

8   This account of René Spitz's observations and description of anaclitic depression and hospitalism is from Mohammad and Sharon Shafii, *Clinical Guide to Depression in Children and Adolescents* (Arlington, Va., American Psychiatric Publications, 1992) pp. 13–16. The classic paper was Spitz, R. A. (1945) "Hospitalism—An Inquiry into the Genesis of Psychiatric Conditions in Early Childhood," *Psa Study of the Child*, 1:53–74.

9   Bowlby, J. and Robertson, J. (1952) "A Two-Year-Old Goes to Hospital," in *Mental Health and Human Development*, Proceedings of the Seminar on Mental Health and Infant Development, Bishop Otto Training College, Chichester, Sussex, England, July 19–August 10, 1952, organized

by the World Federation for Mental Health with support from the World Health Organization, International Library of Psychology, London and New York, Routledge (and posted on books.google.com/), pp. 123–124.

[10] Patrick Russell's notes from his book *100 British Documentaries*, posted on the Robertson Films website (www.robertsonfilms.info/). This documentary film by James and Joyce Robertson (1969) entitled, *John, Aged Seventeen Months, for Nine Days in a Residential Nursery*, has been unforgettable. The Robertsons documented the profound distress of hospitalized children and in the case of "John" (and three other normal children) their care in a pediatric nursery while a parent was admitted to hospital. I saw the film *John* as a medical student and have never been able to get this small boy's disintegration out of my mind.

[11] Robert Karen (1994) *Becoming Attached* (New York: Oxford University Press), pp. 84–85. This is an excellent account of the work of René Spitz and John Bowlby on childhood separation and hospitalism. It is also the best summary I know of the films made by James and Joyce Robertson (see note 10 above). Karen also describes the bitter resistance to these films from the medical and nursing establishment in the UK—and the gradual but profound changes in pediatric hospital policies about parent visits and participation in care they provoked.

[12] From notes compiled by Dr. Inge Pretorious for the Anna Freud Center "Open Afternoon," 17 September 2006, posted on the Internet as "The Hampstead War Nurseries and the Origins of the Anna Freud Centre" at <www.annafreudcentre.org/war_nurseries.htm>. The direct quotation is from a paper by Anna Freud and Dorothy Burlingham (1944) "The Case for and Against Residential Nurseries," in: *Infants without Families: Reports on the Hampstead Nurseries 1939–1945*, Volume III of *The Writings of Anna Freud* (New York: International Universities Press, 1973). For further discussions of the experience of the wartime nurseries, see also Anna Freud (1951) "An Experiment in Group Upbringing," *Psa Study of the Child*, 6:127–168, and I. Hellman (1983) "Work in the Hampstead War Nurseries," *Int J Psa*, 64:435–439.

[13] *Ibid.* The direct quotations (from Anna Freud) are taken from Dr. Pretorious' notes, too, and also come from *Infants without Families: Reports on the Hampstead Nurseries 1939–1945, op. cit.*, p. 220.

[14] See Karen, *op cit.*, pp. 61–62, for another account of the work of Anna Freud and Dorothy Burlingham in the wartime nurseries they created.

[15] Atul Gawande (2009) "Hellhole," *The New Yorker*, March 30, 2009, pp. 38–39.

[16] *Ibid.* Gawande adds that in a similar 1992 study of fifty-seven POWs released from detention camps in Yugoslavia after an average confinement of six months, EEG-like tests revealed similar brain abnormalities months afterward, "most severe in prisoners who had endured either head trauma sufficient to render them unconscious or . . . solitary confinement."

[17] *Ibid.* By "sustained" and "social," Gawande implies that he means enduring personal relationships in which an empathic hearing and mutual understanding—what I here call *recognition*—can take place. Without this "sustained social interaction," he concludes, "the human brain may become as impaired as one that has incurred a traumatic injury."

[18] I put the word in quotation marks, because "recognition" that is grossly inaccurate is, by definition, not really recognition at all.

[19] Many playwrights, Shakespeare among them, create dramatic irony on the stage by means of misrecognition. The joke is that the audience knows of the error. In *The Importance of Being Ernest*, Oscar Wilde calls it "Bunburying" when his character takes on one identity in the country, another in town, and so amuses the audience with the idea of this resulting confusion.

[20] Waugh, E. *Brideshead Revisited* (Boston: Little Brown & Co, 1945), pp. 69–70.

[21] Mariana C., personal communication, 14 March 2004.

[22] Erikson, E. "The Eight Ages of Man," *Childhood and Society* (New York: W. W. Norton & Co., 1950), pp. 247–284. Erikson, a protégé of Maria Montessori's, was also a psychoanalyst who was part of Anna Freud's circle in Vienna before World War II. His description of the psycho-social point of view became a twentieth-century classic.

[23] Miller, A. *The Drama of the Gifted Child* (New York: Basic Books, 1950). Alice Miller, a Swiss psychoanalyst, has argued that children and teenagers who are "gifted" at tuning in to a mother or father's narcissistic needs may find it impossible to live their lives independently, beyond the perimeter of parental expectations and ambitions.

[24] John Bowlby, whose life-work concerned children's early attachments, made this rueful suggestion after he was attacked for insisting that parents needed to take the trouble and time to rear their children. I trust few contemporary parents will miss his irony.

[25] The restoration of a parent–child relationship, once alienation becomes entrenched, is a prodigious task, particularly after a bitter divorce or years of neglect. No reconciliation is plausible without a major, sustained effort. Among students referred for residential treatment at Montana Academy, this is sometimes the presenting problem: a teenager, failing globally, who lacks a close relationship because of parents who have become distanced or excluded from a teenager's life. This alienation makes that adult's participation in parenting all but impossible. In such cases, calling a major time-out in a teenager's life, somehow, making a break from his distractions (e.g., friends, drugs, cell-phones, televisions, iPods, and romantic dalliances) may be the *sine qua non* in restoring a parent's capacity to function. Obviously, a parent has also to suspend the distractions that have been the occasion for alienation—e.g., a demanding career, social commitments, hobbies, travel, addictions, etc. There are other contexts for alienation, too. In some stressed and deprived communities, many fathers are in prison, mothers impoverished and addicted, and adolescent children have become alienated and un-parented. Again, when alienation has become habitual and intractable, restoring parents to their proper roles—or finding surrogate parenting—can be a challenge, or even beyond a parent's capacities. So the prognosis for normal maturation is grim.

[26] See Chapter 8: Case Study: "An Invisible Girl."

[27] No doubt this description and this pace of life will sound familiar to many modern parents.

[28] There are times, however, particularly when setting a determined limit, when parents usefully make the point in public precisely to induce shame. I have done this myself when I thought it necessary. However, it's more often wise not to complicate an act of recognition or make it unlikely to be heard by making it in public—and so humiliating a young person. It's wise to be careful about saying in public what ought to be private communication. See Chapter 7 for a discussion of the context in which to set limits.

[29] This is the fallacy of Von Domarus. For an intriguing discussion of this fallacy, which also appears to be the basis for schizophrenic delusions, see Silvano Arieti's textbook, *Interpretation of Schizophrenia* (New York: Basic Books, 1974). This construction is also the basis for metaphor (as opposed to simile), but not a sound basis for empathy or for parenting.

[30] This loss of a responsible adult, parental point of view and capacity to act is one major reason for parental failures of recognition and limit-setting. If out of her own childhood unhappiness a mother remains identified only with the child-as-victim that she was, she may not be able to stand the slightest distress in her child or participate in setting limits as an adult. She may fail to recognize her son's frantic signal that he needs limits, and

fail (in the face a child's noisy distress) to set limits that a daughter needs, but of course doesn't want. A long series of frustrating experiences with parents has taught me that this isn't a problem of parental stupidity or stubbornness or even ignorance, but instead a failure to hold onto an adult, parental perspective *and also* to see from a child's point of view.

[31] Kegan, R. *In Over Our Heads* (Cambridge: Harvard University Press, 1994). Kegan's remarkable studies and those of his colleagues demonstrate that not all adults (by any means) reach what he calls "3rd-order" thinking, much less 4th-order cognitive maturity. As he demonstrates with a telling clinical history, a failure to achieve fully adult thinking handicaps a parent, particularly in contexts in which American culture fails to provide structural and family support for parental limit-setting. I should point out that we're talking about limit-setting prematurely, inasmuch as this parental task will be taken up directly in later chapters. However, the truth is that we separate them conceptually only for heuristic purposes. In Chapter 9 we put the two core parental tasks back together, where they belong. Here is an example that demonstrates this inter-relationship. A parent who cannot do the one finds it impossible also to do the other very well.

[32] This isn't a new idea. See Miller (1997) *op. cit.*

[33] I trust it will be obvious that *x* can be about erotic behavior, dress, or coiffure or makeup, smoking or about drugs, or about political affiliation. But *x* must be among those decisions parents are ready to concede that a daughter is grown-up enough to make for herself. Here I'm emphasizing what parental recognition of *separateness* might sound like. I'm not suggesting that we ought to take an "anything you decide is fine" approach about every decision a minor might wish to make. Surely for a thirteen- or even a seventeen-year-old, there are moral or practical prohibitions—e.g., sexual intercourse, recreational heroin—that we must insist our minor children comply with, because we're not yet prepared to permit them to make those choices for themselves.

[34] As these comments suggest, recognition and limit-setting are not entirely separate issues. When limit-setting is necessary, recognition provides a constructive and hopeful context.

[35] To some extent this assertion sounds like an anachronism, inasmuch as young people in the West inhabit a permissive, laissez-faire society whose constraints around sexuality and the use of psychoactive substances have become attenuated. Relative to the Victorian society of "No" (e.g., Vienna 1890) in which Freud described hysteria and other neuroses, today's privileged teenagers live in a society of "Yes"—and may be said to be much less conflicted. Perhaps this is why modern psychiatrists rarely see hysteria or other classic neuroses. We live instead in an epidemic of (relatively unconflicted) narcissism.

[36] This is a topic for later discussion. See Chapter 6.

[37] In some families, I've watched parents who only seem able to recognize a boy's naughty motives and behavior and seem willfully to ignore all of his virtues. This is a destructive *mis*recognition, which makes a boy feel that he is bad.

[38] See also chapters six and seven, where we take up limit-setting.

[39] For my summary of adolescent developmental lines and the missing milestones in adolescent immaturity, see McKinnon, J. (2008), *op. cit.*

[40] This is conventional wisdom in psychotherapy, where the immediate context (*you* and *me*) involves the therapist directly. It's one thing for a patient to remember a remote event to do with his father, but quite another when those past feelings, e.g., about a father, surface again within this immediate relationship, as if the therapist stood in for the father. We call this reiteration *transference*. This is where it traditionally has been taught that the most vivid and memorable interpretation (recognition) takes place. Here I'm saying something similar—that recognition of a teenager's thoughts and feelings are

most vivid and compelling when they're recognized here and now, within the relationship between an adult and a teenager.

41 This is a useful simplification. Compared with adolescence, when all previous stages and themes come back into play at once, the exaggeration is a modest one. See Erikson (1950), *op. cit.*

42 *Ibid.* Here I refer to Erikson's observation that the primary task of adolescence, in the course of these reiterations of childhood themes and past crises, is to establish a first cut at an adult identity—and so his term for this essential adolescent turmoil, the *identity crisis.*

43 This was Anna Freud's observation—that in adolescence a teenager replays *all* prior childhood themes, more or less all at once. Also see Erikson (1950), *op. cit.*, re: the identity crisis. This reiteration of so many emotional leitmotifs makes adolescence a very complicated operetta. Perhaps this is also why it can be so difficult to restore harmony and developmental progress when it all goes awry. Yet as Anna Freud and Erikson both have pointed out, it's this reiteration of previous themes that provides a second opportunity to work out prior stage-specific conflicts, historical disruptions in family life or psychological traumas, and so achieve a better pre-adult resolution of conflicts, or experience needed, missed childhood experiences in adolescent versions, or overcome a residual narcissism. Adolescence provides, in short, both a complicated new developmental problem and also a rich, new developmental opportunity.

44 The *psycho-social* developmental line, which I describe from birth through adolescence, comes from the clinical writings of Erik Erikson, *op. cit.*

45 I have summarized a number of these developmental lines in *An Unchanged Mind, op cit.* A brilliant, more sophisticated account of even more of these developmental lines may be found in Kegan, R. *The Evolving Self* (Cambridge: Harvard University Press, 1982).

46 I have numbered these recognition statements to be able to point out that those labeled "1" implicitly refer to the infantile theme of trust (mistrust); those labeled "2" refer to the hot issue of "autonomy"; those labeled "3" refer to issues of oedipal closeness (or guilt-worthy harm); those labeled "4" are about education and mastery; and those labeled "5" describe emerging adult identity. If these aren't readily comprehensible at this point, the following discussions may help to make sense of these stage-related themes.

47 Those familiar with the neuropsychological literature may recognize that this adolescent re-working of all prior psychological leitmotifs takes place in the same developmental moment in which a massive dendritic proliferation, followed by a radical "pruning" of inter-neuronal interconnectedness, reorganizes the adolescent brain. It is hard to resist the inference that the profound neuronal reorganization reflects the psychological reorganization, and vice versa.

48 Cross-contextual thinking is much the same as abstract thinking—an adolescence cognitive achievement; see Kegan (1982) *op. cit.*

49 Erikson's term: *confusion*, or *identity diffusion*, which refers to a failure of identity to cohere, or to become stable, during adolescence.

50 Like all the clinical histories in this book, Lisa's case is a composite, compounded from the histories of many students and families I have known over the years. Yet, if I am successful, readers will recognize the essential truth of this account.

51 Although Lisa's case deliberately emphasizes a lack of recognition, she also (obviously) lacked sufficient limit-setting. When in a later chapter I present another teenager whose parents fail to set limits, it will also be true that they failed to recognize him properly. For (as I will emphasize in Chapter 9), recognition and limit-setting are not really separate tasks. Recognition is necessary to effective limit-setting; limit-setting *is* an act of recog-

nition. To fail to set limits when they need to be firmly set is a failure of recognition as much as a failure of limit-setting. It is only for heuristic purposes that, in Lisa's case, I emphasize the one, in my discussion, rather than the other.

[52] Actually, I left this possibility open by emphasizing her early learning differences and hinting at attentional lapses.

[53] In this book I refer to educational consultants, wilderness programs, therapeutic schools, adventure or experiential activities, emotional growth programs, and other rubric from the range of "alternative" (non-medical, non-psychiatric) programs for troubled teenagers that have evolved over the past few decades. Readers wanting to understand this range of contemporary services might usefully begin with: Paul Case, *What Now? How Teen Therapeutic Programs Could Save Your Troubled Child* (Franklin, Tenn.: Common Thread Media, 2008). For a history of the rise of alternative adolescent programs, see: John L. Santa, Ph.D., "Residential Treatment and the Missing Axis," *Journal of Therapeutic Schools and Programs*, Vol II, No. 1, 2008.

[54] "CBT" refers to "cognitive-behavioral therapy," usually a short-term, structured, educative effort aimed at changing "cognition." Its premise, in part, is that symptoms arise from irrational or wrongheaded "thoughts," which may be corrected.

[55] The "ranch" refers to the rural campus of Montana Academy, a residential therapeutic school located forty miles west of Kalispell, Montana. For more than a decade, the other founders and I along with a team of splendid colleagues have treated troubled teenagers we usually enroll after the successful completion of an initial "wilderness" program.

[56] This is the conceptual basis for the official *Diagnostic & Statistical Manual of the American Psychiatric Association*, Fourth Edition, 1982 (DSM-IV). In essence, it is a compilation (with many more "diagnoses" every edition) of clustered signs and symptoms and misbehaviors, which are dubbed "disorders" and often confused or conflated with "diseases," as if a laundry-list of symptoms were the same as a disease, and as if pharmacological symptom relief were the same as a cure. This would be equivalent to calling belly pain a "disorder" and prescribing morphine to "treat" that symptom. For a recent critical essay on the upcoming revision of the DSM, see an op-ed in the *Wall Street Journal*, 27 March 2010, by Edward Shorter, who is a professor of the history of medicine at the University of Toronto.

[57] Here I'm making a point: that developmental immaturity itself is associated with a variety of signs and symptoms (anxiety, low self-esteem, deflated mood, angry tantrums, etc.), and to treat those symptoms with drugs that might relieve them somewhat without directly treating the underlying developmental immaturity, which is their cause, is one reason for treatment failure. On the other hand, conventional diagnosis and treatment often address a developmental obstacle—e.g., ADHD, primary depression, psychotic illness—and constitute an important first part of a two part-treatment. It's not sufficient to remove an obstacle if there is no follow-through, to get stuck maturation moving again. The removal of a developmental obstacle doesn't usually, in itself, solve the problem of developmental immaturity.

[58] Lasch, C. *The Culture of Narcissism* (New York: Warner Books, 1979), p. 305. This comment comes in the context of Lasch's discussion of the writings of Jules Henry and Arnold Rogow, who thought American parents (of the mid-twentieth century) "alternately 'permissive and evasive' in dealing with the young, because they 'find it easier to achieve conformity by the use of bribery than by facing the emotional turmoil of suppressing the child's demands." They argued that this reluctance makes it "impossible for [the American child] to develop self-restraint or self-discipline; but since American society no longer values these qualities anyway, the abdication of parental authority itself instills in the young the character traits demanded by a corrupt, permissive, hedonistic culture."

59 For a clinical example, see Chapter 8, Case Report: "An Indulged Boy."

60 Lewis, M. "Coach Fritz's Management Theory," *New York Times Magazine*, March 28, 2004. This magazine piece was republished as a slim book: *Coach: Lessons on the Game of Life* (New York, W. W. Norton & Co., 2005).

61 These factors—and many others, including a high incidence of divorce, the obligatory modern two-career family, and ubiquity of drugs—may help to explain the remarkable explosion in alternative (non-medical) adolescent programs (e.g., "wilderness" programs, whose most obvious feature may be an unplugging from the modern media matrix and a distancing from drug sources and pals). By removing a teenager from this modern culture, these programs restore adult control and supervision.

62 These extra-familial interventions are described and discussed in Chapter 10.

63 If they cannot cooperate, children may *not* grow up properly.

64 Here, once more, I use the term "parent" in a general sense, and I mean to include limit-setting outside the home (at school, at the job, on the basketball court) that relies upon other adults. The point stands, however. In the rearing of teenagers, sheer coercive power is not much use without a warm relationship. If a teacher must confront a child's misbehavior, it's one thing if the student loves and respects his teacher, and something else again entirely if they're strangers to one another.

65 A parent who loses those bonds loses clout. Because this is such critical leverage in limit-setting, it's commonplace when teenagers are sent away from home to a therapeutic program or boarding school to expend a lot of time and effort to repair parent–child relationships. Often this is the key therapeutic task. To set limits within this relationship, adults (and sons and daughters, too) must both believe they have something valuable to lose.

66 See Chapter 8, Case II: "A Chastened Girl."

67 For teenagers who think and make decisions like three-year-olds, however, adolescent access to these choices (drugs, alcohol, sex, cars) and risks (sexual predation, gangs, intoxicated drivers, crime, etc.) presents a mortal danger. Some parents have the resources to do what we do routinely for three-year-olds: remove them from those dangers (i.e., to a wilderness program or therapeutic boarding school, where they're supervised closely and the risks are reduced). The hope is that, when they have grown up enough to be trusted to make their own choices in the face of those temptations and risks, then those teenagers can safely return to conventional adolescent lives. This, in a paragraph, is what wilderness programs and therapeutic boarding schools are for.

68 Munich, R. and Munich, A. (2009) "Overparenting and the Narcissistic Pursuit of Attachment," *Psychiatric Annals* 39(4):227–235. The authors describe "over-parenting" as a misguided attempt by modern parents to intrude into teenaged sons and daughters' struggles to try to live their lives for them, and so protect them from consequences and thwart the attempts of other adults to set limits.

69 Wallerstein, J. (2004) personal communication. Judy and her colleagues have written a distinguished sequence of follow-up studies that describe the impact of divorce upon children and teenagers, including: *The Unexpected Legacy of Divorce: A 25-Year Landmark Study* (New York: Hyperion, 2000).

70 Munich and Munich (2009), *op. cit.* The first clinical vignette demonstrates intrusive "over-parenting."

71 We tend to put limit-setting into developmental sequence at Montana Academy, organizing hurdles that students must surmount to complete the program in developmental order—starting with trust and trust-worthiness and moving on to acceptance of reasonable adult authority, and so on. To contemplate this sequence in ethical and spiritual

terms, see Fowler, J. *The Psychology of Human Development and the Quest for Meaning*, (New York: Harper Collins, 1981); and Erikson, E. (1950), *op. cit.*

[72] When this becomes impossible at home—in the midst of modern mass culture, unco-operative neighbors, or simply because parents cannot supervise their teenagers 24/7 to enforce limits they have set, some parents in recent years have sent teenaged children on wilderness treks, emotional-growth outdoor programs, and residential therapeutic schools. For most of these parents, the compelling initial reason for this drastic step is the need to reestablish adult–child relationships in which limits can be set and adult authority acknowledged. Usually with sorrow and at great cost, these parents act upon the second rule, because they cannot otherwise (at home) hope to establish the first.

[73] Again, for an explanation of this assertion, see McKinnon, J. (2008), *op. cit.*

[74] These are lyrics from the pop song, "Love and Marriage," by Sammy Cahn and Jimmy Van Heusen.

[75] Rousseau, J-J. (1762) *Contract Social*, book I, chapter 1, in which Rousseau famously wrote that in society, "L'homme est né libre, et partout il est dans les fers."

[76] Freud, S. (1929) *Civilization and Its Discontents* (London: Penguin, 2002). Freud famously asserted in this work that in human beings neurosis is inevitable, because there is no way to transform an infant into a socialized adult without creating internal conflict.

[77] Kegan cites the studies of ethical development in children by Robert Kohlberg on this point. See *Collected Papers on Moral Development and Moral Education* (Cambridge: Center for Moral Education, 1973).

[78] Thanks, Mom.

[79] Thomas, Dylan. (1934) "The Force that Through the Green Fuse Drives the Flower," *Norton Anthology of English Literature* (New York: W.W. Norton & Co., 1962), Vol. 2, p. 1632–1633.

[80] Chess, S. and Thomas, A. *Temperament and Behavior Disorders* (New York: New York University Press, 1968).

[81] McKinnon, J. (2008), *op. cit.* This is the basic argument.

[82] On the other hand, it's also true that some squeaky wheels may be made to run more quietly, even if an underlying immaturity hasn't been addressed. Some symptoms (stemming from immaturity, I'd argue) are much easier to suppress than others; some kinds of misbehavior (stemming from immaturity, I'd argue) are much harder to ignore.

[83] A new study from the Kaiser Family Foundation reported that "the average young American now spends practically every waking minute—except for time in school—using a smart phone, computer, television, or other electronic device . . . Those ages 8–18 spend more than seven and a half hours a day with such devices, compared with less than six and a half hours five year ago. And that does not count the hour and a half that youths spend texting, or the half-hour they talk on their cell-phones." See Tamar Lewin, "If Your Kids Are Awake, They're Probably Online," *New York Times*, January 20, 2010.

[84] Since the publication of my first book, *An Unchanged Mind*, a number of readers have written to ask how this understanding of immaturity and its remedy might become available to teenagers who don't need, or whose families cannot afford, to send them to alternative programs, such as wilderness treks or residential therapeutic schools. These queries usually end with what seems the obvious question: How about in the public high school?

[85] Douglas H. Heath (1993) *Schools of Hope: Developing Mind and Character in Today's Youth* (Bryn Mawr, Penn.: Cornrow Publishing House, 1999) p. 145.

[86] For a careful, historical account of American high-school drop-out statistics, see Barton, P. *One Third of a Nation: Rising Drop-Out Rates and Declining Opportunities* (Princeton: Policy Information Center, Educational Testing Service, 2005).

[87] For a scholarly account of the correlation between school size and teacher–student relationships, see Heath, D. H. (1993) *op cit.*, pp. 80–83. Heath writes (p. 81): "Large schools reduce the opportunity for sustained relationships to occur between everyone in the school."

[88] The typical limitations in a family's capacity to supervise and set limits for immature teenagers are similar to the limitations (noted above) in our discussion of outpatient therapies. Some parents run out of resources sooner than others, but in the end most employed parents cannot simply drop whatever else they are doing to supervise a stroppy, sneaky teenager 24/7. It can become a full-time job for a parent (or therapist) just to stay in close touch and coordinated with all the other (surrogate) parents (teachers, vice-principals, police officers, coaches, other parents) who also are trying to help. The global nature of the task and the elusive nature of the modern teenager may simply swamp a family's capacity to manage and supervise.

[89] The quality of public residential "treatment" has been a matter of serious dispute in recent years. A major study documented a scandalous incidence of sexual abuse by prison warders and other inmates in jails and prisons holding juvenile inmates. The National Survey of Youth in Custody, representing 26,550 adjudicated youth held nationwide in state operated and large locally or privately operated juvenile facilities, reported that "an estimated 12% of youth in state juvenile facilities and large non-state facilities . . . [have experienced] one or more incidents of sexual victimization by another youth or facility staff in the past 12 months. . . . [Among] thirteen facilities identified as "high rate . . . six had victimization rates of 30% or more." See Kaiser, D. and Stannow, L., "The Crisis of Juvenile Prison Rape: A New Report," *New York Review of Books* blog, 7 January, 2010.

Another study conducted by a task force appointed by the governor of New York and chaired by Jeremy Tavis, president of the John Jay College of Criminal Justice, reported (in a confidential draft report obtained by the *New York Times*) that "New York's juvenile prisons are both extremely expensive and extraordinarily ineffective. . . . The state spends roughly $210,000 per youth annually, but three-quarters of those released from detention are arrested again within three years. And though the median age of those admitted to juvenile facilities is almost 16, one-third of those held read at a third-grade level" (Nicholas Confessore, "New York Finds Extreme Crisis in Youth Prisons," *New York Times*, December 14, 2009). It is also in these state-run "boot-camps" and quasi-military lockdowns and juvenile prisons that other shocking allegations of violence and sexual abuse have been documented.

The same findings are *not* characteristic of private "alternative" programs, where parents electively enroll teenaged children (and can remove them at will) and where the enrolled population of middle-class teenagers is a vastly different sample of the American adolescent population—in clinical diagnoses, rates of addiction, and criminality, for a start. The dramatically different treatment outcomes in these distinctive populations have been reviewed in Behrens, E. and Satterfield, K., "A Multi-Center, Longitudinal Study of Youth Outcomes in Private Residential Treatment Programs," presented at the Conference of Independent Educational Consultants Association, Boston, April 27, 2007. See also Behrens, E. and Satterfield, K. (2008), "Longitudinal Family and Academic Outcomes in [private] Residential Programs: How Students Function in Two Important Areas of Their Lives," *J Ther Schools and Programs*, II(i).

The notorious lack of efficacy in some state-run programs has frequently been generalized carelessly to the private programs, as if the same teenagers, the same problems, the same staffing, the same clinical approaches to treatment, and the same outcomes were characteristic of both populations and both kinds of treatment facilities. As Behrens shows in convincing detail, nothing could be further from the truth.

90 Dishion, T. J., McCord, J., and Pulin, F. (1999) "When Interventions Harm: Peer Groups and Problem Behavior," *Am Psychologist*, 54:1–10.

91 For a thorough history of "alternative" programs in the United States, see Santa, J. (2008) "Residential Treatment and the Missing Axis," *J Ther Schools and Programs*, II(i).

92 See Behrens, E and Satterfield, K. (2008), *op cit.*

93 In those years, one criterion for enrollment at Montana Academy was a successful progress through a wilderness program. For this reason, my sample of young wilderness veterans is skewed. Certainly there are teenagers who don't do well in wilderness, who don't reconcile with their parents, who run away or hold their breaths and get little from the experience. Nevertheless, the transformations that happen in teenagers who do well in wilderness is impressive.

94 In some of the wilderness programs with which I'm most familiar, the therapist commutes into and out of "the field." When back at base camp her task, in large part, is to call parents and educational consultants, keeping all the adults up to date, and helping parents to think through their parts in the process.

95 Presumably not every wilderness program requires these rituals, nor do they all do them in exactly the same way or use the same names for what they do. Moreover, other programs use similar means to structure therapeutic attempts to get parents and children talking straight to one another. In any case, this isn't my point. I'm simply arguing that, whatever the rubric, these common rituals are acts of mutual recognition that repair damaged, distorted relationships and reconcile teenagers and their parents. They are, for many programs, at least as useful as the limit-setting I've also emphasized. In sum, recognition and limit-setting are at the heart of the wilderness experience for both teenagers and parents.

96 I employ the phrase "more honest" because in our experience this is what most immature teenagers manage to accomplish in an accountability letter—something less than the whole truth and nothing but the truth. In the course of the later therapeutic groups held at Montana Academy, for example, students invariably enlarge upon previous self-disclosures of drug use and wretched personal behavior and experience, revealing that their wilderness accountability letters have been partial confessions, elliptical histories, and only relatively candid. This fact doesn't invalidate wilderness attempts to come clean, but only suggests that human beings tend to hold back the worst, if they think they can—a spectacle all too common on television and in the newspaper when politicians are caught with their pants down. This behavior is surely the more common among childish teenagers, whose highest guiding moral principles don't yet include abstract ethical concepts, such as integrity.

97 In this section I illustrate with examples from the therapeutic boarding school I know best, which is Montana Academy. Each of the nation's residential therapeutic schools is distinctive, however, in emphasis, in the particulars of rules, procedures, staffing, and theory. Yet there's enough that's similar about them to warrant using one rubric (therapeutic boarding school or residential therapeutic school) to refer to them all. Moreover, I trust that my examples, albeit drawn from only one, will help to make sense of them all. I don't refer to Montana Academy and its particular diction and norms, except for general illustrative purposes. Certainly other therapeutic boarding schools provide splendid experiences for teenagers and their families. When parents decide the fit is better at another school, presumably that school will do a better job than we would do. In sum, this book is intended for all parents rearing normal teenagers or struggling with immature teenagers. In particular, I hope Chapter 10 will prove to be of use to parents of students enrolled in wilderness programs and in other therapeutic schools. It is *not* meant to be a commercial for Montana Academy.

[98] The odds of a healthy adult losing this childhood developmental achievement (continence) are remote, but not zero. An adult may become incontinent again, if the stress is enormous. For most grown-ups this won't happen even during acute worries about a divorce or after news of a diagnosis of cancer. But combat veterans used to describe as a commonplace a soldier's incontinence during battle. And presumably most of us would lose it under torture.

[99] The day before I wrote this sentence, a sixteen-year-old boy was referred to Montana Academy who'd been successfully toilet-trained at age three, but developed enuresis at four, immediately after his parents adopted and brought home a five-year-old "brother." His incontinence persisted for more than a decade, despite multiple pharmacological attempts at a remedy.

[100] Robert Kegan (1994), *op. cit.*, has demonstrated in systematic studies that adults in midlife, in substantial numbers, remain stuck in an earlier stage of psychological development, and so remain grossly immature, and not likely to finish growing up anytime soon.